RAVING UPON THAMES

An Untold Story of Sixties London

ANDREW HUMPHREYS

First published in 2022
by Paradise Road

A CIP catalogue record for this book
is available from the British Library.

ISBN 978-0-9935702-3-0

Edited by Chris Wright
Proofread by Omer Ali
Book design and layout by Gadi Farfour
Cover illustration and design by Jem Panufnik © 2021
Endpaper maps by Gadi Farfour

Printed by TJ Books Ltd, Padstow, Cornwall

www.paradiseroad.co.uk

For Arthur, Giorgio and Harold

'I've heard a lot about that place, it's full of bleedin' layabouts, ban the bomb types! And drugs! What do you all wanna join the likes of them for? They're all up to no good. Bloody reds, the lot of 'em.'

A warning to Don Hughes to stay away from Eel Pie Island, recalled in his book *Friday on My Mind*

CONTENTS

INEVER MEANT TO WRITE THIS BOOK: I only wanted to read it.

My wife and I moved to Richmond from Soho in 2007. We had been living in a studio flat off Leicester Square, which was exciting as long as you didn't spend too much time at home where, month by month, the walls squeezed in ever closer. Not that things could get any tighter in the bedroom, which was, in reality, a corner of the living room with plasterboard partitions to hide the bed – lying on it, you could touch all four walls simultaneously. We knew Richmond only barely, from occasional fair-weather visits to its vast and rambling park. Our idea of the town was exemplified by a conversation a friend overhead on a train pulling into Richmond station: 'Nick, I didn't see you there! Coming back from town?'

'Yes, the theatre. The Albery.'

'What did you see?'

'See, darling? I was in it!'

Richmond was where old luvvies went to take the final curtain. It has greying actors like other boroughs have pigeons. There's a reason for that: the borough of Richmond upon Thames is green and beautiful and twenty minutes from the West End by train. My wife and I were drawn by the sense of space, the clean air, parks, riverside walks and, unlike Soho, shops that sold useful things, like fresh fruit and veg. Richmond might not have had the entertainments and buzz of Soho but you didn't run the risk of interrupting a drug deal every time you stepped outside your front door.

But the gulf between Richmond and Soho wasn't always so great. Our first clue that underneath the village greenery and English Heritage aesthetic the borough of Richmond upon Thames harboured a grungier strand of history came shortly after moving in, when the pub opposite the train station closed for renovations. On the protective boards the builders fitted over the windows was a large image of a grooving young Mick Jagger and a short text explaining that in the early 1960s this was the site of the Crawdaddy club, where the infant Rolling Stones played a weekly residency.

While I've never been a fan of the Stones, growing up I was an avid reader of the weekly music papers. I first moved to London, in the 1980s, because of its live music scene and I eventually ended up working for *Time Out*, with its pages and pages of weekly live music listings. So how was it that I'd never heard of the Crawdaddy? It turned out there was a lot I didn't know.

Sessions of idle googling led to *Comstock Lode*, a music zine published between 1977 and 1982 that ran to ten issues, all edited and largely written by someone called John Platt. Platt's passion was 1960s West Coast American psychedelic music and Beat-era writing, but also British R&B. Issue seven included an extended piece on the Richmond and Twickenham music scene of the '60s. The reason for this seemingly incongruous inclusion – alongside pieces on San Francisco psychedelic rockers Country Joe and Quicksilver, and Grateful Dead poster artist Stanley Mouse – was that Richmond upon Thames was Platt's home turf.

Platt was brought up in the area and in his late teens began working for the local libraries department. Away from the day job, he became recognised for his music writing and went on to co-author books on the Yardbirds and Mitch Mitchell, of the Jimi Hendrix Experience. Platt also wrote a very good by-area history of the London music scene, and was a consultant on the TV series *Rock Family Trees*. In 1993, he moved to New York, where he worked on book and TV projects to do with Cream and Eric Clapton.

All of which is to say, John Platt knew his stuff. His piece on Richmond and Twickenham provided a backstory to the Rolling Stones and the Crawdaddy, and also covered the Stones' replacements at the club, the Yardbirds. It detailed the heady musical happenings on nearby Eel Pie Island, the early local jazz and blues festivals, a folk haunt called the Hanging Lamp, alternative-arts workshops, hippie communes and something called Colonel Barefoot's Rock Garden. Blimey.

Platt was of the opinion that when it came to musical activities the Thames Valley area – meaning the towns along the Thames from Putney through Richmond and Twickenham to Kingston – was, in the 1950s and '60s, as important an area as Soho, Liverpool or San Francisco. He felt it had never been given the recognition it deserved. His *Comstock Lode* piece was an attempt to set the record straight. The feature, part potted history, part personal reminiscence, ran to a meaty 7,000 words, but it left me wanting to know more. Perhaps Platt had once had plans to expand the story into a book, but we'll never know: he died of cancer in his adopted home of New York back in 2001, at the age of just forty-eight.

So, I asked another music journalist to write the book instead. I have a small publishing company specialising in non-fiction books about London. In 2015, we were about to launch our first titles and I felt a book reclaiming Richmond and Twickenham as the Haight-Ashbury of London would be a great addition to our list. The journalist turned me down. I approached a second candidate, the chief music critic of a national newspaper, who just happened to have been brought up in Richmond. He was busy with a memoir. A third well-respected music writer listened politely and also said no.

In 2016, Giorgio Gomelsky, first manager of both the Rolling Stones and the Yardbirds, and founder of the Crawdaddy club, died. A second key figure, Harold Pendleton, organiser of the Richmond-based National Jazz and Blues Festivals, passed away the following year. I decided I'd better get on with writing the book myself before there was nobody left to interview. As it happens, it's a fantastic story and I'm truly grateful to those three music journalists for leaving it to me to write.

I wasn't around at the time the events in this book happened – born fifteen years too late and 175 miles to the north. So I'm indebted to all the people who were there and who agreed to be interviewed for this book. I wish I could have talked to more people, but then the book would never have been finished. Only a handful of those I contacted declined to be interviewed, almost all women: I wonder if that says something about how the female experience at the time differed from the men's? I was delighted to discover that many of those with whom I spoke remain as defiantly non-conformist today as when they thumbed their noses at the world from the terrace at L'Auberge or dancefloor at Eel Pie Island. To all of you, I hope this book does a decent job of portraying the extraordinary times you lived through.

Thank you Judy Astley, Vanessa Barnes, Geoff Barker, Ron Bartholomew, Nat Bocking, Fraser Botwright, Henry Boxer, Roy Buckley, Gary Cowan, Dave Cousins (The Strawbs), Jim Cregan (The Ingoes, Blossom Toes), Alan Cresswell (Riverside Jazzmen), Peter Crisp, David Dadswell, Bob Danks, Martyn Day, Wendy Edmonds, Paul Endacott, Ray Everitt, Chris Faiers, Sue Fischer, Peter Flower, Karina Gabner, Simon Goode, Stephen Goy, Gillian Green, Martin Greene, Geoff Grimes, Steve Hackett (Genesis), Oliver Harries,

WITHOUT WHOM...

Peter Hogan, Markus Holler, Robin Hunter, Simon Kirke (Free, Bad Company), Tim Large (Dave Anthony's Moods), John Lethbridge, Loretta Leu, John Lucas, Paul Lucas (The Tridents), Terry Marshall, Don Martin, Barry May, Alan 'Alf' Maynard, Les McCallum, Jim McCarty (The Yardbirds), Aurie McKay, Frank McConnell, Peter Moody (The Grebbels), Diana Morris, Keith Mulberry, Richard Newman, Tom Newman (The Tomcats, July), Leo O'Kelly (Tír na nÓg), Angie Page, Barbara Pendleton, Nick Pendleton, Anthony Phillips (Genesis), Mark Pickthall, Vivienne Pirog, Peter Polish, Brian Ranken, Colin Richardson, Mike Rivers, Andy Roberts, Brian Rutland (Grove Jazz Band), Mark Rye, Jon Sadleir, Paul Samwell-Smith (The Yardbirds), Roger Sharp, Grenville Sheringham, Alan Sherriff, Ian Shircore, Caldwell Smythe, Paul Stewart, Subi Swift, Graeme Taylor (Gryphon), Tony Thorne, Rob Tolchard (The Others), Alan Turner (Gary Farr & the T-Bones), Pete Turner, Nick Tweddell (The Muleskinners), Bob Wagner, Gina Way, Weed, Kevin Westbury, Heather 'Fluff' White, Nigel White, Annie Wiggins, John Williams (The Authentics), David Wills, Alan Winter and Andrea Wordsworth.

Andrew Humphreys, October 2021

Melody Maker

April 13, 1963   Friday 6d

BEAT BATTLE HOTTING UP
PAGE EIGHT

Harry James band tour

HARRY JAMES, whose Basie-styled outfit is the talk of the American big-band jazz scene, is a strong possibility for a tour of Britain next spring.

A cable this week from MM New York correspondent Ren Grevatt reveals that the latest band exchange involves the famous trumpet-leader.

Says Grevatt: "James, in Hollywood, is known to be considering a British tour for his band. Dates mentioned would be April or May of 1964.

"No contracts have yet been drawn but tradesters close to the James band feel the odds are better than ever that the tour will happen.

Sell-out

"It would be the second major band tour to jell for Britain in recent weeks. Stan Kenton is already booked for the latter part of the year."

Harold Davison, who is handling the Kenton deal, told the MM on Monday: "We are negotiating for Harry James, but I cannot say anything more at this early stage."

A trip to Britain has been mooted for some years, but the nearest James got was when his powerhouse band played Berlin in 1957. Then, the band "went like mad" during two sell-out concerts at the Sportplatz.

● JAMES—April

Gerry jumps to No. 1

● *A victory leap from Gerry and the Pacemakers celebrates the top pop news*

First record hits the jackpot

HE's done IT. Who? —Gerry Marsden. What?—Topped the MM Pop 50 with his first record.

Exactly a month and a week after "How do you do it" was released, it has sold close on 100,000 copies and leapfrogged into the No 1 spot.

It's another triumph for beat-breeding Liverpool, and talent-tapper Brian Epstein, manager of Gerry and the Pacemakers, and the Beatles, among others.

Snap news this week was that the single will be released in America within the next few weeks.

And Gerry with the group will soon be starting to record titles for their first LP—featuring songs written by them and the Beatles.

Gerry and the group scored a London success at the plush Pigalle Restaurant on Sunday, and on Monday caused a minor traffic jam in the West End, when a streetful of fans spotted the 'pint-sized popster coming out of a tailor's.

Gerry worked for British Railways before turning professional to go to Germany with his group.

Now he has a complete summer date book—in Margate, Weston-super-Mare, Southend, Bournemouth, Jersey and Guern-sey—a top spot in the BBC "Pop prom" concert at the Albert Hall, on May 9, and fresh radio and TV dates coming in every day.

The group got their break when Parlophone's George Martin saw them performing in a Liverpool ballroom.

Just before he went on stage at a concert in Parkstone, Dorset, Gerry commented to the MM: "I feel great. We keep pinching ourselves to make sure we're not dreaming—it's all happened so fast.

"The boys are thrilled. It's more shock than anything. They never really thought it would make it."

Future plans? Gerry mentioned that there was something in the air about a concert at Blackpool with Sammy Davis—"but nothing definite yet."

Gerry, who plays guitar, piano harmonica, and bass, is accompanied by his brother Freddy Marsden (drums and vocals), Les Maguire (piano, guitar, vocals), and Les Chadwick (bass guitar, vocals).

CARNABY STREET... KING'S ROAD... RICHMOND UPON THAMES

London's soporific southwest suburbs receive a jolt of music-led social revolution

IT'S SUNDAY 14 APRIL 1963. Conservative Harold Macmillan, born when Victoria was on the throne, is Britain's prime minister. Harold Wilson is the recently elected leader of the opposition Labour Party. Britain is still bristling at French president Charles de Gaulle's veto of its entry into the European Economic Community three months earlier. There are two TV channels. Showing on BBC1 that night is the *The Black and White Minstrel Show*, followed by *Perry Mason*. 'How Do You Do It?' by Gerry and the Pacemakers is the country's No.1 single. Cliff Richard's *Summer Holiday* tops the album charts. Two places lower is the Beatles' debut album *Please Please Me*, released just three weeks earlier. In a further three weeks it will hit the top spot, where it will remain for thirty weeks, launching not just Beatlemania but arguably the youth-led revolution of carefree excess, self-exploration and sexual freedom known as the Sixties. For the moment, however, it's grey, cold and raining in black-and-white London.

The miserable weather has not deterred the crowds from turning up at the Crawdaddy in Richmond. It's not much in the way of a club – 'Crawdaddy' is just the name given to Sunday evenings in the back room of the Station Hotel. But there is an electrifying buzz about the resident band, who've been playing here for the last seven Sundays. They're called the Rolling (or Rollin') Stones.

For the moment, the band is Richmond's best-kept secret, although they're not local: vocalist Mick Jagger and guitarist Keith Richards are southeast London boys, raised in Dartford; drummer Charlie Watts and bassist Bill Wyman are from north and south London, respectively; the group's leader, Brian Jones, is from Cheltenham. Only the pianist Ian Stewart is from this side of town: born in Scotland but brought up in Sutton, in Surrey. Until recently Stewart has been responsible for hustling bookings because he's the only one with regular access to a phone – it sits on his desk at Imperial Chemical Industries. That's why most of the band's gigs have been out this way: at the Ealing Club, the Red Lion in Sutton, the Ricky Tick in Windsor. Of all the gigs, though, the Crawdaddy is the one that feels like home, largely because it's run by Giorgio Gomelsky, the Stones' de facto manager. Gomelsky works hard at promoting the club, turning Sunday nights in Richmond into an event, building a fanbase, making a name for the band. It's paying off. Every week sees a bigger crowd than the last.

The Stones play R&B, rhythm and blues, the new rival sound to Liverpool's popular Merseybeat. Both channel the style and energy of Black American music and they're united in a shameless idolisation of Chuck Berry and Bo Diddley. From here, though, the northerners veer toward the sentimental and showbiz, aping Everly Brothers harmonies and Motown 'la-la-las'. R&B is rawer, chasing the sound back to the cotton fields of the southern states through artists like Muddy Waters, Howlin' Wolf and John Lee Hooker, old black guys with gravelly voices and beat-up guitars. The Beatles warble 'I Wanna Hold Your Hand', the Stones come on with 'I Just Want to Make Love to You'.

Cool they may be, but the Stones are still a bunch of unknowns playing covers in the back room of a pub, while with a hit album and hit singles, the Beatles are the biggest entertainment story in Britain. So on that wet April Sunday as the Stones launch into their second set at the Crawdaddy and bassist Bill Wyman notices four shadowy figures being ushered to the front of the room, his eyes widen as he realises, 'Shit, that's *the Beatles!*'[1] Keith Richards has a similar reaction: 'We're whacking our show out and everybody's having a good time, you know. I suddenly turn around and there's these four guys in black leather overcoats, standing there. Fuck me! Look who's here! They've come to check us out, man.'[2] Mick Jagger was too embarrassed to even look at the visitors.[3]

The Beatles were similarly impressed by what they saw. 'It was a real rave,' said George Harrison. 'The audience shouted and screamed and danced on tables.'[4] John Lennon thought the Stones were more radical than the Beatles. Ringo Starr recalled thinking the Stones were great. 'They just had presence. And, of course, we could tell – we'd had five weeks in the business, we knew all about it!'[5] A dissenting opinion was offered by Neil Aspinall, the Beatles' personal assistant, who was also present at the Crawdaddy: he thought the Stones were 'okay', no worse or better than an average band at the Cavern in Liverpool. 'They could do their stuff and that was all you needed to do. A lot of people couldn't.'[6]

The Beatles stuck around until the end of the set and then the two groups went back to a flat on Edith Grove in Fulham, where some of the Stones lived. From this first meeting, the Beatles and Stones remained both friends and rivals. A few months later, Lennon and McCartney would gift the Stones their first hit single, 'I Wanna Be

Your Man', a throwaway track that became a Ringo song when the Beatles recorded it for their second LP, *With the Beatles* ('We weren't going to give them anything great, were we?' said McCartney). When the Stones released their debut album, it knocked *With the Beatles* off the top of the charts, where it had sat for twenty-one weeks. The Stones then stayed top for twelve weeks until their record was displaced by *A Hard Day's Night*, the Beatles' third album. The pattern was set for the bands to duel it out for the remainder of the decade, the Beatles selling more records, the Stones enjoying greater credibility among those who liked their rock'n'roll spiked with attitude.

Britain is a small place, so up-and-coming bands are bound to cross paths sooner rather than later. Still, it's surprising that this first get-together of the two most influential groups in pop history happened not in a West End recording studio, Soho club or King's Road boutique, but in a nondescript pub, where the tarmac and brick of London give way to the woodlands and meadows of Surrey. The story of how this came about is one this book sets out to tell.

If supplying the setting for this nervy first encounter was Richmond's sole contribution to the great history of British popular music then it would amount to little more than an unguessable question in a pub quiz. But the Rolling Stones' Crawdaddy residency – and the Beatles' visit – is only part of a larger scene.

If you were a teenager in 1963 (the year according to Philip Larkin's 'Annus Mirabilis' that sex was invented in Britain), then Richmond upon Thames was a very good place to be. You could also catch the Rolling Stones every Wednesday at Eel Pie Island in neighbouring Twickenham. The 'Island' was a tiny enclave in the middle of the Thames, home to a scattering of boat-builders' yards and shack-like homes among the trees. On the far side, was an old hotel with a ramshackle ballroom where bands played. 'It was like breaking into a haunted house and doing a gig there,' says Tom Newman, guitarist with the Tomcats and July. 'It was such an unlikely place,' says Twickenham-born DJ and presenter Annie Nightingale, 'and that was what made it so attractive.' A bearded, pipe-smoking maverick named Arthur Chisnall ran the Eel Pie Island music club as a semi-experimental sanctuary for teenage wildlife. It was where every parent told their offspring not to go, with the result that they flocked there in droves. It was just the bands, a bar and lots of young people (nobody ever seemed to get turned away for being underage) drinking, dancing, smoking, chilling on the grass outside – rave culture thirty years before its time. And what bands. Following the Stones, the Island became an incubator for British R&B, a regular gig for the likes of Cyril Davies and his All-Stars, the Tridents with Jeff Beck, and John Mayall's Bluesbreakers with Eric Clapton. It even played host to some of those old original American bluesmen on their visits to England.

Around this time, sixteen-year-old Andrea Hiorns, from Brentford, wrote a letter to her American pen pal, Candi:

Wednesdays are good days. I go to my Island. I must tell you all about it, it is an important part of my life. It's in the River Thames. You cross a steep bridge over the river and pay a toll of 4d to an old lady called Rose. Then walk along a winding road with bungalows on either side. There's lots of trees and it's dark and mysterious. You turn a bend and see a large decrepit hotel with a crumbling facade. You hear loud blues music. Walk through the gates and you are in another world. All material cares disappear and we are the only people who exist.

There's a large converted barn, you go down some steps after conning your way in with 6d – it's usually 3/6d – your wrist is stamped and you go down. It's very dark with just red and green lights. Long John Baldry is singing with his band at one end of the hall. The walls are white, flaking and full of cobwebs, with cartoons, murals and names painted all over them. People dance there crazily. Next door is the pub, where we and the musicians all congregate, we con drinks and play the jukebox and talk to everyone. I often go there on my own but always end up meeting someone I know to dance with.

Outside there is a long strip of grass down to the river with large stone nuts and bolts lying around and convenient bushes where couples make love and smoke hash. It's the coolest place in England, there's nowhere else like it.

Back in Richmond, UK festival culture was being born. Starting in 1961, the playing fields sandwiched between the Royal Mid-Surrey Golf Club and the Old Deer Park, home of Richmond and London Scottish rugby union clubs, were the setting for the National Jazz Festival. This was the brainchild of Harold Pendleton, president of the National Jazz Federation and the man behind the Marquee jazz club in London's West End. The summer festival was a chance for some of the bands that played the Oxford Street basement to get out into the sunshine for a weekend. In 1963, Richmond faves, the defiantly non-jazz Rolling Stones, stole into the line-up and ran away with the show. Partly as a consequence of their success, in the following years so many non-jazz artists made it onto the bill – the likes of Spencer Davis, Graham Bond with Jack Bruce and Ginger Baker, Manfred Mann, the Moody Blues, the Yardbirds, Animals and the Who, plus the Rolling Stones again – that the event was well on its way to becoming the UK's first annual rock festival (the Isle of Wight festival wouldn't happen until 1968 and the first festival at Glastonbury was 1970).

'We were so blasé about it all,' recalls Ian Shircore, from nearby Hanworth. 'Sunday night we'd be hanging out at L'Auberge and someone would say, "Are we going to the Island tonight?"

"Who's on?"

"Clapton, I think."

"Nah, we've already seen him twice this month.'"

L'Auberge was a coffee bar at the foot of Richmond Hill and, along with the Crawdaddy, the Island and one or two pubs, it was one of the hubs of the local scene. There was a scattering of other popular hangouts in and around nearby Twickenham and Kingston but Richmond was at the centre of the action. This was a prosperous satellite town (locals take offense if you call it a suburb) with a buzzing high street, lots of cafés and pubs, ABC, Gaumont and Odeon cinemas, a famous riverside ice-rink, and abundant parks, greens and public gardens for al fresco gatherings. It offered a plentiful supply of large Victorian houses, rapidly being split up into countless affordable flats and bedsits. Many of these were occupied by students from the handful of local art schools, teacher-training colleges and a military musical school. It all added to a lively air of shabby gentility that, as the Sixties progressed, nudged toward full-on bohemianism. 'There was always music drifting out of windows,' remembers local girl Angie Page, 'and you could walk into a house and sit down with people smoking and you didn't even have to know them.' Richmond may not have been as hip as Soho or Chelsea but, unlike those places, young people could afford to live here.

'I remember going to Richmond with my parents on a Saturday afternoon,' says Tony Thorne, from Teddington. 'There would be a procession coming up the main street from the station, and it would be beatniks and art students, probably from all over London.' A couple of years later Thorne was a L'Auberge regular. 'There was a kind of axis between Soho and Earl's Court and Richmond. People would come to Richmond, especially at weekends, and head for L'Auberge and hang out and exchange news and information and gossip. Then they'd go off to gigs, like Eel Pie Island.'

R&B, the music most associated with the area, was a short-lived phenomenon that had peaked by 1965, but it led to blues, rock and psychedelia, while its beatnik fans – some of them, anyway – morphed into Mods, hippies and freaks. The Richmond scene flowered. It was the flipside to Soho; one was back alleys and basement dives, neon-lit and manic, the other laid-back, open-skied, Arcadian. But they shared the music, the fashions and an appetite for mid-altering substances. Richmond was the first police district in London to receive its own dedicated drug squad. It was a very nice place for bad habits.

As the Sixties progressed, Richmond and its environs were where Rod Stewart was discovered busking on a station platform; where the members of Cream first shared a stage; where the Who road-tested tracks from *Tommy*; where Mick Jagger and Ronnie Wood jammed with David Bowie; where singer-songwriter John Martyn was recorded for a live album that lay undiscovered for forty years; and where the future Elvis Costello gave his first public performance.

Liverpudlian-Irish post-punk Costello seems an unlikely name to be linked with Richmond but between the ages of five and sixteen he was Declan Patrick MacManus (born in 1954), living in East Twickenham, on the north side of Richmond Bridge. Many years later, in a magazine interview, Costello recalled his time in the borough: 'The Rolling Stones were playing nearby, at the Station Hotel in Richmond. The Who were at Eel Pie Island. The Yardbirds lived in the next street. I'd see [Fleetwood Mac founder] Peter Green in this record shop I used to go to. I was living in rock'n'roll central, although I didn't think so at the time.'[7]

Costello wasn't the only one who failed to recognise the rave-up happening on the Thames at the time. The April 1966 issue of *Time* magazine ran a cover story titled 'London: the Swinging City'. This story famously began the process of mythologising the Sixties even as it was happening. It glamorised the boutiques of Carnaby Street and King's Road, the dinner parties of Kensington and clubs of Mayfair. 'Not everyone looks upon London's swing as a blessing,' the authors noted. 'For many who treasure an older, quieter London, the haystack hair, the suspiciously brilliant clothes, the chatter about sex and the cheery vulgarity strike an ugly contrast with the stately London that still persists in the quieter squares of Belgravia or in such peaceful suburbs as Richmond.'

To get a sense of just how wrong *Time* got it, let's return to the Crawdaddy on the night the Beatles dropped in. Also in the audience that Sunday was an eighteen-year-old guitarist from Surrey named Eric Clapton. He'd just joined a band called the Roosters. In less than twelve months he'd be joining another band, a Richmond-based outfit called the Yardbirds. Two more future Yardbirds, Paul Samwell-Smith and Jim McCarty, were also at the Crawdaddy that night. When the Stones move on from Richmond, it's the Yardbirds that will take over their Sunday-night residency. Over the next five years, the band will launch the careers of not just Clapton, but also his replacements, Jeff Beck and Jimmy Page – three guitarists who drew up the blueprints for British rock music. If a sinkhole had opened up and swallowed the Station Hotel that night, the Sixties would never have happened.

This book, then, is the untold story of how 'peaceful' Richmond, Eel Pie Island and neighbouring Thameside suburbs launched the Rolling Stones and the Yardbirds, nurtured R&B, and became a centre of bedsit bohemianism and haunt for the likes of Clapton, Beck and Page, Rod Stewart, David Bowie and Ronnie Wood. Far from sitting out the Sixties, this was a playground for musicians and their switched-on audiences, who fed off each other to launch many of the sounds that powered the myth of the Swinging City.

CHAPTER 1

OFF THE COAST
OF TWICKENHAM

An island in the Thames with a raffish reputation is established as an offshore outpost of jazz

'**G**RAND JAZZ BALL" said *Melody Maker*'s advertising column. "Fully Licensed – Cy Laurie's Jazz Band – Eel Pie Island." I hadn't heard Cy Laurie at the time, but I liked the sound of Eel Pie Island. It seemed to go with "Gut Bucket" or "Honky Tonk". It had the right feel to it.' This is George Melly writing in *Owning Up*, the first of his four volumes of autobiography (Melly was never short of something to say). Melly is a recently demobbed naval seaman now working in a London art gallery devoted to Surrealism, and an addict who trawls the less thumbed pages of the *A to Z* in search of venues where he can get his fix of 'filthy jazz'. Which is how he finds himself in Twickenham, crossing the water to Eel Pie Island. He describes the long grass and luxuriant weeds, the decaying

FACING: Eel Pie Island from the air in 1949. The hotel and ballroom are on the right-hand side of the Island, facing Ham, midway along its length.

17

weather-board bungalows and, at the centre of the Island, the time-worn hotel lifted from the pages of Tennessee Williams. It's a warm summer evening and the blistering paintwork catches the setting sun. The sound of the band inside, playing a turn-of-the-century pimp's lament, 'My Bucket's Got a Hole in It', carries across the water to the Surrey shore.

Melly recalls that there were about twenty people at the Grand Jazz Ball that night, in those days a perfectly respectable number, he remarks. He doesn't make clear when exactly 'those days' were, but other sources point to 1948. Emboldened by a few pints at the bar, Melly asks clarinettist and bandleader Cy Laurie if he can get up and sing a number. Laurie says okay, and Melly pushes his luck by hogging the stage for several songs. At the end of the evening Laurie asks him if he wants to join the band. Melly recalls how he went home in a state of rapture. He would be far from the last person to leave the Island that way.

No one is exactly sure when Eel Pie Island got its name. Historically, it was the Parish Ayte, Goose Ayte or Twickenham Ayte – an *ayte*, or *ait*, being a small river island. But the associations with leisure and entertainment go way back. An early seventeenth-century map of Twickenham shows the centre of the Island marked 'hath been a boulding alley'. As early as the mid fifteenth century, London had roofed bowling lanes – King Henry VIII was an avid and snobbish player, who banned the lower classes from the game. Around 1737, the Island gained a tavern, called first the Ship Inn then later the White Cross. This place became famous for its pies, filled with eels, a fish that was then plentiful in the Thames, providing a cheap and nutritious staple for London's poor, and this is almost certainly how the Island gained its name.[1]

In 1830, the pub was demolished and replaced by the Eel Pie Island Hotel, which quickly became a popular destination for day-tripping nobility and gentry up from London. Nine years later, in *Nicholas Nickleby*, Charles Dickens wrote of such an excursion: 'It had come to pass, that afternoon, that Miss Morleena Kenwigs had received an invitation to repair next day, per steamer from Westminster Bridge, unto the Eel-pie Island at Twickenham: there to make merry upon a cold collation, bottled beer, shrub [a type of punch], and shrimps, and to dance in the open air to the music of a locomotive band.' The hotel is also highlighted in John Fisher Murray's *A Picturesque Tour of the River Thames*, first published in 1845: 'Upon this aite a house of entertainment has been erected; and here the river steamers are accustomed to land great numbers of holiday folks, desirous of the delights of pure air, and solicitous to banquet upon eel-pies, for which the tavern is famed.'

Forty years later, *Dickens's Dictionary of the Thames*, compiled by Charles Jnr, notes that Eel Pie Island is now out of vogue and the eels formerly so abundant are almost completely gone from the Thames due to pollution. This might explain why, in 1891, the hotel and its grounds, which covered almost the entire middle third of the otherwise undeveloped island, were sold. The buyer was Andrew Pears, of Pears Soap – which had a factory in nearby Isleworth – who leased out the hotel's sizeable vegetable garden to William Sergeant, who built a boathouse and slipway on the site. A dance hall was added to the hotel in 1898, a year before it was sold on again. The good times returned in the first decade of the new century, with one paper reporting that on a summer Sunday the hotel might serve upwards of 2,000 meals, but the Great War killed the trade and the hotel was again put up for auction, in 1919. It was described as having fourteen bedrooms on the two upper floors, various sitting rooms and lounges on the ground floor, and a tea garden in extensive grounds. The next three decades are sparsely documented but the business changed hands several more times. There were still dances, such as the one reported in *The Era* of 15 June 1927, in which the Queen's Dance Band, 'a popular five-piece combination', entertained a big crowd on Whitsun Monday, accompanied by a 'demonstration of the Heebie-Jeebies' given by Audrey Phillips and George Porter. There may have been some long-term residents in the rooms on the upper floors but, from contemporary accounts, the place had become neglected and the grounds were wild and overgrown. Which is the state it was in when, in 1951, the hotel was bought by a local businessman named Michael Snapper.

Born in Chelsea in 1908, Snapper started his professional life working in his family's antique business.[2] He later migrated west to Kingston upon Thames where he established his own antiques emporium at 146 London Road, which, as an unabashed self-promoter, he called Snapper's Corner. Later, he also acquired a neo-Gothic manor house with corner turrets and high ecclesiastical-style windows, also on London Road, and this became Snapper's Castle. He'd always had a flair for the extravagant. In his youth, he owned a pair of performing bears. He also trained German shepherds for film work. Snapper and his dogs appeared on BBC TV in 1936 – one of them, Coona, could recognise the letters of the alphabet, while another dog, Mikeve, made it into the *Guinness Book of Records* for the highest jump by a dog (nine feet six inches). Snapper was also an enthusiastic ice-skater (he reputedly tried to teach one of his bears to ice-skate) and collected vintage cars. Boating was another interest and it was in his capacity as a founding member of the London River Yacht Club (est 1950), while searching for a suitable site for a club headquarters, that Snapper found his way to Eel Pie Island.

No one knows why Snapper bought the Eel Pie Island Hotel. It was too big to serve as a clubhouse. Most likely it just appealed to the entrepreneur in him – or the showman. Soon after the purchase, he filed plans to build an outdoor roller-skating rink on the site and

Michael Snapper and partner, and Snapper's well-balanced
German shepherd, Mikeve.

to turn the ballroom into a casino, but the local council refused permission. It did grant an alcohol licence for the hotel, so he could at least have a functioning bar. There are Twickenham locals who recall going to the hotel for tea around this time, but it is unlikely there were any guests in residence given the state of the place. It also seems the ballroom was no longer seeing much use, not if Brian Rutland's memories are accurate.

Rutland, who grew up in Isleworth, was a teenage jazz fan who took up the trumpet and formed the Grove Jazz Band, named for the street where he lived.[3] The band started out playing in his parents' garage before graduating to gigging at local pubs, eventually landing at the Queen's Head (now the Barmy Arms) on Twickenham

Embankment. They were soon pulling in a larger audience than the pub could accommodate, so when somebody mentioned that the hotel on the island opposite had got its licence back, Rutland went over to see Michael Snapper. Rutland remembers this being some time in early 1956. Snapper was happy to have the musicians restore some life to the ballroom, as long as they brought a drinking crowd with them. The 1950s were witnessing a boom in jazz clubs run by musicians taking it on themselves to find somewhere to play. Across London, scout huts, community halls and the backrooms of pubs rang out with the sounds of Dixieland and ragtime. Now, Brian Rutland had the Eel Pie Island Hotel.

When the band checked out the ballroom, they found it full of broken chairs and tables, and old bedsteads. 'It looked as though it hadn't been used for fifty years,' says Rutland. Snapper made it clear that if the band wanted to play there, it was up to them to clean up the place. The first show was a well-attended and boozy success, and the Island gigs became a weekly event. All was going swimmingly until a couple of months into the residency, when a man approached Rutland and told him that he needed to look for somewhere else to play. This was Arthur Chisnall. Rutland recognised him as someone who'd been at a couple of shows. He stood out because he looked to be at least fifteen years older than everybody else. 'I don't know why he was mixing with us, but he was. Anyway, he suddenly saw an opportunity because everyone was catching on to jazz and it was getting very popular, and so he took over.'

Chisnall was an employee of Michael Snapper and looked after one of his shops in Kingston. He doesn't make the most charming of entrances into the story, elbowing Rutland's band off the Island, but Arthur is no longer around to give his own version of what happened. Still, the result was that Brian Rutland and the Grove Jazz Band left and found themselves a new gig elsewhere. Today, he

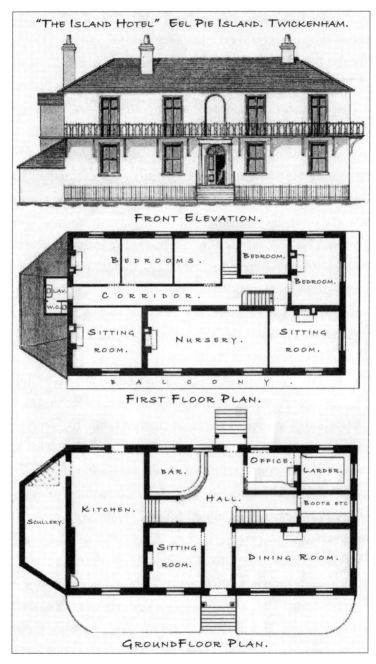

Plans for the Eel Pie Island Hotel as it was originally built in the 1830s, with two floors. At some point before the middle of the 20th century, a third floor was added.

says of the Eel Pie Island Hotel, 'I am convinced if we hadn't gone over there, nothing would ever have happened'.

With the help of friends, Chisnall picked up where Rutland had left off. He replaced the Grove Jazz Band with the Terra Buona Jazz Band. There was no cover charge and no advertising – letters were sent out to student unions at local colleges, but otherwise it was all word of mouth. They expected a few dozen people to turn up but they came in their hundreds. Within weeks, Chisnall had to introduce a door fee to pay the bands who, seeing the size of the crowd, were no longer satisfied with just playing for beer. He also began paying a £3 weekly rent to Snapper. The hordes of teenagers streaming onto the Island to drink and dance quickly met with resistance from local residents. The local police station became involved and told Chisnall that if he wanted to continue he needed to run things in a more orderly fashion. They suggested he set up an official club with registered members.

On Friday 10 August 1956, the official Eelpiland Jazz Club was launched. Members, who paid 2s 6d to join, were issued an Eelpiland Passport, a small folded document printed with the legend: *We request and require in the name of His Excellency PRINCE PAN all those whom it may concern to give the bearer of this passport... any assistance he/she may require in his/her lawful business of jiving and generally cutting a rug.* Pan signed himself 'Prince of Trads' – that's 'trad' as in traditional jazz.

At this distance, it's hard to appreciate how central trad jazz was to late 1950s alternative youth culture. It was born out of a nerdy British passion for the recordings of a select group of early 20th-century musicians, largely from New Orleans, such as Joe 'King' Oliver, Edward 'Kid' Ory and Jelly Roll Morton. In 1950s Britain, rock'n'roll was hogging the mainstream: Bill Haley's 'Shake, Rattle and Roll' had hit the British charts in 1954, and 'Rock Around the

Clock' made number one in November 1955 and again in January 1956. Elvis Presley's 'Heartbreak Hotel' and 'Blue Suede Shoes' were both Top 10 in the UK charts in May 1956. But many saw rock'n'roll as gormless teddy boys gleefully barging grannies off the pavement on the high street. Trad, by comparison, was cool. In the opening scene of the 1959 film *Look Back in Anger*, Richard Burton as 'angry' Jimmy Porter establishes his nonconformist credentials by blowing jazz trumpet in a youth club. Trad attracted a hip and educated audience given to duffle coats, jeans and straggly hair. They were weekend beatniks, spiritually free and footloose, even while catching the No.667 home to mum and dad. Thanks to its significant student fan base, trad inevitably became associated with left-wing politics and anti-establishment movements. With the clarinets and real ale went CND badges and Ban the Bomb posters. Trad bands set the tempo for the anti-nuclear Aldermaston marches when they began at Easter 1958, in which thousands of demonstrators tramped the fifty-two miles from London to the Atomic Weapons Research Establishment in Berkshire. As a result, the national press was determined to link jazz fans with any sort of delinquent behaviour. Two headlines from *The Times* in 1960 – 'Jazz Fan Charged with Burglary' and 'Jazz Fan Charged with Murder' – prompted *Jazz Monthly* to complain it had 'yet to see "Butterfly Fancier Charged with Larceny" or "Stamp Collector Charged with Rape".'

In the late 1950s, Kingston School of Art student John Stephens joined an anti-apartheid march that formed on Twickenham Green.[4] He followed it through the town centre and onto Eel Pie Island, where the band at the head of the march, Ken Colyer's Jazzmen, took to the ballroom stage and played on. Won over by what he heard that day, Stephens became an Island regular. He couldn't have had a better introduction, because when it came to trad, nobody was held in higher esteem than Ken Colyer. He formed one of the first New

Members of Eelpiland were recognised by their passports, issued by His Excellency Prince Pan. There was supposedly no admission without a passport.

Orleans-style bands in the UK, the Crane River Jazz Band, named after the river that ran through Cranford, out near Heathrow, where they rehearsed. In 1952, Colyer had done what no other English jazzman had, which was go to New Orleans and play with some of the Black American musicians revered by British jazzers. According to George Melly, Colyer came back from New Orleans 'like Moses coming down from Mount Sinai with the tablets of the law' and, thereafter, every note he blew was sacred. But Colyer's importance to British music extends far beyond jazz.

At the White Hart pub in Cranford, in the interval between sets by the Crane River Jazz Band, Colyer would bash out American folk songs on a guitar, accompanied by kazoo, washboard and double bass. While he was in New Orleans, two of the former Cranes – clarinettist Monty Sunshine and guitarist/banjo player Tony 'Lonnie' Donegan – along with trombonist Chris Barber (who we'll meet again shortly), went into a studio and during the session recorded a couple of their interval songs and in so doing changed music in Britain forever. Released in December 1955, 'Rock Island Line' and 'John Henry' launched the musical revolution that was skiffle. Easy to play, needing only cheap guitars, washboards and home-made broom-handle basses, it became a nationwide phenomenon. John Lennon and Paul McCartney started out in skiffle bands, as did so many other UK musicians in the next decade. Colyer also holds a significant place in the annals of the Island – on 10 August 1956, his band was the first to play Arthur Chisnall's Eelpiland Jazz Club, kicking off almost a decade and a half of musical history.

At this point, it is worth pausing to describe the Island. It is small: only a third of a mile long and skinny. It sits in the Thames just off Twickenham Embankment, and the river flows around in channels about the width of a four-lane road on either side. With a good arm you could lob a cricket ball across. The hotel sat roughly midway along the Island on its south side, facing Ham Lands on the Surrey bank (Twickenham is in Middlesex and the river is the border between the two counties). In the mid 1950s there were about forty homes, mostly wooden shacks and bungalows, linked by a path that ran along the spine of the Island. Both ends of the Island were covered by woodlands, small wildernesses, supposedly maintained as nature reserves and off-limits. As well as the hotel, there was Brocks Tea Garden on the Ham side, whose guests mostly arrived by boat, and a hut and moorings belonging to the Twickenham Canoe Club. On the Twickenham side were several boatyards, engineering workshops and slipways, and a pontoon for Thames Launches, a pleasure steamer company that had also recently diversified into small-scale shipbuilding.

Schoolboy Robin Hunter lived on the Island as a child between 1953 and 1959, in a wooden house raised on bricks against the flooding to which the eastern end of the Island was susceptible, especially during high spring tides.[5] He remembers it as a cold, damp place during the winter, with a lingering aroma of mud and rotting river plants. The Thames at this time was still an artery for barges, typically filled with coal, wood and rubble, and hauled by tugs with funnels that belched clouds of black smoke. The river's secondary use was for industrial waste disposal. As a consequence, the water was toxic. 'The tidal reaches of the Thames constitute a badly managed open sewer,' The Guardian reported in 1959.[6] Two years earlier, in 1957, the Natural History Museum had declared the Thames to be biologically dead. While on the Island, Hunter developed severe asthma – which quickly cleared up once the family moved away to a house on dry land.

There was also the problem of access. The Island could only be reached by boat, which usually meant the chain ferry on which passengers stood as they were hauled across. Out of ferry hours, or to avoid the tuppence fare, the Hunter family had two small dinghies in which to scoot over to the slipway at the foot of Water Lane, which ran from the Embankment up to the High Street, passing an as yet un-redeveloped bombsite (on 19 June 1944 a German V1 doodlebug hit Water Lane, killing six people).

It took a particular sort of person to appreciate Island life. Eccentric would probably be the word. Robin Hunter recalls one resident, a keen sailor, who would raise and lower the Union Jack each day on the mast he'd erected in his small garden. He remembers another looking like a seedy fairground clown, with hair sticking out below the hat he always wore; he lived in a tumbledown shack with three Great Danes. Roy Buckley, whose family moved onto the Island in 1948, when he was seven years old, remembers a neighbour who was referred to as the 'Countess'; she kept a couple of Samoyeds, large herding dogs with thick, white coats, whose hair she would collect and spin to make scarves and shawls.[7] He also recalls that the most easterly house on the Ham side was occupied by a former dancer from the Folies Bergère in Paris.

The Eel Pie Island Hotel was equally encouraging of eccentricity. Poet and critic John Lucas gives this description of his first visit as a jazz-loving student in 1956: 'We left the pub and walked the few yards to the chain ferry where a long queue had formed, everybody dressed pretty much alike. We crowded onto the ferry and a minute later stepped off it, this time onto the Island, the two of us borne along by fellow revellers. There was a feeling of carnival in the air. The path along which we shuffled was leading us to an old ramshackle hotel that stood on the far side of the Island. It looked shut up and on the verge of collapse, surrounded by the river on one side and, on the other, ragged unkempt bushes and shrubs which might once have formed the hotel's grounds, though they had long since run to seed, like the hotel itself.'[8]

The ballroom was a large barn of a building on the right side of the hotel as you approached from Twickenham. The entrance was on the water-facing side: up a few steps into a lobby, where clubbers showed their passports and paid the entrance fee, then down another short flight into the ballroom itself. Inside was a cavernous space with arches on one side and a long bar on the other. At the far end was a stage, slightly set off to the left. Above it was an odd mezzanine area with windows that overlooked the hall. There was little in the way of decoration, and everything was covered in dust and grime. Trumpeter Mike Peters, of the New Orleans Stompers, remembers there was a glorious arched window looking out on the Thames that had lost most of its glass. One winter evening there was a blizzard blowing outside and the Sandy Brown Band played in overcoats, hats and gloves while snow drifted across the stage.

After Ken Colyer and his band inaugurated the Eelpiland Jazz

Club, they were followed by, among others, George Melly, back on the Island as frontman with the Mick Mulligan Jazz Band, and Sandy Brown, regarded by many as the most original clarinettist of his time, who played the first of many Island gigs in January 1957. A session the following month featured no fewer than three bands: Cy Laurie, Bill Brunskill's Jazzmen and the Alpha Jazzmen. The special triple bill was to celebrate the opening of a footbridge connecting the Island with Twickenham Embankment. Previously, visiting musicians had to cram themselves and their instruments onto the chain ferry. Mike Peters described this as 'a decidedly dodgy affair, like the D-Day landings but without the gunfire'.[9] Trombonist Mel Henry, who played on the Island as part of the University College Jazz Band, recalls their drummer losing some of his kit on the crossing.[10] At the end of the night it was doubly tricky because everyone was drunk and there might be hundreds wanting to get off the Island by way of a vessel that could accommodate no more than a dozen. After 3pm on 9 February, everyone could walk across.

The bridge was commissioned and paid for by Michael Snapper at a cost of £6,000. At the opening, it was blessed by the vicar of nearby St Mary's Church and by a rabbi, after which the local mayor cut a ribbon stretched between the handrails, while Captain LJ Lovell, in command of a Port of London Authority launch, led a small flotilla below the bridge. Eelpilanders danced from Twickenham Green, along the high street and over the bridge to give an impromptu jive session outside the hotel before piling into the ballroom where the three bands all played. The more dignified members of the community toasted the occasion inside the hotel. Arthur Chisnall and Cy Laurie avoided each other.

Chisnall had by now been running his Eelpiland Jazz Club for six months, with sessions every Friday and Saturday night. His success had, it seems, prompted Snapper to approach Cy Laurie,

The Eel Pie Island Hotel viewed from the Ham shore, as it was in the Eelpiland era. The dance hall is the structure with the rounded gable, to the left of the main building.

promoter of his own popular West End jazz club, with a proposition to take over running music at the ballroom. Presumably Snapper thought a more experienced operator might bring in more money and be able to pay more rent. The first Chisnall knew about it was on the Saturday before the bridge opening when a second band turned up unannounced and said they'd been booked by Cy Laurie. During the following week, the two promoters negotiated an agreement: Chisnall would continue to hold sessions on Friday and Saturday nights, and Laurie could have the rest of the week. However, a month later the local newspapers were reporting that Laurie's midweek sessions were drawing audiences in single figures. He accused Chisnall of waging a campaign against him in Twickenham, persuading regulars not to turn up. It was probably true. It certainly worked because Laurie stopped booking bands for the Island. Relations were evidently patched up at some point because the clarinettist was back appearing with his own band on the Island in 1959 and 1960. By this time word had gotten round that the hotel was a top place for trad. Ken Colyer came back regularly, even recording a live album on the Island in May 1957, and there were appearances from scene leaders Kenny Ball, Acker Bilk, Terry Lightfoot and the goonishly retro Temperance Seven, all of whom would become household names within the next couple of years, all scoring hits in the UK singles chart. Not that this would necessarily turn out to be a good thing – trad's foray into family favourites territory would result in younger fans deserting it in en masse. As Humphrey Lyttelton later reflected, 'The worst thing that ever happened to jazz was when it suddenly invaded the pop field. It was like a rabbit invading a python.'[11]

But that was years in the future. Back at the Eelpiland Jazz Club, in 1958, the Riverside Jazzmen, led by local clarinettist Alan Cresswell, of East Sheen, asked if they could play on Sunday, a night that the ballroom wasn't being used.[12] Chisnall said he couldn't pay them but he wouldn't charge them for using the hall. The band began by treating it as a fun rehearsal session until, over the weeks, the audience grew and Chisnall started charging on the door – as he did on Fridays and Saturdays – out of which he now paid the band what Cresswell remembers as a fair wage. Because they were local and reliable, Chisnall also had the band play interval slots on other nights for some of the bigger name artists. According to Cresswell, the Riversiders kept a regular weekly slot, either on a Sunday or Wednesday, right through until early 1963, which means that they probably played the Island on more occasions than any other band.

Cresswell remembers turning up one weekend to find a new addition to the dance hall: adorning the wall behind the stage was a huge mural, a colourful and cartoonish depiction of six winkle-picker-wearing jazzers (clarinet, double bass, trumpet, drums, banjo and trombone). Created by eighteen-year-old Paul Harris, a former Kingston School of Art student, the mural immediately became part of the visual identity of Eelpiland. Cresswell also recalls the long bar, presided over by Jack Marrs who, in contrast to the crowd, was always suited and who kept a neat goatee beard. He served Flowers bitter and Watney's Special out of a row of a dozen barrels, and the area around the bar was always slopping with beer. But what Cresswell remembers most – what everyone remembers most – is the dance floor. It was sprung: laid on woven wooden battens so, like a taut drum skin, it would give dancers an extra spring in their step. Except the floor was never meant for the wildly exuberant skip jiving and stomping they went in for on the Island. As an army of feet pounded the floor in time with the music it would buck up and down like a giant trampoline. 'You felt like the floor was going to collapse and we were all going to go into the river,' said John Stephens, a club regular from the 1950s.[13] Just walking across the room while the band was playing was like being on deck in stormy seas – it was impossible to make it from the bar to the other side of the room with a full pint.

The audiences weren't as big as they would become later, so there was plenty of room for dancers to show off. Enthusiasts had their own favourite spots. Boys without girls danced by the arches, couples in the middle. Regulars knew which parts of the floor bounced most and monopolised them. John Lucas conjures up nights at Eelpiland in *Next Year Will Be Better*, his memoir of life in England in the Fifties: 'At one point in the evening I wandered over to the far side of the rackety old ballroom, my back to the whirl of bodies, the jeans and check shirts, dirndl skirts, flying beads and pony tails, and looked from a smeared window as light faded above the elms and, below, the Thames, glistening in oblongs of light cast by the hotel, made its way toward London. Behind me, the sprung

Eelpiland stalwarts, the Riverside Jazzmen, with band leader Alan Cresswell, far right.
Behind them is the mural painted by Kingston School of Art student Paul Harris.

floor shook and thumped to a number that may have been "Muskrat
Ramble". New Orleans on Thames, I thought.' Ken Colyer once said
something similar about the Island to his band: 'This is as close as
you will get to New Orleans in England, the atmosphere and the
feel is here,' he told them. 'I have never experienced it as strongly
anywhere else.'[14]

There were occasional experiments with types of music other
than trad jazz. Chisnall booked a few modern jazz acts, although
this was never likely to please because of the antagonisms between
the traddies, with their gospel of New Orleans, and their arch-
enemies, the moderns. The sharply dressed moderns, or modernists,
soberly tapped their toes and chin-stroked to the free-form bebop
of improvisers like Charlie Mingus and Charlie Parker. As the *Daily
Mirror* explained, 'Mod enthusiasts are usually in their 20s and do a
job of some kind'[15] – as opposed to trads, who were more likely to

be students. 'Trads mostly look on Mods as a lot of slickly dressed phoneys pretending to get intellectual pleasure where none exists.' As with the rift between traddies and rock'n'rollers, this one was driven by social status as much as musical tastes. It was more of a working-class thing to like modern jazz, while jiving to trad was a very middle-class form of rebellion. Chisnall booked saxophonist Bruce Turner, who when he appeared with Humphrey Lyttelton at Birmingham Town Hall was famously greeted with a sign reading, 'Go home, dirty bopper'. It's likely the reception probably wasn't much warmer on Eel Pie Island, which although draped in rebellion and bohemianism was middle class to the core.

Other musical experimentation included at least one booking for Diz Disley, who was a short and gleeful Welsh-Canadian guitarist in the Django Reinhardt tradition, and who George Melly described as having 'the face of a satyr, en route to a cheerful orgy'. Melly also recalled Disley had a 'built-in anti-success mechanism', turning up at gigs without his guitar and missing deadlines (he was a professional cartoonist) because he was in a jail cell. Skiffle, the bastard child of traditional jazz, also featured at Eelpiland in the early days, but – true to its origins – it was almost always as an interval act.

According to a *Twickenham Tatler* article, in July 1961 Eelpiland membership stood at 8,500, with many more names on the waiting list. This made it one of the biggest jazz clubs in the country, according to the report. Parents of one girl, the article said, admitted to feeling somewhat bewildered by the fashion and musical tastes of their young daughter but conceded that they respected her judgment in these matters. The man behind the club, said the article, referring to Arthur Chisnall, was 'slightly bewildered at the success of something that started life as a personal affair'. So who exactly was this bewildered individual?

DOW
AMONC
TH
DEAD-
BEATS

CHAPTER 2

THE EEL PIED PIPER

A jazz club for social deviants and a laboratory for psychological research – and all bad press is welcome

WHEN THE POET-CRITIC JOHN LUCAS VISITED EELPILAND IN 1956, working the door was a taciturn man with a pipe protruding from his heavily bearded face, dressed in a ragged blue sweater, equally worn grey trousers and open-toed sandals. He collected the entrance fee and rubber-stamped wrists.[1] While he wasn't effusively welcoming, he seemed benign enough. This was Arthur Chisnall, the Eel Pied Piper.

James Arthur White Chisnall was born on 3 June 1925 at 33 Birkenhead Avenue, in Kingston upon Thames in Surrey. He never knew who his father was, but memories of his mum sending him to a neighbourhood shop with notes (and telling him to keep hold of them if the grocer's wife was there) led him to believe it might have been the guy who stocked their larder. He left school at fourteen and worked in the carpet department of a Kingston department

FACING: A pair of Eelpiland ravers photographed at the club in September 1960 by Peter Hall, and published in a controversial story in *Weekend* magazine.

store before joining the Royal Engineers in 1942. He was posted to North Africa, where he took part in Operation Bertram, creating dummy tanks and gun batteries in the desert to hoodwink German army intelligence in the run up to the Battle of El Alamein. After the war, he returned to Africa in the employ of the British government, part of an ultimately failed attempt to cultivate peanuts in colonial Tanganyika, intended to solve cooking oil shortages back in the UK.

In 1951, back in England, Chisnall managed to secure a hardship bursary for a year's residential study at Coleg Harlech, a progressive adult-education college in North Wales. He took a course in social science, then headed back to Kingston, where he found work in a shop owned by Michael Snapper – not Snapper's Corner but another, smaller junk shop on Richmond Road. At Harlech, Chisnall's classes would almost certainly have included discussion of a new and puzzling creature: the teenager. The classes would have examined the concept that defined a generation of post-war social commentary, that of the 'alienation' of these teenagers from their parents and society at large. This obviously chimed with Chisnall, who decided to set up a youth club, where he could put what he learned at college into practice. Plenty of teenagers from the local art school used to come into his junk shop to buy secondhand jazz records, so the club had to have music. His employer happened to own the perfect venue in the hotel on Eel Pie Island.

There is an eight-page document among Arthur Chisnall's papers, now kept at the Eel Pie Island Museum in Twickenham, titled 'A Therapeutic Jazz Club in England'. It's a draft of an article by American psychologists Charles and Mariann Winick.[2] Charles was a pioneer in the study of drug addiction, and at the 1957 Newport Jazz Festival he organised one of the first public forums to discuss drug use among jazz musicians, with Dizzy Gillespie and Duke Ellington as panelists. The therapeutic jazz club discussed in the paper is Arthur Chisnall's Eelpiland, which during the course of its eleven-year lifespan was considered so revolutionary that it attracted the interest of respected New York-based academics and was discussed in the *International Journal of Social Psychiatry*.

For Chisnall, the jazz element at Eelpiland was secondary. It was a lure to attract the kids, along with a secluded location, a bar and a lack of authority figures. Chisnall's idea was to pack Eelpiland with the well-educated, middle-class youth of Richmond and Twickenham ('high communicators' in the parlance of the Winicks), and introduce among them a number of less fortunate kids ('low communicators'). Door staff would regulate the intake, making sure there were never too many 'low communicators' in the club on any given evening.

Get past the psychobabble and the whiff of snobbery, and it sounds like a sensible way of avoiding trouble. Don Hughes's *Friday On My Mind*, his account of growing up a Mod in nearby Hounslow, makes clear how easily violence could flare up in clubs, which were often flashpoints for local turf wars between groups of rockers, Teds and Mods. There was a no-gangs rule at Eelpiland, enforced by security that was low-key but muscular enough to ensure the policy could be enforced if necessary.

Chisnall ran the door himself, at least in the early days. It was a way of seeing who was turning up. He was particularly attuned to anyone who looked like they might be a runaway, a dropout or a misfit – a kid with problems. His intentions were to help them reorient their lives. His methods were ad hoc and unorthodox, possibly ill advised. He turned his own home into a refuge. Roger Sharp was about sixteen when his father kicked him out of the family home in Isleworth. He was wandering along when a grey minivan pulled over to the kerb. It was Arthur Chisnall. He recognised Sharp from the club and asked him where he was going, and if he needed a

Pipe-smoking Arthur Chisnall, photographed during his Eelpiland days. Despite running a hugely popular jazz club, his interests lay with social-working rather than music.

lift. Which is how Sharp ended up sleeping on the sofa at Chisnall's flat at 293 Sheen Road, on the borders of Richmond and East Sheen. The flat had a spare bedroom but that was already taken by Tony Watts, who was the banjo player with the Riverside Jazzmen, and his girlfriend Susie Shahn (the daughter of American artist Ben Shahn). According to Sharp, Chisnall never took any money from his lodgers, but he didn't like them to loaf around, either. Watts paid his way by working as a handyman and general assistant at

Eelpiland, while Shahn worked in the cloakroom. 'Having escaped from my brutal father, I thought living with Arthur was great,' says Sharp. 'He was generous but he never made you feel that you were a recipient of charity.'

Jack Lambert was another lodger. Raised by an alcoholic mother in Hampton, he left school at fifteen with no qualifications and began working as a messenger boy at Waterloo Station. One day in Twickenham, he saw a jazz band parading down the high street en route to Eel Pie Island and he followed them. 'I don't remember when I became aware of Arthur,' Lambert recalled, 'or when he became aware of me, but I do remember him not taking money from me to get in and asking me if I would stand by the door to check for stamps on people's wrists.'[3]

By this time Chisnall had bought a spacious three-storey house at 31 Waldegrave Gardens in Strawberry Hill. He invited Lambert to move in. Were times more innocent then? Perhaps in the Sixties there was nothing strange in a single man in his thirties inviting vulnerable teenagers to come and live with him. Sharp, and others who were 'rehomed' at Waldegrave Gardens, are adamant that Arthur had no sexual interest in any of his lodgers. He was hands-off in every respect. Despite spending several years living under his roof, Sharp says Chisnall was an elusive person even in his own home. 'Arthur never vouchsafed any details about himself and he couldn't handle anything that was too emotionally involving. He spent hours in the bath, smoking his pipe. He liked a single malt and he relaxed a bit if he had a drink. But he was remote.'

Chisnall occupied just two of the rooms in the house, using one as a bedroom, another as an office. 'He had no possessions except for a change of socks, a car and – an extravagance for him – two telephone lines,' says Lambert. 'He didn't see it as a home but… as a sort of halfway house for Islanders in need of somewhere to park.'

Other bedrooms accommodated a regularly changing procession of needy lodgers. These included Ian Armit, his wife and their two baby girls. Armit was a pianist who played with Humphrey Lyttelton, Alexis Korner and Long John Baldry, but his wife had serious mental issues that overshadowed Armit's musical career. Another lodger, Louis, believed he was Van Gogh and painted in such thick impasto that someone who bought one of his works claimed forty years later that it had only just dried. Arthur Buss was one of the last of the long-distance tramps who roamed the country pushing a rusty old pram full of junk: he'd show up at Waldegrave Gardens every year when it started to get cold and settle in for the winter. 'He used to say, "All you need in life is a topper hat and a wallet full of money",' says Roger Sharp, who shared a tiny room in an extension at the back of the house with his girlfriend, Wendy.

According to Sharp the people offered shelter at Waldegrave Gardens were 'all buggered up, couldn't get on with life', which occasionally brought turmoil to the house but was rarely dull. Sharp remembers a couple Chisnall brought in from Soho, who were addicted to amphetamines and moved in with a bag full of pills. They knew Quentin Crisp and invited him for dinner. 'He turned up in this lilac mohair jumper and multicoloured fedora,' says Sharp. 'I'd made baked potatoes. He picked his up and said, "Oh, a potato. Do you know I haven't eaten a potato since the end of the Second World War." He was living on Complan protein drinks.'

Jack Lambert thought that most of the residents at Waldegrave Gardens probably should have been either in rehab or receiving psychiatric care. He recalled one of the lodgers assaulted Chisnall. It didn't deter him and he continued to do things his own way. 'He never lost his cool,' says Lambert. 'His self-discipline was remarkable.'

As well as providing a refuge, Chisnall sent some of his wards back to school. Coleg Harlech had been a turning point in his own

Chisnall bustles through Eelpiland, where he plucked out the alienated and under-achieving and, through his contacts, helped them into education or employment.

life, and he was keen to provide the same experience for others. With money raised from raffles and events at Eelpiland, Chisnall provided funding for the education of around twenty Eelpilanders. Jack Lambert was one beneficiary, Roger Sharp another. Lambert eventually decided he wasn't suited to academia and dropped out. Not sure what to do next, he applied for a job at a children's playground and was offered the position. It proved a good fit and over the next decade Lambert became an authority on adventure playground design, co-writing the first noted book on the subject, published in 1974. By this point, he no longer lived at Waldegrave Gardens, but his affection for Chisnall never dimmed. 'Arthur was a kind of father figure to me,' he said.

Another success story involved a young man called Neale Pharoah. As a teenager he'd been thrown out of the family home by his abusive father. He inhabited a series of bedsits, flitting between dead-end jobs, sponging off girlfriends and shoplifting, until he was caught trying to cash a bogus cheque and given three months in a detention centre. On his release, Pharoah was taken in by Chisnall, who somehow wangled him a place at Ealing Technical College. Chisnall also suggested Pharoah write about his experiences. The result was an article, entitled 'The Long Blunt Shock', which ran in *New Society* magazine in September 1963. Pharoah wrote a follow-up about casual drug use, 'He Gets Out of It', published in February 1964. The articles led to an invitation to appear on a BBC radio programme. The BBC interviewer, Wilfred De'Ath, later turned their conversations into a book, published in 1966 as *Just Me and Nobody Else*. The publisher proclaimed the book to be, 'A vivid and vital clue to the understanding of a generation now on the threshold of manhood.'

Chisnall's knack for fostering such opportunities was rooted in his talents as a networker. Although reserved on a personal level, he saw it as part of his mission to cultivate relationships with influential people, such as politicians and members of the clergy, some of whom he persuaded to visit his club. One of these people was Leslie Wilkins, then deputy director of the government's Home Office Research Unit. Wilkins was a statistician and criminologist, and an early proponent of the idea that criminalisation of drug use would only benefit organised crime. Chisnall managed to interest him in his Eelpiland experiment. In a subsequent memoir Wilkins would write, 'Arthur would have been accepted today as an imaginative "outworker" and probably also accepted by legitimate social work authorities. He was ahead of his time, outworkers had not been invented, or perhaps they were his invention.'[4]

Wilkins was introduced to Chisnall by Gordon Pask, an occasional visitor to the Island. Pask was a polymath and cybernetics pioneer – and much more. According to an obituary (he died in 1996), his research spanned biological computing, artificial intelligence, cognitive science, logic, linguistics, psychology and artificial life.[5] His work was sponsored by governments and industries on both sides of the Atlantic, but also extended to a collaboration with fringe theatre producer Joan Littlewood and radical architect Cedric Price (on a fantastical but never realised project called the Fun Palace). In the 1960s, Pask's non-profit Systems Research Ltd was operating out of rooms above a launderette on Hill Rise in Richmond. Chisnall sent his lodger Roger Sharp over to the offices, where he was put to work on collating performance data for the US Air Force. Chris Whitehouse (now known as Weed) was another Systems Research employee around this time. What he remembers most is Pask's eccentricity: 'His belief in fairies, his professed fear of the man-eating woodlice which lurked in nearby Richmond Park, and the vast number of rituals that had to be performed (regardless of the company he was in) to placate the former and ward off the latter.'[6] Pask gathered many of the subjects for his psychological experiments from L'Auberge, the cafe at the bottom of Hill Rise, and the Eelpiland Jazz Club.[7] Chisnall was happy to open his club to researchers: his members were also interviewed for Michael Schofield's report *The Sexual Behaviour of Young People*, published in 1965.

While he mingled with interesting and influential people, Chisnall's informal brand of social experimentation seems to have been conducted without official recognition or support. There is nothing in his papers that indicates the involvement of the local council or government, or of any charitable or religious body.

As Eelpiland approached its fifth anniversary, in June 1961, *News of the World* ran a story on the club.[8] The reporter was given the job of stamping wrists at the door while chatting to Arthur, who was taking the money. 'You must realise that what goes on in this place is the latent desire among the young to get away from regimentation,' says Chisnall. 'Then what am I stamping their wrists for?' replies the smart-alecky journalist. 'Here was a side of the jazz cult not generally known,' reads the article, noting that Eelpilanders included budding architects, accountants, doctors, engineers and students, and that these youngsters 'all seemed highly intelligent'. That night, along with the jazz, the newspaper reports, there was to be an address by John Stonehouse, Labour MP, on Africa (the Stonehouse who would unsuccessfully fake his own death in 1974 and be exposed as a spy in the pay of Soviet Czechoslovakia). June Lawson, a trainee fashion designer from North Wembley and veteran of Ban the Bomb marches is quoted explaining how young people differ from their parents: 'We're rebels,' she says.

For every positive media story about Eelpiland, there was another that delighted in portraying the club as a den of sordidness in the suburbs. Step forward *Weekend* magazine, source of a lazy and lurid piece titled 'Down Among the Dead-beats', which ran in September 1960. 'Elephants wash. Pigeons wash. Flies wash. Cats wash,' it begins. 'But not THESE cats.' It continues: 'When the Saints Come Marching in, will they reek of oakum and armpits? Will they have hair like spun yarn, beards like spinach, and eyes like rissoles in the snow?' But it was the line 'jazz played by hep musicians who are often doped to the eyebrows', accompanied by a photo of Alan Cresswell's Riverside Jazzmen, that had the band's agent instructing the solicitors Guillaume & Sons of Salisbury Square, EC4, to threaten legal action against Associated Newspapers unless an apology and damages were forthcoming. There was more trouble. The full-page splash photo that led the article was of two 'Beat' girls leaning against the wall, one with a bare midriff, hip cocked, coolly

Happy dancing 'dead-beats' in an image from the *Weekend* magazine article that led to sackings, legal threats and questions in the House of Commons.

eyeing the photographer; the art desk had touched in their eyes with white to give them a demonic flash. Another photo showed couples necking in the grass. Two clubbers reportedly lost their jobs as a result.[9] Chisnall wrote letters of complaint and managed to get the issue brought before Parliament by the left-wing MP for Salford East, Frank Allaun.

In the weeks following the *Weekend* article, more newspaper coverage followed. Most amusing of the lot was a sketch by playwright, columnist and Twickenham Riverside resident Jeremy Sandford that ran in the *Observer*.[10] In it, he visits the club and chats to some of the regulars, including someone named Ray: "'They had some pictures of this place in the papers," said Ray. "It was very sad really. Next day we were besieged by businessmen. Left their Bentleys on the shore, you know, and their chauffeurs. With neatly furled umbrellas. Queuing in the bushes."

"What were they queuing for?"

"Dunno. Some of the pictures were, you know, luscious. Neckin' in the bushes."

"Did they get in?"

"Don't suppose so.'"

Chisnall always denied that Eelpiland encouraged these arboreal fumblings, which was a bit rich given he issued membership passports in the name of Pan, horny god of the wild, consort of frisky nymphs and satyrs. Talking about the Island, jazz singer George Melly reckoned you could 'almost see the sex rising – like steam from a kettle'. It was very difficult not to get laid on Eel Pie Island, he told BBC Radio 4 in 2006. John Lucas, meanwhile, recalls the giggling and grunts coming from the bushes, 'audible evidence of what were known as knee-tremblers'.[11] In *A Hero for High Times*, Bob Rowberry, the man who first sold acid to RD Laing, who stole jewellery from Joni Mitchell and who owned the cat after which Procol Harum were named, says he had sex with a girl in a pile of coats at Eelpiland – and who wouldn't believe him, given that this is one of the least outlandish claims he makes in the book.

There were also probably drugs around, but nothing too heavy at this stage. Lucas mentions that the evening air around the hotel was heavy with the scent of hash. But Chisnall was skilled at walking the line between rebellion and criminality. If he or his helpers caught anyone with a joint inside the club, they were told to take it outside. On at least one occasion, when one of the club's doormen identified an undercover policeman lurking among the punters queuing to get in, Chisnall introduced himself and made a point of inviting the copper to have a good look around. The police would always leave disappointed at the lack of customers for the charge room.

As for the negative press, that was part of the plan. Every time a newspaper stoked outrage over the supposed sex, drugs and wickedness on the Twickenham island, hordes of kids would show up looking for a piece of the action. Among these fresh arrivals, inevitably, would be a smattering of the lost boys and girls Chisnall had set up the club to help. In this way, in the words of John Lucas, he made Eelpiland 'one of the great, good places of the Earth'.

JAZZ

SATURDAY 10 AUGUST

TUBBY HAYES QUINTET · JOE HARRIOTT QUINTET · RONNIE ROSS QUARTET with BILL SAGE · JOHN WILLIAMS BIG BAND
2—5.30 pm   Admission 5/-

CHRIS BARBER'S JAZZ BAND · OTTILIE PATTERSON · ALEX WELSH BAND · HUMPHREY LYTTELTON BAND · DILL JONES TRIO · RUSTIX · GINGER JOHNSON'S AFRICAN DRUMS plus 'Rhythm and Blues' with GRAHAM BOND QUARTET · GEORGIE FAME GROUP and Liverpool's 'MASTERSOUNDS'
6.30—11.30 pm   Admission 10/-   All-day ticket 12/6

SUNDAY 11 AUGUST

NATIONAL AMATEUR JAZZ CONTEST—Final Heats and Awards
12 WINNING BANDS FROM SEMI-FINALS HELD ALL OVER BRITAIN Judges: Humphrey Lyttelton, Chris Barber and Joe Harriott (Sponsored by CARRERAS makers of GUARDS Cigarettes)
2—5.30 pm   Admission 5/-

ACKER BILK'S PARAMOUNT JAZZ BAND · TERRY LIGHTFOOT'S JAZZMEN · FREDDY RANDALL BAND · BLUE NOTE JAZZ BAND CYRIL DAVIES' 'Rhythm and Blues' ALL STARS · LONG JOHN BALDRY · THE ROLLING STONES · THE VELVETTES
6.30—11.30 pm   Admission 10/-   Week-end ticket 20/-

3rd NATIONAL JAZZ FESTIVAL

Sponsored by The **EVENING NEWS & STAR**

At the beautiful grounds of the Athletic Association

RICHMOND

SURREY. TRAVEL BY BUS, TRAIN OR TUBE. FREE CAR PARK
30 MINUTES FROM THE WEST END BY UNDERGROUND

TICKETS NOW AVAILABLE FROM N.J.F BOX OFFICE, 18 Carlisle Street, W.1
KEITH PROWSE, 90 New Bond Street, W.1 (HYD. 9000), Branches and Agents

MARQUEES · REFRESHMENTS · CLUB HOUSE · LICENSED BARS

VAIL & CO. LTD. LEEKE STREET, W.C.1   TER 2548

CHAPTER 3

A GARDEN PARTY IN RICHMOND

The birth of UK festival culture and the blossoming of R&B, and what a Lancashire accountant had to do with it

O N A MARCH EVENING IN 2015, heritage guide and music buff Alan Sherriff gave a talk to Richmond's local history society. His subject was the impact of the National Jazz & Blues Festivals that were held at the Richmond Athletic Association Grounds from 1961 to 1965. Largely forgotten by all but a handful of nostalgists, these were some of the first popular outdoor music festivals to be held in Britain, early forays into the fields with instruments, amps and lighting rigs. They set live music off on a path that would tramp its muddy way to the Isle of Wight, Hyde Park, Glastonbury and beyond. The Richmond festivals began as a showcase for trad jazz but rapidly evolved to embrace blues and rock, so that over the five years the likes of Ken Colyer's Jazzmen and the Tubby Hayes Quintet gave way to the Rolling Stones, Yardbirds and the Who. By the time of the fourth festival, BBC cameras were present, and performances from the fifth festival were broadcast live on Radio Luxembourg and captured in colour for American TV. Fans travelled to Richmond from all over the country. Sherriff told his audience that, as a teenager, he came down from Newcastle specially for the 1965 festival, joining an audience that (briefly) included half of the Beatles, to see a line-up of Long John Baldry, Julie Driscoll, Rod Stewart, Jimmy James and the Vagabonds, Spencer Davis and the Animals, among others.

People who make up the membership of local history societies tend to have experienced a bit of history themselves. It's not surprising that in the Q&A session that followed the talk the first three people to put their hands up to speak had attended the festivals. One gent had even performed on stage. He didn't have a question, instead he wanted to pay tribute to the man who had founded the festival more than half a century earlier, Harold Pendleton. The mic then passed to a man who was obviously too young to have been around back then, who stood to say, 'My name's Nick Pendleton. And just to say Harold Pendleton's sitting here right next to me.'[1]

It's telling that the man who not only has a strong claim to launching the UK's multimillion-pound music festival industry, but who also founded the world's most famous music venue (the Marquee, which gave the Rolling Stones their first gig, hosted the residency that propelled the Who to fame, and staged early shows by Jimi Hendrix, David Bowie, Led Zeppelin, Elton John, Pink Floyd, Queen, the Police, the Jam and the Sex Pistols, among others), a man who music manager and author Simon Napier-Bell has called 'one of the most important people in the history of British rock', should go unnoticed at an event celebrating his achievements.[2]

The unassuming Harold Pendleton was born in Southport, Lancashire (now Merseyside), on 17 June 1924. His parents, George and Ada, owned a chain of bakery shops. George was a fan of western films, an enthusiasm that he passed to his son, sparking a lifelong interest in American culture, and particularly jazz. Southport is just up the coast from Liverpool, then a port teeming with transatlantic shipping. The Pendletons had friends who were merchant sailors and a young Harold would ask them to bring him jazz records from America. George wanted to make sure Harold had a proper profession, so he had him articled as an accountant. What Harold wanted, however, was not to be found on the Lancashire coast and, at the age of twenty-four, he quit Southport for London. Arriving at Euston Station, so the story goes, he boarded a bus for the West End and asked to be dropped off 'where the action is'. The conductor suggested Soho, so Harold hopped off at the top of Charing Cross Road, where he found his way to Dobell's jazz record shop. There was one other customer flicking through the stock and Harold asked him if he knew any good jazz clubs; he did and he was going to one that night if Harold wanted to come along – this was Chris Barber, a trainee actuary, soon to become the leader of one of the UK's most popular jazz bands. Barber would become a lifelong friend and collaborator, and Pendleton would later manage his band.

As well as being music fanatics, both were businesslike men in the generally shambolic world of jazz. While holding down day jobs, they began promoting jazz nights at clubs around the West End, including at the basement Creole Club on Gerrard Street in Chinatown. (A few years later, Ronnie Scott would open the first iteration of his eponymous jazz club in the basement of another Gerrard Street address.) With Barber's support, Pendleton became treasurer of the National Federation of Jazz Organisations of Great Britain, formed in 1948 to promote jazz around the country. Within a short space of time, frustrated that a steering committee split between traddies and modernists did nothing but squabble itself into inertia, Pendleton managed to have himself voted chairman.

Harold Pendleton, who trained as an accountant in Lancashire before his love of jazz led him to London, where he took over the presidency of the National Jazz Federation.

He gave up the day job in the City to run what was renamed the National Jazz Federation (NJF). The work involved promoting concerts and editing the weekly *Jazz News* magazine from offices at 18 Carlisle Street in Soho. Although the NJF's remit was to support jazz in the UK, the best musicians were in America, and so it made sense to Pendleton to bring those musicians over so their UK counterparts could learn from them. In this he was bamboozled by the protectionist approach of Britain's Musicians' Union, which banned foreign artists from performing in the UK and thereby, in its view, taking gigs away from home-grown talent. When Pendleton attempted to bring over brilliant New Orleans clarinettist Sidney Bechet, the union blocked him on the grounds that Britain had no shortage of clarinet players. Pendleton's way around the restrictions was to bring over 'singers', a category of artist that fell outside the union's rulings. Which is how blues pianist Memphis Slim and gospel singer and guitarist Sister Rosetta Tharpe were able to tour England. Later, Pendleton and Barber were also able to bring over a number of African-American blues artists, notably Muddy Waters and Howlin' Wolf, to play landmark concerts that would inspire a generation of British musicians.

In 1958, Pendleton was approached by the owners of the Academy Cinema on Oxford Street who were losing money running a failing jazz club in the basement: would he be interested in taking it over? The space in question was known as the Marquee ballroom, so called because of its circus tent decor, which had been created by photographer and designer Angus McBean (now best remembered for shooting the cover of the Beatles' debut LP *Please Please Me*). As it happened, Pendleton was on the lookout for somewhere to start a new jazz club, and so on Saturday 19 April 1958 the first 'Jazz at the Marquee' event launched with Jamaican-born alto saxophonist Joe Harriott. To begin with, the club ran only at weekends, but Pendleton and Barber kept expanding the bill until there were bands seven nights a week. Barber himself had a regular Wednesday slot with his band – a guaranteed full house after 1959 when their cover of Sidney Bechet's 'Petite Fleur' was released as a single and sold more than a million copies. One feature of the Marquee's programme that was revolutionary at the time was to present both trad and modern jazz; leading British modernists the Johnny Dankworth Orchestra were given a Sunday night spot.

It was largely due to Barber's influence that the Marquee became the West End stronghold of the fledgling British rhythm and blues movement. It was a former member of Barber's jazz band, guitarist Alexis Korner, who established the country's first regular R&B night, in March 1962, out in Ealing. Within weeks, with Barber's encouragement, Pendleton gave Korner and his band, Blues Incorporated, a Thursday night residency at the Marquee – Thursday being the worst night of the week because it was just before payday. For the first R&B night at the Marquee the whole of the Ealing Club made an expedition to Oxford Street, which in terms of numbers was still only a fraction of what the Marquee could hold. At this point, R&B was a one-band movement with few fans and little in the way of public recognition, yet within eighteen months it would ambush trad jazz, and boot it from the mainstream and into the realm of 'specialist interest'.

The revolution began at the Marquee. In July, Korner's band was invited to make an appearance on BBC Radio's *Jazz Club* programme. This clashed with their engagement at the Marquee, so Korner asked one of Blues Incorporated's two regular vocalists, Long John Baldry, to do the club gig. He also made a call to a young slide guitarist who had been showing up at the Ealing Club to jam with the band. His name was Brian Jones, and Korner asked if he could get together a few regulars from the Ealing Club and make up a support band. Jones obliged by roping in sixth-form student Mick Jagger and part-time postman Keith Richards, along with piano-playing shipping clerk Ian Stewart, Richards' art-school friend Dick Taylor on bass and possibly Tony Chapman on drums.[3] Jones gave the impromptu group the name the Rollin' Stones, after a Muddy Waters track. On 12 July 1962, the Stones made their debut at the Marquee. They played several more support slots at the club that summer before being sacked by Pendleton, supposedly for not being 'authentic' enough – although Christopher Sandford's *The Rolling Stones: Fifty Years* says that the falling out came when Pendleton referred to the band as 'greasers' within hearing of Keith Richards, who took a swing at him and got the band barred from the club.

That was 1962. For the beginnings of Harold Pendleton's involvement with the Richmond Athletic Association Grounds, we need to rewind several years. In 1956, jazz fan Edward John Barrington Douglas-Scott-Montagu, otherwise known as Lord Montagu, decided he wanted to hold a music festival in the grounds of the chateau-like family home at Beaulieu, on the edge of the New Forest in Hampshire. His inspiration was probably the Newport Jazz Festival, which had debuted on Rhode Island in the US two years earlier. He approached Pendleton, in his role as chairman of the National Jazz Federation, for help and together they launched the Beaulieu Jazz Festival. But then they fell out and Pendleton withdrew his support. Montagu went solo and held a second festival the following year.

Pendleton had stepped away because he had issues with how the event was run. His misgivings were borne out in 1960 when that year's festival was the occasion for what the press delighted in calling the 'Beaulieu Riots'. What exactly happened that July day is disputed but it resulted in twenty ambulances and five fire engines tearing across the baize-like lawns of the stately home.[4]

The trouble started during the headline set by Acker Bilk. When we last encountered him, the Somerset-born clarinettist was playing student parties on Eel Pie Island. Since then, he'd been given a makeover that dressed him in the Edwardian campery of waistcoat, bowler hat and goatee, along with marketing campaigns that insisted on addressing him as 'Mr Acker Bilk' and silly advertising slogans, such as 'An Acker a Day Keeps the Bopper Away'. He was now an unlikely proto-pop star, with chart-topping singles and legions of nutty fans uniformed in army boots, fur coats – or in some cases fur loincloths – and bowler hats daubed with Bilk's name. At Beaulieu, Bilk arrived at the stage in a Model T Ford, courtesy of the Beaulieu Motor Museum. As he played, a stage invader managed to clamber up the lighting gantry behind the band, inspiring others to follow his lead. A small army crashed onto the stage, smashing up gear and climbing the rigging. Someone grabbed a microphone and demanded 'free beer for the working man'. Elsewhere, someone set fire to a building. The BBC, which was broadcasting the event live on television, abruptly ended its coverage with an anxious, 'Things are getting quite out of hand'. A reported thirty-nine people were injured, three of them seriously. Two were subsequently jailed for assaulting police officers.

Some said the fracas was incited by bearded trad fans taking on modern jazzers. Others claimed it was nothing to do with music and it was started by working-class yobs up from Portsmouth and Southampton. Whatever the cause, the incident was met with outrage in the pages of the *Bradford Telegraph and Argus*: 'The near riot at the Beaulieu Jazz Festival on Saturday... was a disgraceful affair. There are those who criticise Africans and who say that such people will never be fit to govern themselves. But a tribal dance to the sound of a tom-tom has a more civilised air than this modern wreck and roll to the beat of the jazz drum.'[5] Sunday paper *The People* was more specific in identifying the culprits: 'Blame these 4 Men for the Beatnik horror – their cult of despair is driving the teenagers to violence,' it told its readers, accompanying the piece with large mugshots of American Beat figureheads Jack 'the Hobos' Prophet' Kerouac, Allen 'the Hate Merchant' Ginsberg, William 'the Ex-Drug Addict' Burroughs and Gregory 'the Crank Poet' Corso.

Harold Pendleton blamed the organisers. To provide TV cameras with an unobstructed view, the paying audience was held well back

At the 1960 Beaulieu Festival, a performance by Acker Bilk was interupted when fans ran riot, invading the stage, climbing the lighting rigging and generally causing mayhem.

from the stage but only by a single rope. During Acker Bilk's set the crowd surged, the rope gave and there was a rush forward. Because the stage wasn't raised, the momentum from behind sent those at the front barrelling into the band and its gear. Despite the mayhem, Lord Montagu was game enough to go ahead with a sixth Beaulieu festival the following year. This time, alongside genuine jazz fans there was an element that turned up in anticipation of another ruckus, and they made sure they got one. In the aftermath, the disillusioned peer of the realm told the *Daily Mail*, 'There will never again be a jazz festival at Beaulieu.'

There was some good to come out of the final Beaulieu festival. That was the year a sixteen-year-old CND badge-wearing, guitar-carrying, shaggy-haired Rod Stewart snuck into the festival and there, while chaps in bow ties and waistcoats vigorously blew trumpets and trombones, lost his virginity to an older woman. In his autobiography, Stewart is candid enough to recall how disappointed she was by the brevity of the experience. Years later the encounter inspired the words to 'Maggie May' ('The morning sun, when it's in your face really shows your age'), which ends with Rod supposing he could collect his books and get on back to school, or find himself a rock'n'roll band that needs a helping hand... the latter is just what he did and he found that band at Eel Pie Island – we'll come back to that later.

Pendleton was irritated by Beaulieu because it gave jazz a bad name. His answer was to organise his own festival – although, for obvious reasons, finding a venue wasn't going to be easy. The solution came, in a roundabout way, out of an office romance. Barbara Coombs started working for Harold in 1953, first as a secretary, then book-keeper and eventually business partner. Somewhere along the way the pair became romantically involved and they married in 1960. Her father was the chief at Richmond fire station, on Kew Road, which required him to conduct safety inspections at the nearby Athletic Association Grounds. As a thank you, the directors were in the habit of sending him tickets for the annual Richmond Royal Horse Show. The year they were married, Harold and Barbara were invited along. It was while at the event – and bored rigid by the whole thing, remembers Barbara – that it struck Harold that he might have found his festival site. The committee at Richmond turned him down at first, but six months later changed their minds. Pendleton later claimed it was because they'd taken out insurance on the main grandstand and hoped that festival-goers would do a Beaulieu and burn it down, and they'd get new facilities out of it.

A small ad in the 19 August 1961 edition of *Melody Maker* announced the inaugural edition of the NJF's National Jazz Festival, set to take place on the weekend of 26–27 August. It was informally

Ad for the first National Jazz Festival, held in Richmond in 1961. The trumpet and chair logo remained even when, in later years, the festival was taken over by blues and rock.

promoted as the 'Marquee's garden party' and the line-up drew on artists who regularly played the Oxford Street club. Pendleton's intention was to showcase jazz to a wider and more diverse audience.

As the first jazz fans arrived at the turnstiles on Saturday morning, workmen were still finishing the stage. Dismiss any thoughts of the Pyramid stage at Glastonbury – back in 1961, the main stage at Richmond resembled a raised bus shelter. An amateur band from Luton kicked off the proceedings with a fanfare parade through the town. The first act appeared after lunch: Don Rendell, who'd played in the band backing Billie Holiday on her 1954 tour of England, along with his quintet. He was followed by Jamaican free-jazzer Joe Harriott, then multi-instrumentalist Tubby Hayes and, topping the bill for the afternoon, Johnny Dankworth. In the evening, the stage was given over to trad, culminating in headliner Chris Barber, with his wife Ottilie Patterson on vocals. At 11:30pm, the lights were extinguished and many of those who'd travelled from outside London for the weekend retired to a makeshift encampment of tents pitched beside a nearby railway embankment. Sunday

1962 NATIONAL JAZZ FESTIVAL RICHMOND 28-29 JULY

ATHLETIC ASSOCIATION GROUNDS
Kew Foot Road - Richmond - Surrey
REFRESHMENTS AND (on Saturday only) LICENSED BAR

SATURDAY 28th JULY   2 p.m. till 11.30 p.m.
CHRIS BARBER'S JAZZBAND
with OTTILIE PATTERSON
HUMPHREY LYTTELTON BAND
ALEX WELSH & HIS BAND
BRUCE TURNER'S JUMP BAND
BOB WALLIS
AND HIS STOREYVILLE JAZZ BAND
COE-PICARD QUINTET
GERRY BROWN'S JAZZMEN
KEITH CHRISTIE - WALLY FAWKES
CYRIL PRESTON'S JAZZ BAND

Other SPECIAL ATTRACTIONS will include the
FESTIVAL BIG BAND
directed by KEN MOULE and AL FAIRWEATHER

SUNDAY 29th JULY   2 p.m. till 11.30 p.m.
KENNY BALL'S JAZZMEN
JOHNNY DANKWORTH QUINTET
TERRY LIGHTFOOT'S JAZZMEN
JOE HARRIOTT QUINTET
DICK CHARLESWORTH BAND
TUBBY HAYES QUINTET
FORRIE CAIRNS & THE CLANSMEN
RONNIE ROSS QUARTET
SONNY MORRIS
AND THE CRANE RIVER JAZZ BAND
DON RENDELL QUINTET

Don't miss the SPECIAL APPEARANCE of the
OMEGA BRASS BAND
directed and led by KEN COLYER

SATURDAY 15/- SUNDAY 15/- WEEKEND 25/-
TICKETS AVAILABLE NOW FROM N.J.F. BOOKING
OFFICE—18 Carlisle Street, London, W.1 (please enclose
stamped addressed envelope). Usual ticket agencies and
through local Jazz Club

The festival's second edition featured Humph, Chris, Johnny and Kenny (Lyttelton, Barber, Dankworth and Ball), the four recognised leaders in the field of British jazz.

was all trad; highlights included Dick Charlesworth and His City Gents, performing in morning suits despite the hot weather, Ken Colyer and, as the closing act, Terry Lightfoot and His New Orleans Jazzmen (all, incidentally, Eelpiland regulars).

Despite the relatively small crowd (around 7,500), there had been trepidation around the borough in the run-up to the festival. *The Richmond Herald* reported that residents were worried it would attract the sort of rowdies who'd wrecked Beaulieu. The paper quoted one unnamed local as saying, 'Richmond should set a pattern of how to treat these undesirables. They should be collected together by the civil authorities, given a wash, and held until reclaimed by their parents at a cost of a £50 fine.'[6] Pendleton reassured the good people of Richmond that he was providing a special security force of 'strong-arm men' to quell any outbreaks of 'rowdyism and raving' and anyone who turned up improperly dressed would be refused admission.[7] 'We don't want any loincloth and bowler-hat types here,' said a festival spokesman. In fact, as the *Herald* noted afterwards, the festival was trouble free. The audience nearest the stage were seated, just like at the opera at Glyndebourne, and listened to the music in appreciative silence. As one interviewee pointed out, they were 'true jazz fiends and not Teddy boys and girls' – although *The Richmond and Twickenham Times* could not refrain from repeatedly referring to the attendees as 'the unwashed'.[8] Still, Harold Pendleton could confidently declare that there would definitely be another festival the following year.

The second National Jazz Festival, held 28–29 July 1962, was a near reprise of the first, with many of the same artists, plus the Humphrey Lyttelton Band and Kenny Ball's Jazzmen. With Barber, Dank, Humph and Ball, the festival boasted most of the key figures in British jazz at the time, both trad and modern. Ten thousand turned up to hear them play. Local newspapers once again seemed almost disappointed at the lack of anything other than jazz to get excited about. The headline in *The Richmond Herald* was 'No Trouble Jazz Festival'. The only bit of bother, it reported, was the off-key noise of aircraft passing low overhead on their descent into

Heathrow. Bands had to pause on several occasions and wait until the racket had died down before starting up again. Ignoring the air traffic, *Melody Maker* called it the 'Quiet Festival'. It claimed that a reporter from one of the national papers had asked Don Read, the man charged with handling the media, when the riots would start: 'Will 8:30 suit you, old boy?' replied Read. Another newspaperman, *Melody Maker* claimed, offered £20 to security staff to start a punch up. Deprived of any real cause to vilify the festival-goers, the local press contented itself with poking fun at their long hair and the difficulties in distinguishing between boys and girls.

Come 1963 and the third edition of the festival, it was still a casual affair. John Clark was a member of the Richmond Jazz Club and of a Duke Ellington-inspired small band called the Rustix Jumptet, who played the festival on the Saturday night. 'Because we knew several of the promoters of the National Jazz Festival we were asked to provide "security". [Band member] John Woods took his ancient boxer dog and we were concerned that if it growled people would see it had no teeth.'⁹ A low paling fence was all that kept the crowds out and there were no staff on site overnight except Clark and a colleague, who slept in the beer tent. But there was something stirring in the air. The first hint had come the previous August when a last-minute addition saw Alexis Korner's Blues Incorporated add the first non-jazz notes to the festival bill. This year, the creep of R&B bands onto the schedule at Pendleton's Marquee was reflected at Richmond, with the appearance of the Graham Bond Quartet and Georgie Fame Group on Saturday (even if their names appeared on posters at half the point size of the jazz acts) and, the following day, the Cyril Davies 'Rhythm and Blues' All-Stars with Long John Baldry and the Velvettes. Not to be confused with the Motown Velvelettes, this lot was a female South African vocal trio who had come to England touring with a production of *King Kong: A Jazz*

Musical, about the tragic life of African heavyweight boxing champ Ezekiel Dlamini. Also appearing Sunday night, right at the bottom of the bill, was the band that thirteen months earlier had debuted at the Marquee, the Rolling Stones.

The Stones were not invited to play the main stage. In fact, except for the Cyril Davies All-Stars, none of the R&B acts appeared on the main stage. Instead, they played in the bar room of the rugby clubhouse, on the edge of the playing fields. *Bexleyheath and Welling Observer* reporter Chris Welch (who the following year would join the staff of *Melody Maker*) was present for the performance by the Graham Bond Quartet. This was keyboardist and saxophonist Bond with Jack Bruce on bass, John McLaughlin on guitar and, on drums, a wild-eyed Ginger Baker – not so much a percussionist, wrote Welch, as 'a concussionist, knocking out fans and fellow musicians alike with an ear blasting, passionate performance on a drum kit that he'd made himself.'[10] On Sunday evening, Welch was back out in the crowd listening to the weekend's closing act, Acker Bilk and His Paramount Jazz Band, when the PA announced that the Rolling Stones were about to play in a marquee on the far side of the field. Acker Bilk had recorded the UK's biggest-selling single of 1962 with 'Stranger on the Shore', while the Stones were bottom of the bill, with a debut single that had barely made a mark on the charts that June, yet 'the whole audience turned round and ran towards this tent,' says Welch.[11] While it would take the rest of the country another twelve months to catch on ('It's All Over Now' would reach No.1 in the charts in July 1964), the Stones had already amassed a sizeable and fanatical fanbase in and around Richmond and Twickenham. The reason for that was down to a Caucasian impresario called Giorgio Gomelsky.

CHAPTER 4

DOING THE CRAWDADDY

The unprecedented, incontestable, inexhaustible purveyors of spontaneous combustion, the Rollin' Stones – and the equally incomparable Giorgio Gomelsky

IT IS SURPRISING THAT NO ONE HAS YET WRITTEN an English-language biography of Giorgio Gomelsky – although there have been two in French. Perhaps we shouldn't be waiting for a biographer and the job should be given to William Boyd or some other similarly gifted novelist with a talent for rollicking good tales of protagonists whose sweeping life stories blur the lines between reality and fiction, and involve a succession of cameos by famous characters from history. In this fantastic adventure, the quixotic Gomelsky pursues an elusive ideal through three acts, one each set in the cities of London, Paris and New York. He is a bear-shaped, dark-bearded, twinkling-eyed, deeply baritoned, rapid-talking, blue sky-dreaming, flash car-driving filmmaker, entrepreneur, hustler, talent spotter, marriage-broker and midwife. He introduces the

FACING: A wrinkle-free, nineteen-year-old Mick Jagger performing at the Crawdaddy, at the Station Hotel in Richmond, in early 1963.

Beatles to the Rolling Stones, Jimi Hendrix to Johnny Hallyday, and the Yardbirds to lasagne. He's given to making absurdly gnomic statements: 'Three things that most fascinate people are water, fire and watching pigs.'[1] He bestows on Eric Clapton the nickname 'Slowhand'. He sets spiritual jazz fusionist John McLaughlin on his path to Miles Davis, and Kevin Godley and Lol Creme on their way to 10cc. He nurtures progressive rock in France and becomes a godfather to post punk in the Bowery. Possibly. Other versions are available. What is not in dispute is that by the time any of his protégés hit it big, Gomelsky had already exited stage left. He'd been dumped, gazumped or lost interest and moved on. He always claimed this never bothered him and that he had greater goals.

He made a memorable first impression. 'The first time I met Giorgio Gomelsky,' says former PR man Greg Tesser, 'I thought I was in the presence of Grigori Rasputin. His hair was greasy and wild, and he waved his hands around like some demented tic-tac man at the Derby.'[2] Pat Andrews thought he was 'wonderful, so tall and exuberant, like he'd just stepped out of a Hollywood movie.'[3] Lasting impressions weren't always so favourable: musician Brian Auger, who Gomelsky managed for a time, said he was a con man.[4]

Giorgio Gomelsky was born on 28 February 1934 in Tiflis (later Tbilisi) in Georgia, then part of the Soviet Union. Typically, where Giorgio is concerned, not everyone agrees on even this most basic fact. Gomelsky's life is an eight-decade accumulation of tall tales, improbable claims and shrugged 'who knows?' Some sources, including Gomelsky's obituary in *The New York Times*, say that he was born aboard a ship as it sailed between Odessa and Genoa. You want this to be true because it makes such a perfect beginning to the story of a man who was perpetually restless.

His father was a doctor and his mother a French-speaking milliner from Monte Carlo and until the end of his life Gomelsky spoke with an indeterminate Georgian-French-Italian accent that made him sound like some Central European count as played by the great Peter Ustinov. In 1938, the family fled the persecution of the professional classes by fellow Georgian Josef Stalin, travelling first to Syria, then Egypt, then Italy, before finally settling in Switzerland. Giorgio later claimed he became a jazz fan around the age of ten or eleven after finding a stack of records in an attic and hearing tracks like Duke Ellington's 'Take the A Train' and Louis Jordan's 'Ain't Nobody Here but Us Chickens'. He subsequently became hooked on the late-night jazz programmes broadcast on American Forces Network radio. With a group of friends, he founded a jazz appreciation society and formed a trio in which he played drums. When he was in his teens, his parents divorced and his mother, who designed hats for Claude Saint-Cyr in Paris, left Switzerland to run the company's shop in London. She sent her jazz-loving son copies of *Melody Maker*, which gave him a window on the British music scene and a hipster's English vocabulary.

Once his schooling was done, Giorgio joined his mother in London; this was 1955. He had an idea that he wanted to make a living by playing jazz, or writing about it, or making films about it or... something. According to his own account, the young Gomelsky – now just into his twenties – launched himself on London by opening a coffee bar off the King's Road. He also found his way to the Soho offices of Harold Pendleton's National Jazz Federation. 'He used to hang around for hours with his broken English,' recalls Barbara Pendleton, 'and we couldn't get rid of him. He was like part of the furniture.' She remembers that he wanted to make a film about jazz in London but the union told him he couldn't film unless he was a member and he couldn't become a member until he'd made a film. Gomelsky was around for the early years of Pendleton's Marquee club and would have caught some of the first appearances

The product of a peripatetic childhood that exposed him to varied cultures, Giorgio Gomelsky was a man who could come up with three impossible schemes before breakfast.

by Alexis Korner's Blues Incorporated, Britain's groundbreaking first R&B outfit. It was either at the Marquee, or afterwards at a pub, that Gomelsky first met Brian Jones.

Whether or not jazz fan Gomelsky liked the new R&B sound, he saw potential in it. He felt the Marquee was missing a trick by not putting on more bands playing this kind of music and he decided to set himself up as a promoter running his own R&B nights. He came to an arrangement with the management of the Piccadilly Jazz Club in Ham Yard (formerly Cy Laurie's Jazz Club) and set up some gigs there for Alexis Korner. 'Harold heard about this and feels I'm trying to steal his thunder,' Gomelsky told interviewer John Strausbaugh in 2015, 'which, of course, is not true.'[5]

'Double-crossing shit he was,' says Barbara Pendleton. 'Then he had the nerve to stand outside the Marquee with leaflets for his shows.' Gomelsky backed off and set about finding a new venue, as far away from Soho and the Marquee as possible. Some friends, members of the Rustics Jazz Band (soon to become the Rustix Jumptet), were running a club in the back room of the Station Hotel pub, out in Richmond. Gomelsky knew Richmond from the NJF jazz festivals, which he'd attended to shoot film of Chris Barber and his band. He went out to take another look. From Soho, Richmond would have felt like a distant backwater, but it was on the Underground network (if at the far western end) and the Station Hotel could not have been more convenient: exit the station and it was right there, over the road. 'They have this nice room in the back of the pub with phony palm trees, a stage with wooden, cut-out music quavers on the back wall and a small white grand piano,' recalled Gomelsky.[6] 'The place held about one hundred, 150 people at most, but I thought the odd juxtaposition would be hilarious. A palm court blues orchestra!'

The Ealing Club had already shown that R&B could succeed out in the suburbs. Five miles south of Ealing, at the Station Hotel, Friday night was jazz night and Saturdays rock'n'roll, but Sunday was free and Gomelsky grabbed it. He borrowed five quid from his friend Ronan O'Rahilly to pay for the rent and the printing of a hundred flyers. O'Rahilly ran the Scene Club in the West End and in 1964 would found pirate station Radio Caroline. One account has O'Rahilly meeting Gomelsky for the first time at a Stanislavski method-acting class, which sounds very Giorgio, but it's more likely the pair met through Alexis Korner, whose band, Blues Incorporated, O'Rahilly managed.[7] The first Gomelsky booking for

Sundays at the Station Hotel was the Dave Hunt R&B Band, who he knew from their appearances at the Piccadilly Jazz Club. Until recently they had been a trad outfit, the Dave Hunt Confederate Jazz Band, but they were now hastily adapting to new musical fashions. They had just landed themselves a guitarist, Ray Davies, who played his first gig with them at the Piccadilly in December 1962. Early in the New Year, the band, including Davies, began their Richmond residency. For whatever reason, Davies's tenure was a short one: his last performance with the Dave Hunt Band was 10 February.[8] Less than a year later, Ray and brother Dave, along with Mick Avory and Pete Quaife, were making their debut as the Kinks at Oxford Town Hall. Davies's last gig with Hunt was also the band's last in Richmond. The winter of 1962/63 was extremely harsh with blizzards over the New Year and snow blanketing the country for weeks afterwards. Equally harsh was Gomelsky's response when the snow caused Hunt and his band to miss a gig the following week: he immediately replaced them with one of the acts that had supported them at the Piccadilly, the Rolling Stones. Gomelsky was obviously looking for an excuse to drop Hunt and replace him with a better band and he'd found that band the previous week.

The Stones were finding it hard going. In early 1963, R&B remained a hard sell in West End clubs, which, at this point, continued to favour jazz. The band were relying on two residencies: one at the Flamingo Club on Wardour Street in Soho and the other at the Marquee, where, after their earlier dismissal by Harold Pendleton, they'd secured another support slot. But in January they were canned by the Flamingo for being too rock'n'roll and sacked from the Marquee, where they were going down a storm, after asking for a pay rise. The double blow left them scratching around the suburbs, with the only regular gig being the Ealing Club, which was fine if they could get a busy Saturday slot, but they were more often playing midweek to audiences in single figures. They badly needed more gigs.

Around the same time, after six months of chopping and changing line-ups, the Stones had tied down Bill Wyman as their regular bass player and Charlie Watts as their drummer, joining Brian Jones, Mick Jagger, Keith Richards and Ian Stewart. Jones was keen that his friend Giorgio Gomelsky should see this new version of the band, which he finally did in early February 1963. Gomelsky later recalled the occasion in an interview with author David Dalton: 'I went to see them in Sutton, at the Red Lion. I liked what they were doing. I said, "Listen, I promised this guy I would give him a job but the first time he goofs, you're in." And then came that famous day. Dave Hunt had a terrible problem getting everybody together, he just wasn't together, and the next Sunday they didn't turn up… So Monday I called Ian Stewart: "Tell everybody in the band you guys are on next Sunday."'[9]

The Stones had played in Richmond before. In the weeks either side of Christmas 1962, they had done six Saturday shows at the Sandover Hall, a small community centre on Ormond Road, near L'Auberge coffee bar. These shows variously featured Ricky Fenson or Bill Wyman on bass, and Tony Chapman, Steve Harris, Carlo Little or Charlie Watts on drums. One source claims that it was the 12 January 1963 gig at the Sandover Hall that saw the first pairing of Bill Wyman and Charlie Watts as the rhythm section with the Stones – although there would be a further two weeks of musical chairs before Wyman and Watts took up their posts permanently. Someone who saw the Stones at the Sandover Hall remembers learning of the gig from a flyer stuck on a lamppost, and that there were fewer than twenty people in the audience. Beyond that, all other details are lost – even the venue itself is gone, destroyed by fire in May 1964.

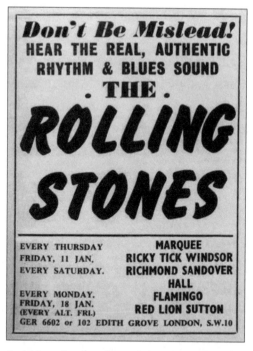

An ad from the *Jazz News & Review* of 9 January 1963, which advertises the Rolling Stones' brief Saturday residency at Richmond's Sandover Hall.

For the Rolling Stones' debut show at the Station Hotel, on Sunday 24 February 1963, Gomelsky claimed all of three people showed up.[10] He later admitted that the misspelled flyers he'd pasted around town reading 'Sunday night, 7:30pm Rhythm and Bulse' hadn't helped. He liked to tell interviewers how Brian Jones had come up to him and said, 'Giorgio, there's six of us and three of them, should we play?' and how he replied, 'Brian, how many people do you think can fit in here? A hundred? Okay, well then, play as if there were a hundred people in here.'[11] Bill Wyman says it was more like thirty people. However many, it wasn't a lot. That changed quickly.

Take a look at the UK charts the week the Stones debuted at the Station Hotel. At No.1 was 'Wayward Wind' by yodelling balladeer Frank Ifield, a Woolworth's Slim Whitman. Filling out the rest of the

Top 10 were the likes of Bobby Vee, Del Shannon, Frankie Vaughan, Cliff Richard and close-harmony trio the Springfields. Wholesome, treacly, dull. Three years into the Sixties and musically it was still the Fifties. The exception, lodged at No.2, was 'Please Please Me', the self-penned second single by the Beatles. While the song owed much to Roy Orbison and the Everly Brothers, it was fresh and dynamic. It pinned back the ears of the music business and set young girls screaming. It was the launch of a sea change in British music and the people watching those first Rolling Stones gigs at the Station Hotel would have felt that this was part of that new scene, too. 'Somebody said to me there was a group playing down at the Station Hotel,' remembers Gina Way, then a Richmond schoolgirl. '"Group" was the new buzzword. The Beatles were a group and there were lots of groups on the Liverpool scene, but I hadn't heard of any groups playing down here before. So we had to go and see.'

The Station Hotel shows took place in a room at the back of the pub with a small, low stage lit by two spotlights – one red, one blue. Starting at around 8:30pm, the band did two forty-five-minute sets with an interval between. There were no Jagger/Richards compositions – the Stones wouldn't start writing their own material for another couple of years. The setlist consisted of covers and songs regularly performed included Chuck Berry's 'Route 66' and 'Memphis Tennessee', 'Little Egypt' and 'Poison Ivy' by the Coasters, 'I'm a King Bee' by Slim Harpo, 'Honest I Do' by Jimmy Reed, 'Walking the Dog' by Rufus Thomas, and a few numbers by the band's favourite artist, Bo Diddley. The Stones weren't the first to play this material, they just did it with more attitude. 'They were rude, they were dirty, they were ugly, they were rebellious, they were nasty,' says local boy Chris Chesney, who would later form his own band Sour Milk Sea (which briefly featured a pre-Queen Freddie Mercury). 'The Stones had balls.'[12]

Seven weeks into the residency, the show on Sunday 7 April pulled in 320 people – more than twice the number the room was supposed to hold. In the beginning, audiences just stood and gawked at the band, so Gomelsky told his young assistant Hamish Grimes to get up on a table and start waving his arms about while shouting 'Yeah! Yeah!' and whistling as loudly as he could. 'Everybody looks up,' recalled Gomelsky, 'and in a split-second they catch on and 200 pairs of arms were undulating like crazy! Man, that was something.'[13]

Arm-waving was about all the audience could manage. Bodies were tightly squashed, leaving no room to dance, so the crowd would shake or 'twitch' on the spot. Boys would take off their shirts and whirl them round their heads. The band often ended the night with a Bo Diddley track called 'Doing the Crawdaddy' (from the 1960 album *Bo Diddley is a Gunslinger*). A chugging crowd-pleaser, it had a call-and-response vocal that had the crowd bellowing 'Look at me do the crawdaddy!' in a deliriously rowdy and cathartic finale. From this, Gomelsky's Sunday night club gained a name – the Crawdaddy.

In the audience on 7 April was Barry May, a young journalist working for *The Richmond and Twickenham Times*. His write-up filled a page the following Saturday and became the first published review of the Rolling Stones. It began: 'A musical magnet is drawing the jazz beatniks away from Eel Pie Island, Twickenham, to a new Mecca in Richmond. The attraction is the new Craw-Daddy Rhythm and Blues club at the Station Hotel, Kew Road – the first club of its kind in an area of flourishing modern and traditional jazz haunts.'[14]

A former member of the Lonnie Donegan fan club and a jazz enthusiast, May didn't have much to say about the music, but his article did capture something of the atmosphere: 'Save for the swaying forms of the group on the spotlit stage, the room is in darkness. A patch of light from the entrance doors catches the sweating dancers and those who are slumped on the floor.' He describes the band's hair 'worn Piltdown-style, brushed forward from the crown' and the sartorial style of the fans with their 'long hair, suede jackets, gaucho trousers and Chelsea boots' – or, in the words of the Station Hotel's old regulars, 'funny clothes'.

According to Bill Wyman, when Brian Jones first saw the review he read it aloud to the rest of the band and then kept the clipping in his wallet for months afterwards. May's reward was a call from *Record Mirror*, who wanted to know are the Stones the next Beatles? And would he like a job as the paper's news editor?

To spread the message, Gomelsky had Hamish Grimes compose a series of extravagantly worded small ads, which he paid to run in *Melody Maker*:

'RICHMOND, Station Hotel: RHYTHM 'N' BLUES with the inimitable, incomparable, exhilarating ROLLIN' STONES' (23 February issue)

'The thrilling, exhilarating, GALVANIC, intoxicating, incomparable ROLLIN' STONES' (9 March)

'The unprecedented, incontestable, inexhaustible purveyors of spontaneous combustion the ROLLIN' STONES' (16 March)

'Untameable wildfire explosion of impetuous RHYTHM 'N' BLUES with insuppressibly stormraising ROLLIN' STONES' (23 March)

'Hyperheterodox RHYTHM 'N' BLUES voluptuousness from tempestuously transporting ROLLIN' STONES' (30 March)

'Unrepressed RHYTHM 'N' BLUES with unmitigating, ebullient, perturbing ROLLIN' STONES' (6 April)

'Stupendously electrifying R&B sounds of unstoppable ROLLIN' STONES' (4 May)

'Warning: R and B sound barrier to be broken by Rollin' Stones' (11 May)

Barry May writes about the 'new' rhythm and blues

JAZZ

Nowadays it means the music that goes round and around—or the Rollin' Stones are gathering them in

The line-up of the Rollin' Stones, with vocalist Mick Jagger, guitarist Keith Richards, and extreme left, guitarist Brian Jones.

A MUSICAL magnet is drawing the jazz beatniks away from Eel Pie Island, Twickenham, to a new mecca in Richmond.

The attraction is the new Craw-Daddy Rhythm and blues Club at the Station hotel, Kew Road—the first club of its kind in an area of flourishing modern a n d traditional jazz haunts.

Rhythm a n d blues, gaining more popularity every week, is replacing "traddypop" all over the country, and even persuading the more sedate modernists to leave their plush clubs. The deep, earthy sound produced at the hotel on Sunday evenings is typical of the best of rhythm and blues that gives all who hear it an irresistible urge to "stand up and move."

Akin to both rock 'n' roll and the skiffle music that raced up and down the charts of three and four years ago, rhythm and blues has been described as "pepped-up" blues and "original American Negro pop-music." But the sound also has its modernistic leaning a fact apparent from some of the material used by t h e thriving rhythm and blues groups.

Traditional jazz as a commercial enterprise is played out, and modern jazz has never been able to command major audiences in this country.

One of the founders of the jazz club, Eelpiland, as it is called, where attempts at presenting both traditional a n d modern jazz have been made, Arthur Chisnell admitted that "things have been quiet." The four and five nights of jazz every week on the island has dwindled to only two—at the weekend

Rhythm and blues can claim to provide almost a

Drummer Charles Watts in action, with pianist Ian Stuart in the background, taking a break on the maracas.

happy medium for young jazz fans. Modernists and "traddies" can be seen side by side at the Station hotel, listening to

resident group, the Rollin' Stones.

From a meagre 50 or so on the club's first night, less than two months ago, attendances have rocketed by an average of 50 a week to last Sunday's record of 320. And the membership book lists more than 700 names of rhythm a n d blues devotees from all parts of London and West Surrey.

Club promoter, bearded Italian film director, Giorgio G o m e l s k y, is thrilled with the success of the club—but fears he may have to close t h e membership list if its popularity continues to rise.

Jazz-lover Giorgio first visited Richmond in August, 1961, when he produced a film featuring the Chris Barber jazz band at the first National Jazz Festival held at the Athletic ground, Old Deer Park.

The Rollin' Stones, a six-piece group, were formed just 10 months ago.

Since then they have played in more than a dozen London rhythm and blues clubs, as well as appearances at the West End Marquee Club.

Semi-professionals now, although the average age of the group is only 20, the daytime occupations of its members are as varied as the instruments they play.

Driving force behind the group is London School of Economics student Mick Jagger, vocal a n d harmonica. He is backed by architect Brian J o n e s (guitar, harmonica, maracas), guitarist K e i t h Richards, an art student, bass guitarist Bill Wyman, a representative, drummer Charles Watts, a designer, and on piano, Ian Stewart.

Although "pop" numbers are sometimes played, songs written and recorded by the American rhythm and blues guitarist Bo Diddley are the Rollin' Stones' favourites. Their appreciation of h i m is carried to the extent of naming the club after a dance Bo Diddley has invented, the "craw-daddy."

The 300 and more in their late teens and early 20s who pack the club on Sunday nights do a dance similar to the craw-daddy. But most improvise on a wildly remote form of the hully-gully, similar to the twist.

For those less inclined to express their feelings physically, the Rollin' Stones also provide visual entertainment.

Hair worn Piltdown-style, brushed forward from the crown like "The Beatles" pop group—"we looked like this before they became famous"—the rhythm section, piano, drums and bass guitar provide a warm, steady

backing for the blues of the harmonicas and lead guitars.

Save for the swaying forms of the group on the spotlit stage, the room is in darkness. A patch of light from the entrance doors catches the sweating dancers and those who are slumped on the floor where chairs h a v e not been provided.

Outside in the bar the long hair, suede jackets, goucho trousers and Chelsea boots rub shoulders with the Station hotel's "regulars," resulting in whispered m o c k i n g, though n o t unfriendly remarks about the "funny" clothes.

Few regulars h a v e taken exception to the pub's new customers, and only a small number have chosen to no longer drink there on Sunday nights.

The Rollin' Stones and the Craw-Daddy C l u b have put the Station hotel on the map, as far as youngsters are concerned.

How sad and unfortunate that it is destined to be soon wiped off the map. Demolished, flattened to the ground and replaced with a brand new public-house.

THE CRAW - DADDY CLUB WILL BE FORCED TO LOOK F O R AN-OTHER WEEKLY STAGE —AND T H E ROLLIN' STONES WILL GO ON ROLLIN'.

The first write-up of a Rolling Stones gig, which appeared in the local Richmond press in April 1963, written by a young reporter who went on to have a career with Reuters.

Even as the Stones were whipping things up at the Crawdaddy, Gomelsky had another wild project in mind: he wanted to make a film with the Beatles. In April 1963, the Fab Four were on the cusp of nationwide stardom. 'Please Please Me', the single, had topped the UK charts, quickly followed by an album of the same name, which had gone top five. Gomelsky claimed to have met the band two years earlier while passing through Hamburg and had been keeping an eye on them ever since. Now, the former aspiring filmmaker had an idea for a script based around a day in the life of the band. On Sunday 14 April, Gomelsky met with Beatles manager Brian Epstein at Teddington Studios, where the group was taping for the pop music show *Thank Your Lucky Stars*.[15] Gomelsky persuaded the Beatles to make the short drive over to Richmond after they finished the day's filming to check out the Rolling Stones.

From Teddington, Gomelsky rushed over to the Station Hotel, where the Stones were setting up. He told them, 'Hey, something good might happen tonight... The Beatles might come!' The band played the first set, took a break and had just launched into the second set when the Beatles showed up. They stayed until the end, waiting while the Stones packed up, and then the two groups headed back to the squalid two-bedroom flat shared by Jagger, Richards and Jones. The Stones played their visitors five demo tracks they'd recorded the previous month at IBC Studios at Portland Place, in a session set up by Gomelsky. It's almost certain that at some point Brian Jones would have shown them the write-up from *The Richmond and Twickenham Times*, which had appeared only the day before. Later that week, on Thursday 18 April, the Stones took up an invitation to see the Beatles top the bill at the Royal Albert Hall for a concert broadcast live by the BBC.

As for Gomelsky's move on the Beatles, they did visit his west London flat for omelettes and a chat.[16] With the help of *Jazz Beat* journalist Peter Clayton, Gomelsky produced a treatment for what he called a Dadaist, off-the-cuff film, which he presented to Brian Epstein. A few weeks later, American film studio United Artists offered the Beatles a three-picture deal and Gomelsky was out. The following year, 1964, Richard Lester's *A Hard Day's Night* hit cinema screens – a film, Gomelsky claimed, that bore a close resemblance to his pitch.

On 24 April, a Wednesday, the Rolling Stones played their first gig at Eel Pie Island. Apparently, Arthur Chisnall had wondered why his Sunday night takings were down so severely and had gone to the Station Hotel to see what was up. His solution was to give the Stones a midweek residency. Gomelsky had also landed the group a regular Sunday afternoon gig at Studio 51 in central London. Based in a cellar on Great Newport Street, just off Charing Cross Road, the place was also known as the Ken Colyer Club, because it was run by the jazz man. But it was owned by a woman called Vi Highland, and Vi and her friend Pat would dispense coffee, tea and sandwiches then, while the band played, retire to their back room to watch television and knit. The Stones would finish their gig here, then head straight over to Richmond on the train while Ian Stewart followed in the van with the equipment.

Meanwhile, Gomelsky hustled. He met *Record Mirror* columnist Peter Jones at De Hems pub, the favoured watering hole of the British music business, just off Shaftesbury Avenue in Soho. Gomelsky persuaded Jones to come out to Richmond to see the Stones. Jones obliged and thought the group maybe had something but he didn't really like R&B. He was at least smart enough to send Norman Jopling, the paper's go-to guy for all things new, out to Richmond on the following Sunday. 'When we arrived,' says Jopling, 'there was a crowd of kids outside the Station Hotel who couldn't get in – the place was packed full.'[17] Jopling and his photographer waved their press cards and pushed through into the back room, where the Stones were part way into their set. 'The noise was already fantastic. It was one of those Bo Diddley songs with a Bo Diddley beat. I'd never heard anything like it in a live act. I'd never felt anything like it. The place shook, everyone in the audience was wet with sweat, the sound was bouncing off the walls, throbbing, utterly irresistible.' Jopling knew the original versions of these songs because he listened to the same imported American records that inspired the Stones. He left the pub with one particular thought going round in his head: 'White people could do it, white people could play the blues.'

The paper with Jopling's review – right up front, on page two – hit the streets on Wednesday 8 May. It was the first mention of the Stones in the national music press (and the first time a group without a record would feature in *Record Mirror*) and it was a rave: 'Maybe you've never heard of them – But by gad you will! The Rolling Stones are destined to be the biggest group in the R&B scene.' It mentioned that the Beatles were fans and that the Stones had been invited to play the Cavern. That afternoon three of the UK's four major record companies called Jopling asking how they could contact the band. Jopling's response was to tell them to talk to Andrew Loog Oldham. Andrew Loog who? Well, a lot can change in a week.

Oldham, not long out of public school and armed with just a brace of O levels and an extraordinary ego, had already interned as an assistant to fashion designer Mary Quant, worked at music hotspot the Flamingo and been one of the first employees at Ronnie Scott's jazz club when it opened in 1959. Recently, he'd persuaded Brian Epstein to hire him and been given the task of helping publicise various Epstein interests, including the Beatles' second single, 'Please Please Me'. Sharp, snappy, calculating and, above all, ambitious, Oldham was Tony Curtis's man-on-the-make Sidney Falco from *The Sweet Smell of Success* transplanted to 1960s London. One day, doing the rounds, he dropped by De Hems to corner Peter Jones and hustle for column inches for his clients. Jones knocked him back but gave him a tip – Oldham should get himself over to Richmond to check out this unsigned and unrecorded band that was about to get a wow of a write-up in *Record Mirror*.

As Oldham says in his autobiography, *Stoned*, he was probably only forty-eight hours ahead of the rest of the pack when, on Sunday

21 April, he boarded a train at Finchley Road & Frognal station, close to where he was still living with his mother, and travelled ten stops south to Richmond to say hello to the rest of his life. He narrates the events as a fable in the making. From the station he crosses the road and heads down the alley leading to the back of the pub. Halfway down the alley he sees two figures arguing: a girl against the wall and a boy pressing his point. 'They were both very earnest, hurt and similar: pale skins, brown hair and flashing eyes. And both very attractive in their similarity, in heat.' Later, he discovers that the alleyway Romeo and Juliet are Mick Jagger and Chrissie Shrimpton, on their first date. Oldham says he didn't know the first thing about R&B, but what he heard when the Rolling Stones played was sex. 'They came on to me,' he writes. 'I was in love.'

He wanted them but, Oldham says, he didn't have the bottle to approach the Stones straight away and went home to consider his next move. One problem was that to arrange gigs you had to be a licensed agent and to get a licence you had to be over twenty-one – Oldham was nineteen, younger even than the members of the band he was eager to manage. He called Brian Epstein to ask if he was interested in a new R&B group but Epstein said no. The fallback was Eric Easton, a grey-haired, grey-suited, old-school booking agent from whom Oldham rented office space on Regent Street. Reluctantly, Easton agreed to go out to Richmond. He didn't get what he saw there but could see that the kids did. After the gig, the oddball couple introduced themselves to the band and got a promise from Brian Jones that he would be at their offices the coming Tuesday. He showed up with Mick Jagger and the following day, Wednesday 1 May, Jones signed a three-year management deal with Oldham and Easton on behalf of the Stones. Five days later, the new management had the group sign a two-year recording deal with Dick Rowe of Decca Records, the executive better known in the business as the Man Who Turned Down the Beatles and who was determined not to make the same mistake twice. Four days later, on Friday 10 May, the band was in the studio, recording their first single, a cover of Chuck Berry's 'Come On'. Talk about moving fast.

And where was Giorgio Gomelsky while all this was going on? The man who had set up the Station Hotel residency, created the hype, whipped up the crowds, funded demo recordings, roped in the Beatles for God's sake, and who considered himself the group's de facto manager (but, crucially, without having the Stones sign anything) – was away in Switzerland attending his father's funeral. By the time he got back, the man who dismissed contracts as 'scratchings on paper' had become the Man Who Lost the Stones.

Speaking in 1995, Gomelsky told an interviewer, 'I thought we had a verbal understanding and felt tremendously let down when they left me. But I never like to work with monsters, no matter how talented. Jagger was organised and ambitious, but selfish. Keith was very spoilt. Jones should have had treatment. His responses were never those of a normal person.'[18] In an interview with author Paul Trynka, Gomelsky's mentor Harold Pendleton was more damning, describing the Stones' leader Brian Jones as 'coldly, cynically evil'.

According to writer John Strausbaugh, both Bill Wyman and Keith Richards would later express remorse over the way the group treated Gomelsky. Richards, interviewed in *Rolling Stone* in 1971, reckoned Oldham and his partner Eric Easton 'fucked Giorgio because he had nothing on paper with us. They screwed him to get us a recording contract.' As Trynka says, Gomelsky was the first of what would be many friends thrown under the bus to satisfy the Stones' ambition.

At the time, Gomelsky seemed to take it on the chin. He agreed to allow the 'monsters' to continue their residency at the Crawdaddy, where they were drawing ever larger crowds. On 13 June, just a few

Keith Richards and Mick Jagger whip up a Crawdaddy crowd, creating a fervour that one journalist described as like a revivalist meeting in the American Deep South.

days after the Stones released their first single, the *Daily Mirror*, the nation's most-read paper, gave the band its first national mainstream press exposure with a story headed 'Twitching the Night Away': *In the half-darkness, the guitars and the drums started to twang and bang. A pulsating rhythm and blues. Shoulder to shoulder on the floor stood 500 youngsters, some in black leather, some in sweaters. You could have boiled an egg in the atmosphere. They began to dance. They just stood as they were. Their heads shook violently in what I can only describe as a paroxysm... Their feet stamped in tribal style. If they could, the dedicated occasionally put their hands above their heads and clapped in rhythm. In its fervour it was like a revivalist meeting in America's Deep South. Responsible for this extraordinary scene in suburban Surrey are five long-haired lads known as the Rolling Stones...*

Note that: '*five* long-haired lads'. It had been six, but one of Oldham's first management decisions had been to can keyboardist Ian Stewart because six members were too many for a popular group. The reality was Oldham thought the older, burly Stewart looked too square. The Soho-schooled Svengali had a vision for the Stones that capitalised on their rebellious and cocksure nature: he wanted to turn them into the anti-Beatles – no suits, no smiles, no making nice to please the grown-ups.

A regular at the Crawdaddy at this time was Hounslow boy Ian McLagan, future member of the Small Faces and Faces. He was first taken there by a friend one Sunday night in May and had no idea what to expect. In his autobiography, *All the Rage*, McLagan recalls the booming bass, chanking guitars and wailing harp that met his ears as he arrived at the pub for the first time. 'The band were rocking out on a Jimmy Reed tune and it sounded so good,' he writes.[19] 'Finally, we squeezed our way in and fuck me, they're not old black guys at all, they're white, young and they're dynamite!' McLagan never missed a Sunday after that, always arriving early to get a spot in front of the stage. Brian Jones and Keith Richards would be sat on stools either side of Mick Jagger who would lean out over the audience, the veins on his neck bulging, hollering for all his worth. Richards spat out licks, weaving in and out of Jones's slide guitar lines, while Wyman's bizarre homemade bass echoed off the ceiling along with Charlie Watts's steam-train drumming. 'I'd see members of other bands hogging the front of the stage like me, making mental notes. The Station Hotel was the place to be.'

The *Daily Mirror* called the Stones London's answer to the Beatles. It was fantastic publicity but not everyone was thrilled. The landlords of the Station Hotel, for instance, were horrified to read about the long hairs fomenting a musical revolution at one of their pubs. They instructed their bar manager to send them all packing. Backstabbed by his band, booted out by the landlords, at this point Gomelsky might just have walked away, except you imagine he was probably making too much money to let go so easily. Instead, he began the search for a new venue, a search that led him – possibly at the suggestion of Harold Pendleton – out of the back door of the Station Hotel and just a verse and a chorus away to the Richmond Athletic Association Grounds, home to Richmond rugby club, site of the National Jazz Festival and location of a clubhouse with a good-sized bar.

The Stones gave their last performance at the Station Hotel on 16 June and their first at the new home of the Crawdaddy two weeks later. Whereas the Station Hotel was only supposed to hold 150 people, the clubhouse could take around 700, which went some way to compensating for its lack of character. It was a large, wood-floored room with windows overlooking the playing fields, a low ceiling and a makeshift stage of planks resting on an unstable base of beer crates. The band gathered pre-show in the rugby club's changing rooms, surrounded by sweaty jockstraps. Geoff Grimes was a sixteen-year-old army rookie stationed in Canterbury and training as a musician. His friend and fellow army musician, Rick McDonald, came from Richmond and the pair sometimes travelled back at weekends, which is when they caught the Stones at the rugby clubhouse. He remembers one week a couple of theatrical types were on stage while the Stones played, pointing into the crowd and shouting, 'That one there!' Those singled out were given tickets for an event to be held a couple of weeks later – which is how Grimes and McDonald came to be among the grooving audience members for the debut of the Stones on the ITV show *Ready Steady Go!*[20]

In May 2004, a unique recording of the Stones at the Crawdaddy appeared at auction at Christie's in London. It was made by brothers Paul and John Lucas, who were members of Chiswick band the Tridents (they later played the Crawdaddy a couple of times and were regulars at Eel Pie Island). They'd gone along to one of the gigs lugging a big old tape recorder with a clockwork motor that had to be wound up, and had asked Brian Jones if he minded if they recorded the band; Jones said it was fine. 'So there we are, standing in front of Brian Jones, and Charlie Watts at the back and Keith Richards over on the righthand side. It was great.' The ninety-minute set, contained on two quarter-inch tapes, included the Stones playing their first hit single 'Come On', along with classic covers such as 'Route 66', 'Roll Over Beethoven' and 'Love Potion No.9'. It is the only known recording of the band's Crawdaddy gigs and it sold for £23,900. An employee at the auction house told Paul Lucas that the buyer was Mick Jagger.

In mid-August 1963, the Athletic Association Grounds were taken over once more by the National Jazz Festival, for its third edition. As the Stones would have been playing the clubhouse that Sunday night, Gomelsky insisted to Harold Pendleton the group be added to the festival line-up. On the day, festival organisers realised that the demand for them was huge, so they were moved from the clubhouse and into a large marquee at the rear of the grounds, meant for people to sleep in overnight or shelter in if it rained. In the tent, compere Bill Carey introduced the Stones as 'Richmond's own' and they kicked into a tight and loud set. One of those at the festival who abandoned Acker Bilk on the main stage to see what all the noise was about at the back was a young Ronnie Wood, who as he approached saw a tent 'bopping up and down, looking like an elephant with its big ass rocking and rolling from side to side.' Even from the outside, Wood said, 'You could tell something good was happening in there.' It was his first time seeing the group he'd join twelve years later. Journalist Chris Welch also watched the performance: 'They were quite aggressive. It was like seeing the Sex Pistols years later.'[21] At the end, Bill Carey went back on stage to announce, 'This has been rhythm and blues, and you have made the Rolling Stones the stars of the festival.'[22]

The Stones continued their residencies at the Crawdaddy and the Island through late September, when Oldham had them booked on a UK tour, sharing the bill with the Everly Brothers and one of their heroes, Bo Diddley. They would return in triumph to Richmond for the 1964 jazz festival, the previous year's bottom-of-the-bill act promoted to weekend headliners. That would be their last public performance in the area until they played the first of their Twickenham Stadium concerts in 2003. But forty years earlier, it had been this corner of southwest London that nurtured the band. In just nine months, starting in December 1962, the committed fan could have seen the Rolling Stones play fifty-seven times in the Richmond and Twickenham area. What the Cavern was to the Beatles, the Crawdaddy was to the Stones. It was where the band honed its act, built a fan base, gained a manager, debuted a first single and attracted the attention of the national press.

In his autobiography *Life*, one of the most startling revelations Keith Richards makes is that he once kept a diary. The entries end, he writes, 'at the exact moment when our future was assured – our getting a regular gig at the Crawdaddy Club in Richmond, from which everything sprinkled out. Fame in six weeks.' It wasn't six weeks, it was more like six months, but it was fast.

'It was Gomelsky who organised us and made those Sunday nights at the Crawdaddy an event, rather than just being a pick-up thing, so that we started getting a name,' Richards has also said. 'He had contacts that we didn't, and he was really good at organising and making something of the Stones, even though it was still on a very small scale. Giorgio was the one who focused it by saying, "Well, we've got to get one place and make it happen there, and then you can build on that," and he understood that people would then come to you instead of you having to go to them.'[23]

Richards calls the Crawdaddy 'our training ground', crediting it as the place where he and the rest of the band got their chops together, where he realised that Jagger could work a stage 'better than anybody in the world – except for maybe James Brown'.[24] Jagger has spoken about their early audiences, 'college people, the art school crowd' who, he says, had their own way of dancing and their own fashions, which changed very quickly: 'We could look at them and go, "Yeah, OK, that's kind of interesting".'

There is an argument that if it hadn't been for the Crawdaddy, there would never have been a 'Jumpin' Jack Flash', and no 'Satisfaction' or 'Paint It Black'. It's a point of view put forward by author John McMillian, who believes it was fortunate for the Stones that they didn't have to grind it out for years in slummy bars the way the Beatles did, otherwise they would never had made it. The Stones, he says, were never bonded enough to weather a prolonged, frustrating period. Jagger would have ditched the band to finish his education, and Wyman and Watts would have gone off in search of better-paying gigs.[25]

Equally as significantly, the raw excitement of the group's performances influenced a whole generation of local musicians who figured if the Stones could do it, maybe they could, too.

CHAPTER 5

HAVING A RAVE-UP

The birdmerising, yardmerising, most blueswailing Yardbirds (with Top, then Eric, then Jeff)

WITH THE ROLLING STONES headed for the likes of the Floral Hall Ballroom in Morecambe, the Queen's Hall in Leeds and Liverpool's Fab Four-stronghold the Cavern Club, the Crawdaddy found itself without a band. Because Gomelsky was still in Switzerland this became the immediate problem of his capable and creative assistant Hamish Grimes, he of the waving arms and 'Yeah, yeahs'.

Grimes first met Gomelsky at a party. When Gomelsky learned that Grimes liked R&B, he invited him to see the group he'd just booked to play at the Station Hotel. Grimes was blown away by the Stones and immediately offered to help out at the club. Born in 1941, Hamish came from a remarkably talented family. His father was Leslie Grimes, political cartoonist for *The Evening Star*, and of his seven children, three worked in the film industry, most notably

FACING: In a publicity stunt engineered by Giorgio Gomelsky, the Yardbirds perform in the garden of Labour peer Lord Ted Willis.

Stephen, a production designer, who regularly collaborated with John Huston, David Lean and Sydney Pollack, and who would go on to win an Oscar for his work on the latter's *Out of Africa* (1985). Brother Bruce was inadvertently responsible for the first bare breasts on British television. He was the art director at the Chelsea Palace theatre on the King's Road, owned by Granada TV. One of the programmes filmed there was weekly variety show *Chelsea at Nine*. An unsteady Billie Holiday gave one of her last public performances on the show in February 1959, shortly before succumbing to cirrhosis of the liver. Another episode featured an African dance group called the Ballets Africains. They had rehearsed earlier in the day fully clothed but with the cameras rolling they trooped on stage with the women wearing only skirts and headscarves. A panicked cameraman shouted, 'They've got bare tits!' Bruce said, 'We'll call it "ethnic". Go for it.' That was Hamish's family. Gomelsky came to look on Hamish as his acolyte and co-conspirator, and the performer of tasks he'd rather not to have to do himself.[1] For example, it was Hamish who had to police the line of hopefuls waiting to see the Stones at the Crawdaddy. 'It was terrible to have to walk down the queue and say, "Look, I'm sorry, but from here on you haven't a chance of getting in",' Grimes told an interviewer in 1983.[2]

In late summer 1963, Grimes took to doing the rounds of the London clubs with the impossibly tall order of finding an act that could generate the same levels of delirium as the Stones. The group that caught his eye had just started a Friday night residency at Ken Colyer's Studio 51 and were called the Yardbirds.[3] Not that Grimes could have had the remotest inkling, but over the next five years the Yardbirds would run up a string of chart hits, break America, where they would be hailed as the crucial link between R&B, psychedelia and heavy metal, and provide a springboard for the careers of the three greatest British guitarists of all time.

As soon as Gomelsky arrived back in England, Grimes took him to see the group rehearse. 'As we're going up the stairs I hear *ta-ta-ta-ta* [getting faster and louder] *TATATATA*,' recalled Gomelsky.[4] 'They're playing a sort of manic accelerando, and it caught my ear instantly. The first thing I told them when the song finally stopped was, "You got the job". The Rolling Stones played their last Crawdaddy gig one Sunday, the Yardbirds played their first the next. No pressure. Before going any further, Gomelsky also had the group sign a five-year management contract. He wasn't going to make the same mistake twice.

As it happened, the new Crawdaddy residents were local to the Richmond area. Chris Dreja (born in Surbiton but brought up in Kingston) and Anthony 'Top' Topham (born in Southall, west London) met at the Kingston School of Art, drawn together by a shared an interest in early Chicago blues. They bought guitars and made an appearance at a school dance, before landing their first paid gig, as part of a five-piece band, at the Crown pub in Kingston. Paul Samwell-Smith (born and raised in Teddington) and Jim McCarty (born in Liverpool but brought up in Teddington) met at Hampton Grammar School, where they were also in a five-piece schoolboy band. Keith Relf (born in Richmond) was another attendee of the Kingston School of Art; he and a friend, Roger Pearce, performed as a duo called the Dreamers, playing gigs around Kingston and Richmond, including at the Vineyard Youth Club – which we'll encounter again later.

In the musical merry-go-round that was the southwestern suburbs of London, the various amateur players regularly crossed paths. Relf and Samwell-Smith came together in the Metropolis Blues Quartet in late 1962. Meanwhile, McCarty hooked up with Dreja and Topham. When the Metropolis Blues Quartet split, Dreja, McCarty and Topham invited Relf and Samwell-Smith to jam at a friend's house in Putney. This was 8 June 1963 and it marks the first time that the five played together, as a result of which they decided to become a group.

They began rehearsing at the South Western Hotel, a pub practically next door to Richmond station and just across the road from the Station Hotel, where most of the band had been to see the Rolling Stones. 'They were a fucking riot! They were amazing,' says Samwell-Smith. 'You'd just shake yourself dizzy with excitement.' (Samwell-Smith and McCarty were also among the few to have seen the Stones at Sandover Hall.) A week or so after that first jam session in Putney, Relf and Samwell-Smith were at Eel Pie Island to see one of their idols, Cyril Davies, performing with his All-Stars. Not lacking in confidence, they approached Davies and asked if their group could play the interval the following week. Incredibly, he said yes. Unlike Alexis Korner who, throughout his career, was known for giving a leg up to younger musicians, Davies had a reputation for being a cantankerous sod. A young Mick Jagger once asked him how to bend notes on the harmonica and was told, 'Get a pair of pliers'. On Sunday 30 June, the group played their first professional gig, which was at the Island.[5] They didn't even have a name – when Davies wanted to know what they were called, so he could introduce them, he was met with an embarrassed silence, until Relf suddenly said, 'We're the Yardbirds'. McCarty says he still doesn't know where the name came from, but Relf had been reading Kerouac's *On the Road*, where the term is used as slang for hobos who ride the rails. It was also one of hip jazz saxophonist Charlie Parker's nicknames. 'Either way,' says McCarty, 'it worked.'

Nobody who was at that gig remembers the support act, but it must have gone well because the newly christened Yardbirds were invited to play the same interval slot when Davies was next on the Island, on 14 July. In fact, after that gig Davies offered them a weekly

Tuesday residency at the Railway Hotel in Harrow, in northwest London, starting that week. This, in turn, led to the slot at Studio 51, which is where Hamish Grimes found them.

To the five suburban kids who made up the Yardbirds, Gomelsky was a larger-than-life character, a man of worldly sophistication. He lived in Kensington, drove a silver Lancia sports car, smoked Sobranies, spoke several languages and, when he invited the band over for dinner, he served lasagne. Most weeks Gomelsky would receive a package of records from America, obscure labels, like the Columbia subsidiary OkeH, and he'd use them to tutor his protégés. 'Boys,' he'd say in a ridiculous bass rumble that could start an earthquake, 'I'm gonna play you something and you will like this!' His tutelage didn't stop with music. Jim McCarty recalls mentioning that he thought he might be in love with some girl and Giorgio telling him to go off and read Shakespeare's sonnets, so he would know for sure. McCarty thought Gomelsky impulsive but brilliant, given to madcap schemes that he'd smash into action before anybody could suggest he might want to give it more thought.

The Yardbirds debuted at the Crawdaddy at the Athletic Association Grounds on Sunday 29 September 1963. The line-up was Keith Relf on vocals and harmonica, Top Topham on lead guitar, Chris Dreja on rhythm guitar, Paul Samwell-Smith on bass and Jim McCarty on drums. Their repertoire included 'Smokestack Lightning' by Howlin' Wolf, 'Good Morning Little Schoolgirl', as recorded by Don Level and John Love, 'I Wish You Would' by Billy Boy Arnold, and Bo Diddley's 'I'm a Man'. The set drew from the same pool of Black American blues artists as the Rolling Stones, but the Yardbirds were careful to select different songs. Predictably, the band was initially greeted by cries of 'We want the Stones', but the catcalls soon gave way to admiration as the crowd quickly realised that this new group was pretty sharp.

There is some irony in the choice of 'I'm a Man', given that guitarist Top Topham had only just turned sixteen – the others in the group were all three or four years older. He was under intense parental pressure to quit fooling around and go to college, and he eventually caved in and announced his departure just a few weeks into the Crawdaddy residency. As it happened, there was an obvious replacement, a fellow R&B enthusiast on the Kingston scene who Topham and Dreja used to trade chords with, and with whom Relf had once almost formed a band: his name was Eric Clapton. A call was made inviting him over to the Crawdaddy to check out the Yardbirds that coming Sunday 4 October.

Like Dreja and Topham, Clapton had also attended the Kingston School of Art, where his oblivious preferences for listening to LPs and getting drunk at lunch in the pub saw him expelled as an undesirable influence. It gave him more time with his guitar. He jammed with friends, including Isleworth-born David Brock, future founding member of space-rockers Hawkwind. Brock and Clapton would often meet up at Richmond's L'Auberge coffee bar, then head off to catch bands at the Island or wander up to Richmond Park, where they would strum guitars, drink cider and smoke weed.[6] In January 1963, Clapton was at the Station Hotel for a gig by the Dave Hunt R&B Band when he ran into a friend and her boyfriend, who was also a big blues fan; this was Tom McGuinness, with whom Clapton formed a short-lived band called the Roosters. They played the suburban R&B circuit, even securing a coveted West End gig at the Marquee, before Clapton and McGuinness moved on to join a Merseybeat outfit called Casey Jones and the Engineers. The band's pop orientation didn't suit and within a matter of months they both quit, which meant Clapton was at a loose end when the invitation came to take a look at the Yardbirds. (McGuinness would join Manfred Mann.)

According to Jim McCarty, the band had Clapton audition for them one afternoon in the rehearsal room at the South Western Hotel. They decided he was at least as good as Top, and two weeks later Clapton made his first official appearance with the Yardbirds at the Star Hotel in Croydon. He played his first gig at the Crawdaddy the following night, Sunday 20 October 1963. In support of the new line-up, manager Gomelsky began advertising again in the weekly *Melody Maker*:

CRAWDADDY CRAWDADDY
R.A.A. Grounds, Richmond
People come flying from
far and wide to hear R&B's

THE YARDBIRDS!!

Between October 1963 and February 1965, Clapton would play forty-five dates with the Yardbirds at the Richmond rugby clubhouse. There is always the risk that people's recollections of Clapton in his early days are retrospectively adjusted for reputational inflation – anyone can spot talent with hindsight. But it was obvious at the time that Clapton brought something different to the band. 'In the beginning,' says Jim McCarty, 'we were a typical band in that all the attention went to our singer, Keith. Then after a while, we noticed a crowd building on Eric's side of the stage. Girls and boys. So, he must have been doing something right, though I'm not really sure exactly what.' Ian McLagan knew: 'What a fabulous player. He played long, brilliant guitar solos that soared. Plus, he looked great. He was a sharply dressed Mod – the real dog's bollocks!'[7] Clapton's look helped define the group's image. Where the Stones had been dirty rockers, the Yardbirds were seen as inscrutably cool. At the same time, their shows were wild, beer-swigging, jump-up-and-down, blues-hollerin' parties. Jim Cregan (who we'll meet again later) was

The Yardbirds, from right to left: Keith Relf, Eric Clapton, Jim McCarty, Chris Dreja and Paul Samwell-Smith – manager Giorgio Gomelsky lurks at the back.

a student at Harrow Art School when a friend introduced him to the Crawdaddy. 'I saw Eric and the Yardbirds several times. Eric played a white Telecaster and he deserved the accolades he got because there was nobody playing like him. And the band had this thing they would do, where Paul Samwell-Smith would walk the bass up an octave, and up again, and it would get more and more frantic, rising to this huge crescendo before he suddenly dropped back into the original signature and the band went back into the song. They called it the "rave-up". It was their trademark. It was brilliant.'

Young guitarist Pete Townshend caught some of the early Yardbirds shows, checking out the competition, and he had his own take on the rave-up, based on the rumour that singer Keith Relf was terminally ill: 'Eric would play faster and faster and Keith, who was asthmatic, would try to keep up on the harmonica, and then Eric would go faster, and Keith would try to keep up and start wheezing, so it looked like Keith was really going to die and it would be Eric that killed him.'[8]

The room had a ceiling supported by steel I-beams, which were low enough that taller audience members could jump up and catch hold of them. 'People used to do that for a better view because the stage was only a foot high and you could only see the tops of the band's heads otherwise,' says Jim Cregan. 'People would hang from the I-beams and sort of dance while hanging, throwing their bodies about. I can't imagine what it looked like from the stage.'

Somewhere along the way, Giorgio Gomelsky (although it could equally have been Hamish Grimes) bestowed on Clapton the lasting nickname of 'Slowhand', because of the slow handclapping of Yardbird audiences as they waited for Clapton to change his frequently broken guitar strings. It was definitely Grimes who hand-drew the Yardbird's jazzy-trippy logo and hand-lettered the ads for Yardbirds gigs that appeared in *Melody Maker* and elsewhere. In 2016, Eric Clapton told an interviewer that he always suspected that it was Grimes, and not fans, who had daubed walls around London

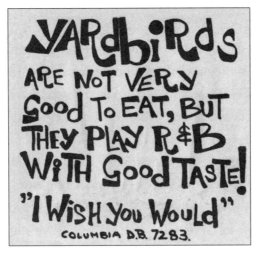

The Yardbirds logo and typography was designed
and hand-lettered by Hamish Grimes.

with the infamous 'Clapton is God' graffiti. If true, it is one of the most inspired bits of music PR ever.

In another top-drawer stunt, Gomelsky and the Yardbirds paid a home visit to Lord Ted Willis, Labour peer of the realm and a prolific writer for film, theatre and TV. One afternoon in the House of Lords, Willis had condemned the music of the Beatles and the Rolling Stones as a 'cheap, plastic, candyfloss substitute for culture'. Gomelsky had the Yardbirds head to Willis's home in Chislehurst, Kent, with photographers in tow, on a mission to present the case for pop and R&B. Rather than telling them all to clear off, the peer – obviously not adverse to a spot of publicity himself – led the group through to the back garden and showed them where to plug in. 'The Yardbirds performed about three songs in our garden,' his daughter Sally recalled, 'and then a neighbour called the police, complaining about all the noise. The police turned up, but because dad was Lord Willis, and had created *Dixon of Dock Green*, they let it go on for a little while.'[9] The following day, *The Daily Mirror* splashed the Yardbirds and Lord Willis love-in on page two. *The Daily Telegraph* also ran the story but repeatedly referred to the group as the Yardsticks.

Along with raising their profile, Gomelsky ramped up the band's workload, adding regular nights at other venues on the R&B circuit. Friday was Edwina's at 133 Seven Sisters Road in Finsbury Park, Saturday night was the Star Hotel on London Road in Croydon – both of these were marketed as Crawdaddy R&B Club nights ('The club that launched the Rolling Stones'). Tuesday or Wednesday was the Ricky Tick club at the Star & Garter in Windsor, while Monday was the Toby Jug in Tolworth, Surrey. In January 1964, the band landed a couple of support slots to Cyril Davies and Long John Baldry at the Marquee, which the following month turned into a regular Thursday then Friday night residency that ran for most of

Fans hang off the supporting I-beams at the Crawdaddy.

the rest of that year, although by late 1964 the band were increasingly away from London touring the UK. Gomelsky bussed willing fans from the Crawdaddy to wherever the Yardbirds were playing to ensure gigs were well attended. Although the members of the group were now earning decent money, Clapton, Relf and Dreja shared a flat together in a house on the South Circular Road in Kew, not far from the Relf family home off Sandycombe Road – handy given that Keith's dad, Bill, the owner of a van, was the band's roadie.

One of Gomelsky's side schemes at this time was working with Chris Barber, Harold Pendleton and the National Jazz Federation to bring American bluesmen over to the UK. Together they hooked up with the German concert agency Lippmann & Rau, which in

1962 had organised the first American Folk Blues Festival, touring a package of Black American artists around Europe, including a single UK date in Manchester. In 1963, the tour included a week of UK shows, including four nights at Croydon's Fairfield Halls. When the festival ended, Gomelsky had news for the Yardbirds: one of the artists, singer and harp player Sonny Boy Williamson, was staying on to tour the UK under his own steam and the Yardbirds were one of the bands he wanted to back him. This was not the original Sonny Boy, writer of 'Good Morning Little Schoolgirl' (he was murdered in Chicago in 1948), but a disciple whose vocal style and harmonica playing were modelled on his namesake. About three weeks later, the Yardbirds played a first gig with Sonny Boy at the Crawdaddy in Croydon and the following night, 8 December, they all appeared at the Crawdaddy in Richmond. They went on to play several more dates together but the first two were significant because they were recorded for an album. What Samwell-Smith remembers is that Sonny Boy was never without his briefcase, which always contained at least one bottle of Johnnie Walker. For the Crawdaddy gigs the band rehearsed with Sonny Boy in the afternoon and by the time they took to the stage in the evening, the whisky had done its work. After the first couple of tracks Sonny Boy went off-piste, abandoning the setlist so the band had to make it up as they stumbled along behind him. Nevertheless, the album was eventually issued, in 1966, as *Sonny Boy Williamson & the Yardbirds*. (Sonny Boy wasn't around to hear it, having died in his sleep the previous year.)

A better live recording, one that captures the ragged excitement of the early R&B scene, was made three months later, on 13 March 1964, when the Yardbirds shared the bill with Long John Baldry and the Hoochie Coochie Men, along with Sonny Boy Williamson. The occasion was to celebrate the reopening of the Marquee, following its move from Oxford Street to Wardour Street, around the corner in Soho. Sonny Boy finished his set wearing a fireman's helmet, presented to him by the club's manager, who was Barbara Pendleton's father and the former chief fire officer of Richmond. The record was put out at the end of the year as *Five Live Yardbirds*, with a cover shot by Hamish Grimes. You can also hear Grimes introducing the band at the start of side one opener 'Too Much Monkey Business' – 'Good evening and welcome, and now it is time for birdmerising, yardmerising, in fact, most blueswailing, Yardbirds….'

In August, it was time for the Marquee's annual weekend jaunt out to the suburbs. What used to be the National Jazz Festival was now, for its fourth edition, renamed as the National Jazz & Blues Festival, with a line-up split about evenly between the two musical styles. The Yardbirds were on the bill, but it wasn't quite the showcase they hoped. On the Friday before the festival, as the group played its regular gig at the Marquee, Relf had to stop because of breathing difficulties. He was rushed to hospital where he was found to have a collapsed lung. So when the band played the festival on Sunday night it was with a stand-in singer. Before then was the much-anticipated return to Richmond of the Rolling Stones, which took place on the Friday night. All that rainy afternoon, the queue had been growing alongside Twickenham Road, until there were some 7,000 soaking fans waiting for the turnstiles to open. When the Stones appeared, girls fainted and the scenes of screaming fans featured in British Pathé News reports screened at cinemas around the country. This never happened with the Original Downtown Syncopators.

On Saturday, the succession of the British jazz stalwarts was pepped up by US blues singer Jimmy Witherspoon, who took to the stage in a mohair suit and bow tie. Later, Witherspoon reappeared to play with the Chris Barber Band. Long John Baldry performed with his Hoochie Coochie Men, featuring Rod Stewart, and they stayed on stage to back the next artist, American pianist and blues

The Rolling Stones are the main stage headliners on a wet Friday night at the fourth edition of what is now the National Jazz and Blues Festival.

singer Memphis Slim. The evening closed with Manfred Mann, who were the day's headliners on the back of their number one single, 'Do Wah Diddy Diddy'.

The Yardbirds were first on the bill on Sunday night. 'It was a strange summer evening,' remembers Paul Samwell-Smith, 'I was having trouble with my amp and I ended up sticking the neck of my bass through the front of it.' Jim McCarty also remembers the band's performance 'being a little bit half-cocked' – possibly because they were missing frontman Keith Relf to illness (his place was taken by stand-ins Mick O'Neill, of the Authentics, and blues enthusiast Mike Vernon). They were followed by Georgie Fame and American jazz pianist and singer Mose Allison who, for many aficionados, was the festival's big draw. The Graham Bond Organisation also performed. At one point the Yardbirds, Georgie Fame and Graham Bond's rhythm section were all up together, so for the first time Eric Clapton shared a stage with Ginger Baker and Jack Bruce, the two musicians with whom he would form Cream the following summer. The festival was closed by the jazz old guard of the Humphrey Lyttelton and Kenny Ball bands.

Attendance for the weekend was around 27,000 and the festival turned a profit, possibly for the first time. Harold Pendleton's rule of thumb was that anything new needed to be given at least three years, because it took that long to create a loyal base and momentum. The trick was not to run out of money in the meantime.

Gomelsky was not doing too badly, either. Although the Yardbirds had to pull out of a national tour because of Relf's illness, Gomelsky had got them on the bill as one of the support acts for the Beatles' three-week run of Christmas shows at the 3,500-seat Hammersmith Odeon. What the Yardbirds didn't have was a hit single. The Rolling Stones had already had a number one in the UK with 'Little Red Rooster', as had fellow R&B bands Manfred Mann (the aforementioned 'Do Wah Diddy Diddy') and the Animals ('The House of the Rising Sun'). The two singles the Yardbirds had put out to date had done nothing, while the album *Five Live Yardbirds*, despite good reviews, also hadn't sold. Early in 1965, Gomelsky told the band that for their next record they had to move away from R&B and try something new. At a meeting at his Lexham Gardens flat, he played the group a song demo by a young unknown from Manchester named Graham Gouldman, who had written it in the changing room of the men's clothing shop where he worked (Gouldman would later become one quarter of 10cc). This was 'For Your Love'. The Yardbirds recorded the song in early February. Samwell-Smith stepped up to production duties and engaged two or three session musicians to help out, including Brian Auger, who led off the track on that most R&B of all instruments, the harpsichord. The twin guitars that had previously driven the Yardbirds' sound hardly featured, coming in only halfway through the track, and then only briefly, before fading back into the mix under clattering bongos and a tight military snare. Perhaps as consolation, the B-side was a guitar-led, 'Green Onions'-like instrumental called 'Got to Hurry'. Easily the most interesting thing about it is the writing credit: Samwell-Smith remembers Gomelsky's voice over the intercom at the recording, saying, 'Hey boys, why don't you put me down as the author on this?' – the rationale being because it was his suggestion they do a bluesy instrumental. So the track was credited to O Rasputin, a Gomelsky pseudonym, and he got the publishing royalties. 'That was definitely dodgy behaviour,' says Samwell-Smith.

Gomelsky would also take credit for the use of a harpsichord on 'For Your Love', claiming it was inspired by his admiration of Wanda Landowska, the famed Polish classical harpsichordist.[10] 'I was the one bringing in all this information. They didn't know about the harpsichord. They didn't know about African music. They didn't know about Arabic music, Stockhausen, Xenakis. In England, they didn't know about this kind of stuff... In Europe we had a better education, so we heard all this stuff when we were twelve, thirteen years old.'[11]

It wasn't just the Yardbirds that Gomelsky says benefitted from his expanded musical horizons. In the same interview, he claims he invited along a sitar player from his local Indian restaurant to the recording of the Yardbird's next single, 'Heart Full of Soul'. The sitar didn't make it onto the record in the end, but friend of the band Jimmy Page happened to be there at the session and he bought the Indian's sitar. The next day he took it with him to the studio, where he played it to fellow guitarist Big Jim Sullivan, who borrowed the instrument and played it for George Harrison. Four months later the Beatles recorded 'Norwegian Wood', commonly held to be the first Western pop or rock record to include a sitar. That's the way Gomelsky told it, anyway.

As keyboardist Brian Auger left the recording session, his parting comment was, 'Who in their right mind is gonna buy a pop tune with a harpsichord on it?' Quite a few people, as it happened. 'For Your Love' was the hit the Yardbirds had been seeking, making the Top 10 in both the UK and America. By that time, however, Eric Clapton was gone.

Playing Christmas variety shows (even if it was with the Beatles) was bad enough, but Clapton absolutely hated 'For Your Love', which he dismissed as 'pop crap'. One afternoon in the week before the record was due to be released he went to see Gomelsky. 'I sat with him in my office in Soho Square,' Gomelsky told an interviewer in 2007, 'and we started a discussion at two o'clock in the afternoon. We didn't even see the day die and at ten o'clock at night we were still talking.' Gomelsky told Clapton nobody was going to stand in his way if he wanted to leave the band, and he did. Within weeks, Clapton found himself a new home where he didn't have to bend from the blues with John Mayall's Bluesbreakers.

If it seems mad that the Yardbirds could be so unconcerned about Clapton walking away, at this point he was just another guitarist, albeit one who took himself very seriously. Yardbird fans might have rated him, but then there weren't that many Yardbirds fans. The same month Clapton left the band, *Melody Maker* ran a multi-part feature on the 'Stars of Beat'. Part one was devoted to Britain's ten top guitarists, listed as George Harrison, Keith Richards, Hank Marvin of the Shadows, Tony Hicks of the Hollies, Hilton Valentine of the Animals, Mike Pender of the Searchers, Keith Hopwood of Herman's Hermits, Dave Davies of the Kinks, Chuck Botfield of the Rockin' Berries and session man Jim Sullivan. No mention of Eric.

As when Top Topham quit, the rest of the group already knew who they wanted as their new lead guitarist. Jimmy Page. He grew up in Epsom, not far from the Yardbirds, was the same age and hung around the same scene – he'd played with Alexis Korner and Cyril Davies, and had been a regular in the audience at Eel Pie Island and the Crawdaddy, where he caught the Yardbirds a few times. Gomelsky knew him – 'Gomelsky knew everybody,' says McCarty – and so the group had their manager ask Page if he'd like to join them. The answer was no. Page was an in-demand session man and he was earning far more in the studio than the Yardbirds could offer. He suggested they check out his friend Jeff Beck instead.

At the time, Beck was with a band called the Tridents. Gomelsky and Grimes caught them playing a sweaty session at the 100 Club, which was close to Gomelsky's office. They were impressed enough to offer the guitarist an audition that week at the Marquee. McCarty remembers the group being unimpressed by his appearance – where Clapton dressed in the tastiest threads he could afford, Beck dressed exactly like the car mechanic he was. 'It was a bit of a shock,' says McCarty. But he could play. 'We tested him on some of Eric's signature numbers,' recalls McCarty, 'and he didn't emulate them, he took them further.' Satisfied, Gomelsky told Chris Dreja to take Beck down to Carnaby Street and get him some new clothes and a decent haircut to bring his appearance more into line with the rest of the band.

Clapton played his last gig with the Yardbirds at Bristol Corn Exchange on 3 March 1965. Two days later, the band released the single 'For Your Love' and that night Jeff Beck made his Yardbirds debut at the Fairfield Halls, Croydon. His first appearance at the Crawdaddy came on 14 March. Some lamented the departure of Clapton ('The day Eric left, the blues left,' says Peter Moody of local band the Grebbels) and it's true that from this point the group began shedding what remained of its R&B roots, but with the maverick talent of Beck in the line-up the band had hit single followed by hit single, peaking both creatively and commercially.

At this point, it's worth pausing to ask a question. Eric Clapton. Jeff Beck. Jimmy Page (who although he turned down the Yardbirds in 1965, would later come back to take up the offer). Between them, the three Yardbirds guitarists would carve out a blues-based rock legacy built on Blind Faith, Cream and Led Zeppelin. All three born and brought up within a loudhailer's distance of each other. What were they putting in the water around here?

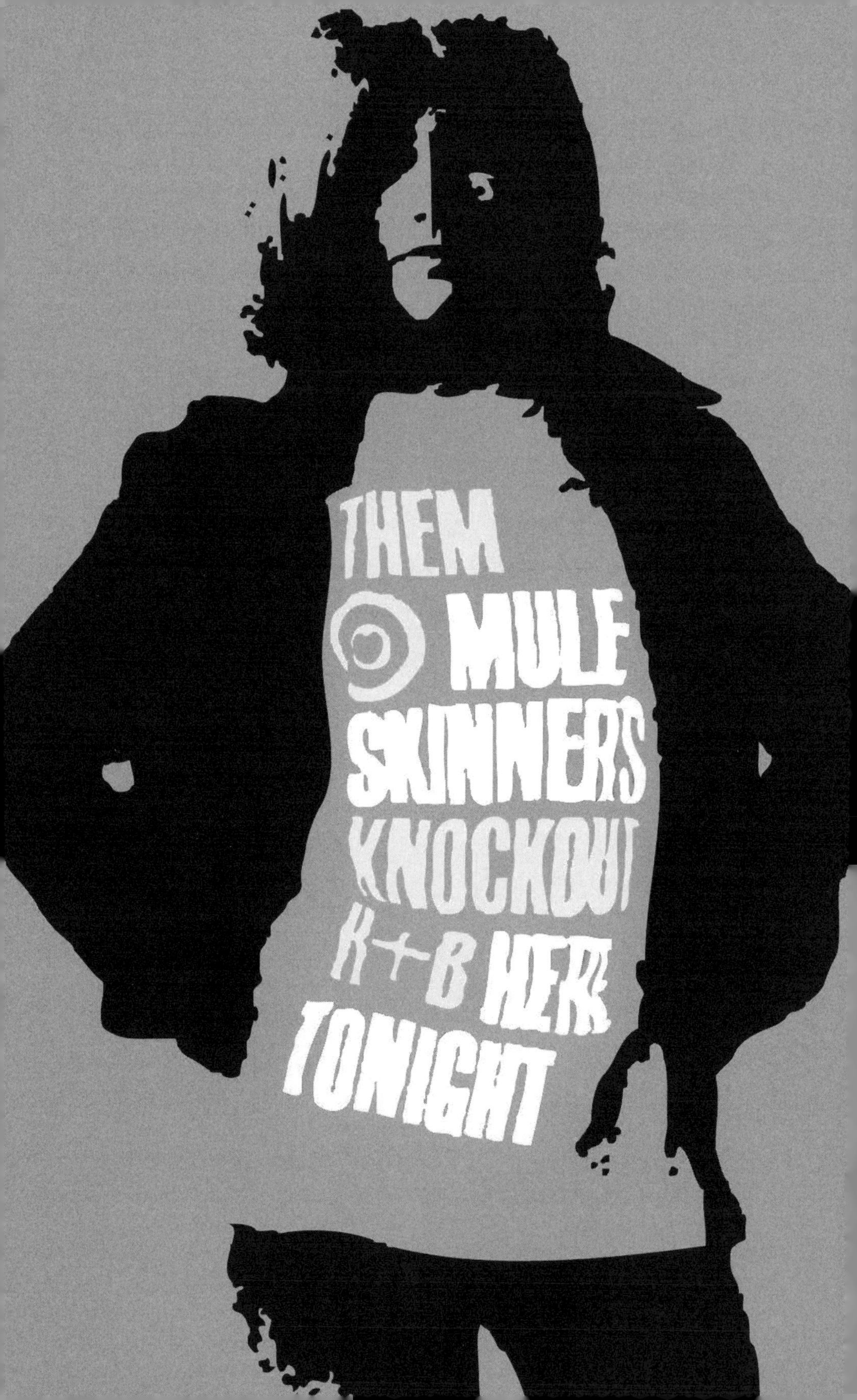
THEM
MULE
SKINNERS
KNOCKOUT
R+B HERE
TONIGHT

CHAPTER 6

STRAIGHT OUTTA HAMPTON

Why Surrey got the blues, and what strobe lights and slipping on marbles had to do with it

IN DECEMBER 2015, US music magazine *Rolling Stone* published its list of the all time '100 Greatest Guitarists' as chosen by a sizeable ensemble of respected musicians and senior music writers. At No.5 they placed Jeff Beck, born June 1944 in Wallington, Surrey. At No.3 was Jimmy Page, born January 1944 in Heston, Middlesex, but brought up in Epsom, Surrey. And No.2 was Eric Clapton, born March 1945 in Ripley, Surrey. Three individuals all raised within twenty miles (and born within fourteen months) of each other, in the bucolic Home Counties southwest of London. What was it about Surrey of all places?

In a roundabout way, the water did have something to do with it. The presence of the Thames is significant. West of London, the

FACING: A poster for the Muleskinners at Eel Pie Island. The band were students at Twickenham Art School, as was poster designer Colin Fulcher (later Barney Bubbles).

ribbon of towns and villages along the river, with their meadows, moorings and slipways, steeples and manors, are possessed of a particularly English beauty. As a result, the area has long been the preserve of the privileged and wealthy. Three or four hundred years ago it was royals and nobles creating landed estates and hunting grounds on which they erected palatial and castellated homes along the water. By the twentieth century their place had been taken by barristers, bankers, stockbrokers and practitioners of other over-rewarded professions. When rock'n'roll hit Britain in the Fifties, the middle-class offspring of the Thames Valley had the cash for expensive electric guitars and drum kits. They were also a brief train ride from the music clubs and coffee bars of London's West End.

Take Hampton, for example. On the north bank of the Thames, west of Kingston, it's best known as home to Hampton Court Palace, the sixteenth-century retreat of Henry VIII. In addition to kings and queens, the town has been the residence of architect Christopher Wren, eighteenth-century actor David Garrick and Xenia Alexandrovna, sister of the last of the Russian tsars, the unfortunate Nicholas II. Anthony Trollope set his 1857 novel *The Three Clerks* in Hampton, and the area features briefly in Dickens' *Oliver Twist* and *Nicholas Nickelby*, and in HG Wells's *The War of the Worlds*.

Then there is the town's hallowed Hampton Grammar School, which dates its foundation to 1557, but is also part of a more recent tradition. 'Hampton School was a cradle for a lot of rock musicians which was a kind of bizarre conjunction, really, because Hampton was a very academic school – and still is,' says alumnus Paul Stewart. 'The headmaster was a vicar, the Reverend George Whitfield, and he had rules about stuff like keeping our hair at a certain length. I think there was a joint feeling among the young guys – because this was a boys-only school – that this was something to rebel against.

The music was part of that. Just before us, a couple of the Yardbirds had gone to the school, Jim McCarty and Paul Samwell-Smith, and another guy called Vic Briggs was around, who went on to play with Eric Burdon. And Brian May came from the school. He was a bit of a nerd. We used to play with him in the back room, you know, trading licks. And another guy called Murray Head. I think the common thing was rebellion against what was going down.'[1]

Some of McCarty and Samwell-Smith's earliest public performances were as part of schoolboy band the Country Gentlemen, playing end-of-term dances at the Grammar. A couple of years later, their spot was inherited by Paul Stewart and a group of fellow Hamptonians, who played as the Others. They built up a devoted fan-base and a circuit of regular gigs, including occasional support slots at Eel Pie Island. In the summer of 1964, the Others recorded their one and only record, a cover of Bo Diddley's 'Oh Yeah', which was released on the Fontana label (before the year was out, parental pressure forced the fledgling musical stars into early retirement). 'We were sort of the ones that got away – that's how people have referred to us,' says Stewart.[2]

While Clapton, Beck, Page and Richards were not grammar school boys, they all came from comfortably middle-class backgrounds. 'How ridiculous that white blues developed in this genteel area of southern England,' says Yardbird Chris Dreja. 'What is a howlin' wolf when you live in Surbiton?'[3] Dreja's one-time bandmate, Top Topham, has suggested that part of the appeal was that blues was the first truly soulful music any of them had heard. Added to which, a lot of the songs were appealingly risqué, with lyrics like 'You can squeeze my lemon 'til the juice run down my leg'. A network of frustrated teenage boys found escape from their mundane suburban lives in the grooves of obscure, hard-to-find albums by Robert Johnson, Sleepy John Estes, Howlin' Wolf and other original blues

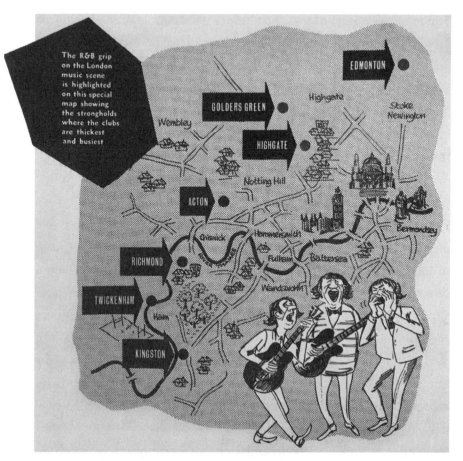

The R&B grip on the London music scene is highlighted on this special map showing the strongholds where the clubs are thickest and busiest

An illustration from the 18 April 1964 issue of *Melody Maker*, accompanying a feature that identifies R&B as a largely suburban London phenomenon.

heroes whose roots lay in Mississippi and Chicago. Just as middle-class students favouring trad jazz over plebian rock'n'roll in the mid-'50s had an indisputable element of snobbishness, so too did the elitist pursuit of sharecroppers' blues over clean-cut, mainstream pop in the early 1960s.

The catalyst for turning a middle-class fanboy obsession into fully fledged national mania was a basement dive down a flight of steps between the ABC Bakery and a jeweller's shop on Ealing Broadway, in west London. Beginning on 17 March 1962, one night

114

a week the Ealing Jazz Club, which had been in existence since 1959, gave the stage over to a bunch of enthusiasts experimenting with Black American electric blues. The sessions were led by guitarist Alexis Korner and harmonica player Cyril Davies. Korner had formerly played with Ken Colyer's jazz band and had met Davies at the London Skiffle Club. The two joined forces to play folk-tinged blues at the London Blues and Barrelhouse Club on Tottenham Court Road but were ejected for turning up with amps. They decamped to Ealing, setting up Britain's first R&B club. Korner operated an open-mic policy that drew every blues enthusiast in the country who could find their way to the Ealing stage. They were all 'trainspotters', according to Mick Jagger, speaking about the early R&B crowd – 'Just a bunch of anoraks. And the girls were very thin on the ground.'[4]

'You didn't go down there to get laid,' agrees Keith Richards, another Ealing habitué.[5] Out of the musicians at the Ealing Club, Korner and Davies put together Blues Incorporated, the UK's first R&B band and a virtual finishing school for the new movement. From this moist subterranean club with condensation dripping from the ceiling, pooling on the stage – 'You were literally stepping in an inch of water in the middle of the all the electrics,' says Richards[6] – the scene exploded.

Blues Incorporated landed a residency at the Marquee, which led to the Rolling Stones' first gig. Shut out of the central London clubs, the Stones established their fanbase out in the southwest suburbs where they lit the touch paper that launched the R&B boom. They hadn't cut any records yet, so the only way to experience the Stones was live. It follows that the many imitators the band spawned would be in the same area: Richmond, Twickenham and the Thames Valley hinterlands – or, as some have called it, the 'Surrey Delta'.[7]

'In 1964 there was more blues music being played in Kingston and

Surbiton than Chicago,' says Greg Tesser, then the publicity manager for the Yardbirds.[8] His claims for Surbiton sound particularly wild given the only local venue was the Assembly Rooms on Claremont Road, but there's no question that there was plenty going on in riverside Kingston.[9] 'Kingston and Richmond were the two key places,' agrees Jimmy Page.[10] 'It was a good scene then, because everyone had this same upbringing and had been locked away with their records, and there was something really new to offer.' In 1964, Coronation Hall, which was a former public swimming baths in Denmark Road, hosted the Yardbirds, Cheynes (featuring Mick Fleetwood), Zombies, and Lulu and the Luvvers. A number of pubs in town had live music, including the Fighting Cocks in London Road, the Swan in Mill Street, the Grey Horse on the Richmond Road and the Crown, which was in Crown Passage. There was also the Jazz Cellar, which started life in a basement but later created confusion on two counts by relocating to upstairs rooms on the high street and ditching jazz for R&B while retaining the old name. And there was the Jazz Boat, which was an old Dutch sailing barge moored just below Kingston Bridge, with a below-deck performance space. That's a lot of live music for a small town.

A couple of years later, when the blues scene was at its height, a journalist writing in *Anarchy* magazine observed, 'Looking at the posters that litter the side streets of central and suburban London, one might be forgiven for assuming that the blues was created by a post-Aldermaston generation of art students rather than by the afflicted negro population of the American Deep South.' [11]

It's notable that even at this early stage (1965), the link between art schools and the evolving music scene was already being made. Later, cultural theorists would devote whole books to the influence of the one on the other. 'If you want to find somewhere from which you could say the whole Sixties culture comes from, it was the art schools,' says Pearce Marchbank, one of the most respected names in British graphic design.[12] 'Art schools were the laboratories that were making rock musicians and designers and painters.'

During the Fifties and Sixties, the loose entry requirements for art school – which welcomed the talented but academically unqualified – offered a way into further education that wasn't university. When John Lennon failed his O levels, Liverpool College of Art offered him a lifeline – 'It was better than working,' he said.[13] 'The simple fact is,' wrote former art student turned rock historian Pete Frame, 'if you have any artistic talent, you can groove along on a grant, go to a few lectures, enjoy an excellent social life, rehearse in any spare rooms, meet similarly inclined students, get posters done for nothing, prepare for stardom.'[14]

Suburban art schools fed the London music scene, including schools in Sidcup (attended by Keith Richards, and Phil May and Dick Taylor of the Pretty Things), Camberwell (Syd Barrett), Hammersmith (Cat Stevens), Harrow (Charlie Watts), Hornsey (Ray Davies, Roger Glover of Deep Purple), Sutton (Jimmy Page) and Wimbledon (Jeff Beck). Obviously, the southwest didn't have any sort of monopoly but it did have three art schools in close proximity – Ealing (attended by Pete Townshend, Ronnie Wood, Thunderclap Newman, Freddie Mercury), Kingston (Eric Clapton, Chris Dreja, Top Topham, Keith Relf, Tom McGuinness of Manfred Mann) and Twickenham (Ian McLagan of the Small Faces).

'It all came out of that art school semi-intelligentsia,' says Chris Dreja, 'that's where the southern blues thing kicked off.'[15] It was at art college that Keith Richards first heard American blues, got his hands on an electric guitar (acquired in a swap for some records) and joined his first band. 'Everybody would bring in their own records and we'd sit around and play stuff like imports,' recalled Pretty Things vocalist Phil May. 'You might buy one record, then the other six bought theirs, so you got to hear seven records, stuff like Slim Harpo, Muddy Waters, Lightnin' Hopkins, Chuck Berry and Bo Diddley. You couldn't turn on a radio or TV and get this stuff.'[16]

Keith Richards recalls a similar experience. 'Guys like Wizz Jones, who was a really good guitar picker, occasionally came round to the art schools, if they wanted a cup of tea,' he says. 'People like Wizz would sit in the john at the school and pass the guitar round. I learned a lot of licks in that john just from guys passing through. We'd go, "Okay, let's cut life class and go to the john." I didn't do well at life class but I became a much better guitar player.'[17] It wasn't just tips on guitar the Stones picked up from art school – in the band's first *Melody Maker* interview, Mick Jagger was asked about their 'giant urchin haircuts': 'Art students and college people have had these haircuts for years,' he explained.[18]

Richards' future guitar partner in the Stones, Ronnie Wood, followed big brothers Art and Ted to Ealing Art College. He explained why to biographer Terry Rawlings. 'Art and Ted would always have their schoolmates over at our house. Artists, musicians and wild bohemians with shades, drainpipe trousers, suede brothel-creepers and big overcoats. They'd have all these nice looking chicks with them and they'd lock themselves in the front room with all their instruments.'[19] Ronnie wanted some of that, the chicks especially. When he finally got there he was unimpressed with the pseudo posturing of the lecturers and his fellow students, but there was one thing art school was good for: 'Almost everyone I knew in Ealing went on to become a professional musician,' says Wood, who palled up with a fellow student to form a group.[20]

Pete Townshend has written that Ealing Art College was a revelation 'in so many ways: socially, creatively, sexually and musically'.[21] In his autobiography, he describes how Ealing offered lunchtime clubs dedicated to bebop, Dixieland, orchestral music and opera, with music played in the lecture hall on a large, high-quality speaker system. He writes about how, soon after he started, a guest lecturer asked the class to draw a line, north-to-south, six inches long, of uniform thickness. After the students complied, the lecturer produced a penknife, pricked his finger and dragged blood across a sheet of paper. '*That's* a line,' he said. Art schools were about teaching students how to think rather than how to paint. Townshend's time at Ealing coincided with that of teacher and theorist Roy Ascott as head of foundation studies. The curriculum Ascott designed was inspired by cybernetics and behavioural sciences and was aimed

Ealing art student Pete Townshend (third from left) participating in a college project involving someone upside down in a telephone box.

at shaking up established patterns. In one session, students were subjected to flashes of light in a darkened room and then let loose to stumble over a floor covered with marbles. Guest lecturers included artist and activist Gustav Metzger, whose auto-destructive art theories later directly influenced Townshend's trademark guitar-smashing. Townshend remembers another guest lecturer being a gay American junkie sax-playing painter – which was a whole lot of firsts for most of the students. Townshend also met Tom Wright at Ealing, stepson of a US Air Force officer stationed nearby, who introduced him to a new world of Black American blues artists, such as Lightnin' Hopkins and Howlin' Wolf.

It's worth mentioning the part American military bases played in nurturing British R&B. An archipelago of these bases lay west and southwest of London. Camp Griffiss was in Bushy Park, just across the river from Kingston, serving as the European Headquarters for the USAAF from July 1942 to December 1944. It remained a US base until October 1963, and American personnel interacted freely with local residents, attending dances and hosting base parties of their own, at which many locals would have heard jazz and blues for the first time. Alexis Korner recruited Ronnie Jones, a black gospel-singing airman from the US base at High Wycombe, to sing with Blues Incorporated.

It was at Kingston School of Art that Clapton met his first real American musician, a folk singer called Gina Glaser, who had travelled the Appalachian Mountains collecting original songs and been part of New York's Greenwich Village scene. He recalls she sang in a clear voice, accompanying herself on guitar in a clawhammer style. To make extra money Glaser posed nude for still-life classes at the school. Clapton was starstruck. Glaser was also a formative influence on two other Kingston art students, the folk guitarist John Renbourn, who made his name with folk-jazzers Pentangle, and singer-songwriter Sandy Denny, later of Fairport Convention.

While the record-buying Kingston art students who frequented his junk shop inspired Arthur Chisnall to launch his Eelpiland club, it was the students from Twickenham Art School who adopted the club as their common room. In its own way, Twickenham was every bit as unorthodox as the art school at Ealing. 'The head of the school was a chap called Osmund Caine,' says former student and Eelpilander Bob Wagner.[22] 'He wasn't interested in whether you had any O levels, he selected students based on their portfolio. One of these chaps we were at college with was a gang leader for a bunch of Mods in Hammersmith. He said everyone he knew ended up in prison except him because he was given this opportunity.' Such an entrance policy – shared by other art schools – resulted in a rich mix of social types and talent, and a haven for oddballs and misfits.

The uniforms of Eel Pie Island, as sketched by Twickenham art student Bob Wagner: 'Jazzers – usually fine-art students; beer drinkers, pipe smokers, sandals; Saturday night crowd. Early Mods – graphic-design students; snappy dressers; Sunday and Wednesday R&B and blues crowd. Rockers – engineering/building day-release students; Sunday and Wednesday rock bands.'

A poster for a night of folk music at the Twickenham Art School in November 1965, designed by student Stephen Goy.

Caine himself was notably odd. He was tall and had a terrifying bellow, possibly honed during his five years with the military police during World War II. He was an accomplished fine artist and some of his best work shares a similar sensibility to that of Stanley Spencer.[23] His wife Mary, who also taught at the school, was a lefty with esoteric leanings: she revived the idea of the Glastonbury Zodiac, a map of the stars on a gigantic scale formed by features in

122

the landscape around Glastonbury Tor, and produced a book and a film about it (the latter narrated by her husband). Osmund was also a prolific designer of ecumenical stained glass and later in life was credited with inventing the bikini. It was 1996 when a London art dealer pointed out that the two-piece swimsuits in Caine's 1938 painting 'Bathing Beach' were bikinis eight years before the French designer Louis Réard introduced the abbreviated swimwear to the world. Caine claimed he'd wanted to paint the women nude but had to think of the 'propriety of the setting', so covered them up in the most minimal way he felt he could get away with.

In 1961, five years before he auditioned for the Small Faces, budding artist Ian McLagan was called before Osmund Caine to show what he could do. It was a Saturday morning and he was one of a bunch of hopefuls who were tasked with painting a composition of their own choosing. McLagan, who played guitar at the time, drew a stage with some guitars leaning against amps – the band were on a break, he told Caine, to hide the fact he couldn't draw people. He passed and entered into Twickenham Art School that September. Echoing Eric Clapton's educational experience, one of the biggest eye-openers for McLagan was the chance to ogle naked women up close in life-drawing class. More significantly (or maybe not), he joined his first band at Twickenham, the Cherokees (the name no doubt inspired by the Shadows' twangy instrumental hit 'Apache' of the previous year). When the cool kids at college caught on to Muddy Waters and Howlin' Wolf, the Cherokees became the Muleskinners, which sounded more bluesy. 'We were never "big time" and most of us weren't what you might call attractive, we were in fact just another more or less unknown 1960s blues band,' recalls the band's harmonica player Nick Tweddell. McLagan incurred the wrath of Osmund Caine when the college head learned that the Muleskinner had spent his sixty quid grant money on an organ.

Stephen Goy, who was a year below McLagan, remembers Caine telling the assembled students, 'The silly boy has wasted his grant money. Do not follow his example!'

One of the most impressive characters at Twickenham, according to McLagan, was Colin Fulcher, who was a couple of years above him but with whom he became friends. Gawky but charismatic, and far ahead of the pack in terms of talent, Fulcher designed a handful of posters and flyers for college events at Eel Pie Island, including one for McLagan's band, the Muleskinners, and another for an end of year dance with music by the Rolling Stones. After graduating, he was talent-spotted and snapped up by the Conran design practice. In the evenings, he began providing lighting for gigs, mixing coloured inks with oil sandwiched between glass slides to create 'bubbles of liquid light', which is how he came to be known as Barney Bubbles. He progressed to working with space rockers Hawkwind, designing their album sleeves, lighting and sets. In the mid 1970s, Fulcher became creative director for post-punk label Stiff Records, producing record sleeves, logos, posters and T-shirts for the likes of Elvis Costello, Nick Lowe, the Damned, and Ian Dury & the Blockheads. Along the way, he also designed the masthead for the music paper *NME* and became a pioneering music-video director, responsible for, among others, the Specials' 'Ghost Town' video. He almost never put his name to his work, preferring to sign himself by his VAT number. Plagued by depression, he committed suicide in 1983 at the age of forty-one.

Back to the question of Clapton, Beck and Page, and why R&B became rooted in the leafy lanes and pastures of the Thames Valley. 'It wasn't just Surrey,' says Grebbels bassist Peter Moody. 'There was a south London blues scene around Streatham, and there were scenes in Manchester and up in Newcastle, but they were nothing like what we had going on'

'Don't underestimate the impact of the Stones,' says Paul Stewart of the Others. 'They had a massive effect on all young musicians, including us.'

'People like Jagger and the Stones were one step ahead of the rest of us,' agrees Moody. 'They were the beginning, basically.'

CHAPTER 7

THEM RIZLA BLUES

Following on from the Stones, Cyril, Ada and Phyllis transform Eel Pie Island into a bastion of R&B

OR THE FIRST SIX YEARS OF ITS EXISTENCE it was the Eelpiland Jazz Club. But by the end of 1962, clubbers would have been letting Arthur Chisnall know that trad was old, dad. According to Roger Sharp, who shared a house with him for years, Chisnall had no particular musical tastes – 'I don't think he liked any kind of music,' says Sharp – possibly because he was tone deaf. He was reluctant to book these new bands with electric guitars and had to be talked into it by the teenagers who helped him run the club. He kept the Saturday and Sunday jazz sessions but added an occasional Wednesday featuring some of the new 'Beat' bands, such as Tony Holland and the Packabeats, Mike Berry and the Outlaws, Cliff Bennett and the Rebel Rousers, and Screaming Lord Sutch and the Savages. All are footnotes in the history of popular music except, of course, Screaming Lord Sutch, who has a sizeable entry

FACING: Eelpilanders pose outside the main entrance to the hotel including, on the far right, regular attendee, the immaculately tailored Rod Stewart.

in the annals of British politics for contesting and losing forty elections, campaigning on promises to provide heated toilet seats for pensioners, abolish January and February (to make winter shorter), and breed fish in a wine lake so they could be caught ready pickled. Anonymous behind their madcap frontman, the Savages were actually a phenomenal band: drummer Carlo Little and guitarist/ bassist Ricky Fenson played early gigs with the Rolling Stones before Charlie Watts and Bill Wyman became permanent hires (Savages pianist Nicky Hopkins would later be a regular session player on the Stones' studio albums). It was Carlo Little who supposedly turned the Stones onto Charlie Watts when they asked him to join the band and he said no because he was earning too much with the Savages. Fast forward to June 1999, and Little and the Rolling Stones are at Wembley, except while the band prepare to play two nights of their No Security tour, Little is earning his living selling hot dogs and burgers from a trailer on the stadium approach.

The Stones are more closely associated with the Crawdaddy, but they played the Island a not inconsiderable twenty-four times between April and September 1963. Their gigs here provided a 'eureka' moment for a young Ronnie Wood: 'I remember the fallout from seeing the Stones' shows there when they were playing stuff like "Walking the Dog" and "I'm a King Bee". We were knocked out. They had a staunch following and that's when I first got wind of them and said: "That's the band I want to be in".'[1]

The Stones' Island gigs were all as part of a Wednesday night residency, except one show on Friday 12 July, when they were hired to play a dance organised by the Twickenham Art School. The student who made the booking was Ian McLagan. One night, while helping the Stones carry their equipment from a gig, he'd asked Mick Jagger for their agent's phone number and, being on the student union social committee, used it to book the band for the college's end of term bash. Naturally, McLagan's own group, the Muleskinners, were the support act. The poster for the gig was designed by Colin Fulcher, the future Barney Bubbles.

'They were just local guys,' says Brian Ranken, a teenage music fan in 1963, who first saw the Stones at the Station Hotel and followed them to the Island. He remembers Mick Jagger announcing that the band had just made a record – 'Come On', released 7 June 1963 – and saying 'We want you to go out and buy it because we need the money.' Tom Newman's memory is that the Stones were not short of cash.[2] Newman's band, the Tomcats, played the Island occasionally and they turned up together one night to check out the Stones soon after the release of 'Come On', which was a number the Tomcats had featured in their sets for years. 'They nicked it from us,' says Newman. 'The Stones had a complete set of new Vox amps,' he says. 'We were so jealous. We were using stuff salvaged from secondhand shops and I had to make our guitar cabinet.'

The Stones appeared with a support act for at least some of their Island performances. A young musician from Hounslow named David Cousins sometimes worked the cloakroom (where he shared shifts with Susie Shahn, Arthur Chisnall's lodger, who also happened to be a talented banjo player and passed on some of what she knew to her co-worker). Cousins and his playing partner, Tony Hooper, persuaded Chisnall to give them a slot. He remembers that when he and Hooper played bluegrass in the interval between the Stones' sets, most of the audience disappeared outside. But those who remained, he says, were appreciative, including Brian Jones: 'Like your music, man,' he told Cousins. Cousins and Hooper would go on to form the Strawberry Hill Boys, the name later shortened to the Strawbs. (After recording with Rick Wakeman and Sandy Denny, and scoring a No.2 hit in 1973 with 'Part of the Union', they're still going today.)

Music fan Brian Ranken was at the Stones gig in late September

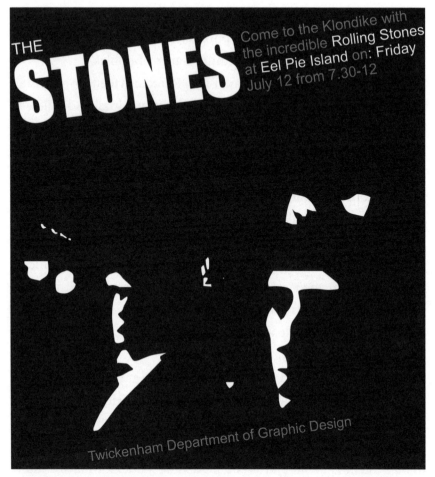

Recreation of a poster for the Rolling Stones' sole Friday appearance on the Island, providing the music for a Twickenham Art School dance – design by Colin Fulcher.

when Jagger announced that this would be their last on the Island for a while because they were heading off on tour, but if it didn't work out they'd be back. It seems to have worked out all right.

The Yardbirds may have replaced the Stones at the Crawdaddy but, despite making their debut at the Island, after those first two performances they never played there again. Around the time he signed the group, Gomelsky came to an arrangement with Harold Pendleton's Marquee Artists Agency, tying the group to a particular club circuit, which didn't include the Eel Pie Island Hotel. Instead, the Island's big drawcard was the man who gave the Yardbirds their break. Starting at the end of June 1963, the Cyril Davies All-Stars had claimed the Island's Sunday night slot. The All-Stars were basically the Savages, only instead of loony Screaming Lord Sutch they were now fronted by the balding, paunchy, badly suited, tetchy and entirely serious Cyril Davies. To a teenage audience, Davies must have seemed ancient (he was thirty-one at the time) and unhip (he looked like a bank manager, although he was actually a panel-beater), but he and his band delivered raw, driving Chicago blues, with harmonica-playing Davies standing at the side of the stage blowing like a hurricane.

Geoff Cole, trombonist with Ken Colyer, remembers crossing the bridge to the Island and being asked by the old lady who collected the toll, 'Is it jazz tonight or them Rizla blues?' If the uncompromising Ken Colyer (or, as the toll lady called him, 'Kelly Collar') had been the spiritual godfather of Eelpiland during the jazz years, then the equally purist Davies – who quit Blues Incorporated when Alexis Korner allowed a saxophone into the band – was the presiding spirit of the R&B years. More so than even the Stones, Davies inspired an entire generation of British blues musicians. Original Yardbirds guitarist Top Topham called him the promoter of the most genuine form of blues the UK had: 'He wasn't a bad imitation, he was the real thing. He influenced us all in a big way.'[3] As an indicator of Davies's stature, Arthur Chisnall paid him more per appearance than Jagger and co.

Sadly, Davies didn't get to see the fruits of his labour. By late 1963, his health was deteriorating rapidly. He'd begun to suffer from pleurisy, but rather than follow good advice and rest, he continued to perform, dulling his pain with drink (according to Keith Richards, Davies 'used to drink bourbon like a fucking fish'). Shortness of breath meant he had to give up the harmonica and vocals, but he continued to play guitar. Some obituaries say he was playing the Eel Pie Island Hotel when he collapsed and was rushed to hospital. What's certain is that he died on Tuesday 7 January 1964, the death certificate citing endocarditis, an infection of the inner lining of the heart. Geoff Bradford, the All-Stars guitarist, later described how he'd been forewarned of this outcome: 'One night,' he said 'we had a gig at Eel Pie Island and this Irish barman said to me, "Yer man's got death sitting on his shoulders." It sent chills through my whole body.'

Leadership of the band was taken over by Long John Baldry, the six-foot-seven vocalist who followed Davies when he split from Alexis Korner and Blues Incorporated. In addition to a seabed-deep, bluesy voice, Baldry had brought some much-needed charisma and wit to Davies's All-Stars. He may have sung about poverty, but in his natty three-piece suits and shined shoes he never looked less than a million dollars. His between-song drollery, delivered in a posh yet gravelly voice, suggested, according to Baldry's biographer Paul Myers, 'Noel Coward doing a comic impression of Winston Churchill.'[4] Baldry was responsible for one of the best descriptions of fellow blues vocalist and friend Mick Jagger, who he said was 'a praying mantis with lips'.

The night after Davies died, Baldry led the band, now renamed the Hoochie Coochie Men, onto the stage at the Island for a tribute show. Afterwards, as Baldry waited on the London-bound platform at Twickenham station, he heard someone wailing on a harmonica and making a decent job of it. 'Gingerly stepping along the platform,' Baldry recalled in characteristically fruity manner in a 1991 letter to a friend, 'I went to investigate the source of this stirring sound, almost tripping over what I thought was a pile of old clothing spilling off a bench. Accustoming my eyes to the gloom, I realised there was a nose protruding from the swathing of a gigantic woollen scarf. "Good evening," I said to the nose. "You strike me as being a bit of a blues fan".[5]

The nose had been at that evening's performance and the two chatted all the way to Waterloo. Baldry was looking for someone to play Cyril Davies's harp parts and he asked the nose if perhaps he'd join the Hoochie Coochie Men for their next gig? The nose said he'd have to ask his mum, and Baldry said he understood and would it help if he came round and spoke to her? Baldry turned up with flowers for mum and within the week Rod Stewart was making his Hoochie Coochie debut – at an all-nighter in Manchester, a day after his nineteenth birthday. 'I owe so much to Long John Baldry,' Stewart writes in *Rod: The Autobiography*. 'He discovered me – on a bench in a railway station, as the perfectly accurate story goes – and he turned me into a singer and a performer.'

It wouldn't be until the next month that Long John Baldry and the Hoochie Coochie Men were back at the Island – with Stewart in the line-up – but from then they played the dance hall regularly through the rest of the year and into spring 1965. Contemporary Eelpilanders remember Baldry well. He was given to referring to his band as Ada Baldry and the Hoochie Coochie Ladies, while Rod Stewart was the Queen of the Mods, or just Phyllis. Baldry's gayness was evident, if not publicly acknowledged, given that homosexuality remained illegal.

Rod Stewart was just one of the Eel Pie faces who made the leap from audience to stage. 'First I went there as a paying customer – riding the Tube down to Waterloo and changing onto the over-ground for Twickenham. That was a pretty length journey to make from Archway, where I lived,' recalls Stewart.[6] The first visit happened when he was going out with an art student named Sue Boffey, who had a friend named Chrissie, who wanted them all to

Long John Baldry performing at Eelpiland. He played the Island as vocalist with the Cyril Davies All-Stars, fronting the Hoochie Coochie Men and as part of Steampacket.

go and see her boyfriend's band on the Island. Chrissie's surname was Shrimpton and her boyfriend was called Mick Jagger. Stewart remembers thinking that the band was great but also having a nagging feeling inside: 'I could do this. My voice is better than that.'

'I saw Rod playing with Long John Baldry,' says Ian McLagan. 'I already knew him from the audience – it turned out we were both trying to shag the same girl. His hair was bouffant and he would wear a three-piece suit, very smart. He stood out.'[7] Even as a performer, Stewart spent much of his time at the bar, drinking and chatting up girls until Baldry shouted for him to come up to the stage. 'The Hoochie Coochie Men would do a set and then when they finished Rod Stewart would get up on stage, pick up Geoff Bradford's Fender Telecaster and play some [John Lee] Hooker,' says Peter Moody of the Grebbels, who occasionally supported Baldry's outfit at the Marquee. 'He probably did three or four numbers. In the second half Stewart would sing with the band. But his solo spots were the best thing.'

In October 1964, Stewart quit the Hoochie Coochie Men to pursue a solo career but two months later hitched himself to Southampton R&B outfit the Soul Agents, with whom he made a handful of return appearances on the Island. In July 1965, Baldry and Stewart were reunited in Steampacket, a soul review supergroup cooked up by Giorgio Gomelsky, which also included organist Brian Auger and singer Julie Driscoll. They played the Island a couple of times that August, and also appeared at that month's Richmond Jazz and Blues Festival. Auger (who lived in Twickenham) remembers that Baldry drew caricatures of all the band members on the walls of the green room above the ballroom stage at the Island. 'I noticed every time I returned to Eel Pie Island,' says Auger, 'we all began to resemble the wall drawings more and more. It was a bit scary.'[8] Incidentally, Driscoll may be the only billed female artist to ever play the Island. There were women who were part of groups – the aforementioned Velvettes, for example, who sometimes backed Cyril Davies – but Driscoll was the only one to be specifically named on one of Arthur Chisnall's contracts. Eelpiland wasn't unique in this – scan the gig listings in *Melody Maker* for the 1960s and early 1970s and, with the odd exception (usually Elkie Brooks or Jo-Ann Kelly), there were few women playing the clubs.

On Sunday 26 July 1964, R&B outfit the Manish Boys made their Eel Pie Island debut, fronted by Davy Jones, who was two years away from reinventing himself as David Bowie. Jones was no stranger to the area – he and his best friend George Underwood regularly travelled from their homes in Bromley, southeast London, to catch bands at both the Crawdaddy and the Island. Jones had

The future David Bowie (second from left) was once a Mod. He played the Island several times with the Manish Boys, and visited regularly to check out rival bands.

only joined the Manish Boys the week before their Island debut (his first gig with them had been the previous night, at Chicksands US Air Base in Bedfordshire). On their second Island date, Wednesday 19 August, the band shared the bill with the Hoochie Coochie Men, as they did again on 7 October and 8 November. The Manish Boys' set around this time included songs like rock'n'roller 'Louie Louie', Herbie Hancock's 'Watermelon Man', and 'Little Egypt', written by Leiber and Stoller, and originally recorded by the Coasters. They also regularly performed Willie Dixon's 'Hoochie Coochie Man', but presumably not at the Island because it would have been bad form for the support act to play the headliner's signature piece. Both bands shared the tiny dressing room above the stage. Changing before one show, Rod Stewart revealed he was wearing knickers. 'We asked him why he wore girl's underwear and he said it was because they were more comfortable,' Manish Boys keyboardist Bob Solly told an interviewer in 2007.[9]

Two years after the Manish Boys played the Island, in December 1966, David Bowie was due to return for a solo gig, but it was cancelled. But the Island left its mark: in 1973, the year after he became a front-cover story with *Ziggy Stardust and the Spiders from Mars*, Bowie released *Pinups*, a collection of covers of songs by mostly British groups, including the Yardbirds, the Who and Pink Floyd. It's a love letter to mid Sixties London and in the sleeve notes he namechecks old favourite haunts, including Eel Pie Island.

By the mid 1960s, Saturday nights at Eelpiland remained reserved for syncopators, stompers and other assorted jazzers, while Sundays and Wednesdays were R&B. A whole host of leading acts made their way out west and across to the Island including Georgie Fame & the Blue Flames, John Mayall's Bluesbreakers (with Bernie Watson on guitar and John McVie – later the 'Mac' in Fleetwood Mac – on bass), the Graham Bond Organisation and the Alex Harvey Soul Band. However, one band truly made the Island their own, and they were the Downliners Sect.

According to guitarist and singer Don Craine, he formed the band as an attempt to meld the music of Cyril Davies with the sex appeal of the Rolling Stones. Except they got it the wrong way round. A Twickenham boy, Craine started the Downliners in 1962, choosing the name as a tribute to Jerry Lee Lewis and his song 'Down the Line'. A disastrous tour of France and several member changes later, the band was relaunched the following year as the Downliners Sect – Craine thought that the addition of the word 'Sect' added an element of mystery. Before long, they were playing eight or nine gigs a week across London, including regular spots at Studio 51, where they were one of the resident bands, along with the Rolling Stones. The Downliners Sect didn't play the Island until late 1963 but Craine had been visiting the hotel since his mother used to take him over for afternoon tea as a small boy. 'There were still people who would row up and have a drink at the hotel,' he remembers. Later, he took to going there on his own to hear rockers like Screaming Lord Sutch and the Savages. On one occasion he went to the island to see the Savages and the band were without their flamboyant frontman; instead there was a tubby, serious-looking guy called Cyril. 'He was fantastic. Seeing Cyril Davies was a life changer,' recalls Craine, who, before the night was ended, became a convert to the blues.

The band's own sets, like many others, were built on R&B standards, although soon they began adding their own compositions (written by their producer Mike Collier), based around simple Bo Diddley riffs. They gave the songs painfully punning titles like 'Sect Appeal' and 'Be a Sect Maniac'. The band was energetic and, above all, fun, and they gathered a loyal following on the Island. According to Craine, Rod Stewart used to get up and do a couple of songs with them and at one point was keen to join, but Craine didn't want another frontman hogging the limelight.

The debut album by Island favourites the Downliners Sect, released in 1964.

They were an excellent live act and at one point were signed to Columbia, but it never translated to commercial success – apart from in Sweden, where the band's second single 'Little Egypt' hit number two in the charts and where they performed to audiences numbering in the tens of thousands. They had too few original songs and their records were willfully eccentric: their second album featured country music, while their second EP, *The Sect Sing Sick Songs*, contained four tracks about death, including their spoof of the Shangri-Las' 'Leader of the Pack' – called, inevitably, 'Leader of the Sect'. While local rivals like the Stones and Yardbirds took flight, the Downliners Sect remained a cult band, a status that probably endeared them to Islanders all the more.

The Tridents, from Chiswick in southwest London, were another Island favourite. They were formed by the Lucas brothers, John (rhythm guitar) and Paul (bass), and their adept reworkings of R&B standards, including an homage to Cyril Davies in the form of a cover of his 'Countryline Special', landed them a steady stream of bookings at venues like the Ealing Club, Crawdaddy, Kew Boathouse, Kingston's Cellar Club and the 100 Club in the West End.[10] In summer 1964, the band's guitarist quit. The Lucas brothers had noticed that the guitarist in the Nightshift, a band that had played some support slots to the Tridents, was a cut above the rest of his mates.[11] His name was Jeff Beck. When Paul Lucas asked would he like to join his band, Beck responded, 'I thought you'd never ask.'

Beck's tenure with the Tridents saw larger audiences exposed to his wild experimentations on the guitar: trilling, hammering, bending, picking, and playing with feedback, distortion and echo. He was aided by Paul Lucas, who rewired the pickups on Beck's Telecaster and built him his first fuzz box. Pushing the limits of technique and technology, Beck's guitar playing sounded like a one-man Apocalypse. He became an Island hero. One early fan was David Bowie, who years later spoke of seeing Beck with the Tridents at the Island and being bowled over: 'He was so complete, so vital and inventive.'[12]

On 25 October 1964, the BBC recorded the Tridents live at the Island for German radio.[13] The following March they went into Oriole Studios in London's West End to cut a couple of tracks, unaware that this would be the last time they would play with Jeff Beck – two days later he made his debut with the Yardbirds. Former guitarist Mike Jopp returned to the Tridents so the band could carry on. Lucas recalls Arthur Chisnall being particularly supportive, booking them extra gigs and offering to buy them new equipment so they could replicate Beck's sound. But, says Lucas, the magic was gone, and the Tridents played the Island for the last time on 28 May 1965 and split soon after. The group and their guitarist are namechecked in the wistful song 'Richmond', written by guitarist Andy Roberts and included on his 1973 album, *Urban Cowboy*:[14]

Remember the nights on the Island
Newcastle Ale on the grass
Jeff on stage with the Tridents
Talking 'bout the past, my love

According to Paul Lucas's diary, the Tridents played at least thirty dates on the Island, but Art Wood always maintained that his band, the Artwoods, played the old hotel ballroom more times than anybody else (Alan Cresswell of the Riverside Jazz Band would argue otherwise). Like many groups associated with the Island, the Artwoods mostly appear as footnotes in the histories of more famous bands. Frontman Art Wood – described as possessing a lived-in face and looking a bit like Sid James – had been one of several singers with Blues Incorporated, the ensemble led by Alexis Korner and Cyril Davies; he was also older brother of the Faces and Rolling Stones guitarist Ronnie Wood. Artwoods keyboardist Jon Lord went on to found Deep Purple, while drummer Keef Hartley began his career as replacement for Ringo Starr in Liverpool band Rory Storm and the Hurricanes and post-Artwoods played with John Mayall, before founding his own Keef Hartley Band and performing at Woodstock in 1969.

Between 1964 and 1967, the Artwoods had a residency at the 100 Club on Oxford Street and signed to Decca, releasing a number of singles and EPs, and one full-length album, titled *Art Gallery*. Along with the Kinks and Donovan, they appeared on the first episode of *Ready Steady Go!* to feature live performances. None of their singles charted but they garnered a reputation as a hard-working, tight live outfit. Guitarist Derek Griffiths remembers life on the road:

Waitress: 'Which band are you?'

Me: 'You won't have heard of us.'

Waitress: 'Oh go on, tell us.'

Me: 'OK. The Artwoods.'

Waitress: 'Never 'eard of you.'

Griffiths remembers one occasion waiting for Art Wood on Twickenham Embankment when a red van pulled up. It belonged to John Mayall's band, who were sharing the bill with the Artwoods that night. The driver hopped out and opened up the back, which was loaded up with a mound of music gear and the protruding feet of someone lying flat on top. The passenger wriggled out, revealing himself as Eric Clapton. He'd been wedged in there since the van left Aberystwyth earlier in the day.

What every musician who played the Island remembers is getting their gear to the venue. Everything had to be lugged from Twickenham Embankment, over the narrow pedestrian bridge and

TELEPHONE: **BRISTOL 27358 (3 lines)**

Peter Burman Agency

10 ST. AUGUSTINE'S PARADE, BRISTOL 1

An Agreement made the 24th day of June 19 65

between Arthur Chisnell Esq hereinafter called the Management
of the one part, and The Steam Packet hereinafter called the Artiste
of the other part.

Witnesseth that the Management hereby engages the Artiste and the Artiste
accepts an engagement to present L.J.Baldry.Rod Stewart.Brian Auger 3
(or in his usual entertainment) at the Dance Hall/Theatre and from the dates for the periods and Julie Driscoll
at the salaries stated in the Schedule hereto.

The Artiste agrees to appear at { 1 Evening performances
- Matinee

at a salary of £ 100

SCHEDULE

1 Day(s) at	Eel Pie Island	on	August 1st	19 65
Day(s) at		on		19
Day(s) at		on		19
Day(s) at		on		19

ADDITIONAL CLAUSES

1. It is agreed that the above named artists shall appear in person.
2. The Artiste shall perform for a maximum of divided into 2 x 1 sessions commencing not earlier than 6.30 and terminating not later than at times by arrangement between Management and Artiste.
3. The Management shall provide first-class amplification, microphone equipment and piano in good condition tuned to concert pitch.
4. Financial settlement for this engagement shall be made with the artist on the night of the engagement.
5. xxxxxxxxxxxxxxxxxxxxxxxxxxxxxxxxxxxxxxxxxxxxxxxxxxxxxxxxxxxxxxxxxxxxxxxxxxxxxx xxxxxxxxxxxxxxxxxxxxxxxxxxxxxxxxxxxxxxxxxx X
6. The Artiste shall not, without the written consent of the Management, appear at any place of public entertainment within a radius of miles of any of the theatres mentioned herein, for weeks prior to and during this engagement.
7. The promoter agrees that any other band performing the engagement(s) described in this agreement shall be composed of members of the Musicians' Union, and in the event of Musicians' Union action arising from the engagement of non-unionists, the promoters shall be responsible for payment of the full fees or percentages as stated in this agreement.

The £100 promised to Steampacket for their debut appearance on the Island was the
highest fee paid to any artist to this date – most headliners went away with £50. It's an
indication of the popularity of Long John Baldry and Rod Stewart with Eelpilanders.

LONDON CITY AGENCY (JCD) **LTD.**

Theatrical Agents & Managers
Licenced Annually by CITY OF WESTMINSTER

189 WARDOUR STREET, LONDON, W.1.   REGent 3378/9

Directors   J.T. Jones
B. Dunning
R. Kingston

This Agency is not responsible for any non-fulfilment of Contracts by Proprietors, Managers, or Artistes, but reasonable safeguard is assured.

This Contract is subject to the conditions of the Arbitrators Award, 1919.

An Agreement made the......17th......day of......January....1967.

between ......Art. Chisnall...................... hereinafter called the **Management** of the one part, and ......~~~~~ BLACKHILL ENTERPRISES........... hereinafter called the Artiste, of the other part.

Witnesseth that the Management hereby engages the Artiste and the Artiste

accepts an engagement to { present ......The Pink Floyd......................
to appear as......known......................

at the Venue on the dates for the periods and at the salaries stated in the Schedule hereto.

SCHEDULE

Cheque to London City Agency (JCD) ltd., within three days

The Artiste agrees to appear at a salary of......£75.0.0. each Performance ~~(Cash settlement to be made with the Artiste during or immediately after the performance)~~

for......1.2......performance(s)   of...2 X 45 mins......duration

between the hours of...7.45.. and.11.15..p.m and..............and..................

......Day(s) at.Eel Pie Island............ on. Wednesday 1st March 1967
Twickenham
......Day(s) at. Eel Pie Island............ on. 29TH MARCH..........196.7
Twickenham
......Day(s) at......................on any Wednesday during 196..
March or April
......Day(s) at......................on please state..........196..

1.   The Artiste shall not, without the written consent of the Management, appear at any place of public entertainment within a radius of .... miles of any of the Venues mentioned herein, for .... weeks prior to and during this Engagement.
2.   It is agreed that the following persons will appear at the performance.. ....The Pink Floyd......................
3.   The Management is to be responsible for the provision and cost of microphones, amplification equipment, chairs and other commonplace props, and piano in good condition tuned to concert pitch.
4.   The price of admission shall be not less than.........................per person in advance, and.............. at the door.
5.   The Management shall supply the Artiste or his representative with full facilities to check advance sales and Commencing Ticket Numbers, and shall provide a full accounting of Admission Money at the conclusion of the performance.
6.   Where musicians are booked through this agency, the Management agrees that any other band performing the Engagement(s) described in this agreement shall be composed of members of the Musicians' Union, and in the event of Musicians' Union action arising from the engagement of non-unionists, the management shall be responsible for payment of the full fees or percentages as stated in this agreement.
7.   The commission required by this Agency from the Artiste/Sole Agent is ....per centum of the fee shown herein.
8.   The Artiste or his representative, now or in the future, agrees to pay a like commission to this Agency for any further engagements at any venue for the same Management, or through the same Booking Agent, during the next Twelve Months, howsoever arranged.

ADDITIONAL CLAUSES

This marks the first appearances of 'the' Pink Floyd on the Island. A week after their second appearance the group were on *Top of the Pops* for the first time, performing debut single 'Arnold Layne'.

143

along the winding pathway to the hotel. 'In those days we had a lot of gear,' recalls Griffiths. 'We had a Hammond organ and big Leslie speaker that goes with the Hammond, and all the amps and the PA. Art had a little minivan and it would fit over the bridge. Just. I'm not sure if he was even supposed to be driving over it – it was a footbridge.'[15] When the Graham Bond Organisation played the Island, the band used a large rowing boat to ship Bond's Hammond over the water rather than lug it over the bridge.

After setting up, the band could retire to the room above the stage, have a few drinks and get stoned while the ballroom filled up. The space was small and would often become crowded with friends and hangers-on. 'Yeah, all sorts of things went on in the band room,' says Griffiths. 'Bands used to use any receptacle they could find to pee into because it meant saving yourself the long journey down the stairs to the toilets at back of the hall and back again. There were the inevitable accidents. I can still see [Artwoods bassist] Malcolm's face now as this noxious liquid dripped through the ceiling above him onto the stage.'

The main band usually did two sets, with support acts playing the interval. As the evening went on, the room would become increasingly rammed. No one is sure exactly what the dance hall's capacity was, but it was claimed that on the busiest nights as many as a thousand people packed themselves into the rickety wooden building. Everyone smoked, and a greyish-yellowish fug shrouded the room. 'It was a fantastic atmosphere,' says Griffiths. 'When you looked out from the stage people were pogoing on each others' shoulders.' The only downer for the band was that at the end of the night all the equipment had to be got back over the bridge again.

Tim Large was the guitarist with Dave Anthony's Moods, a Bournemouth band who gave up the seaside for a crack at London in 1965. They were taken on by Ken Pitt, manager of Manfred Mann (and soon to handle David Bowie). Pitt got them repeat gigs at a host of venues, including on Eel Pie Island. 'Two or three trips across the bridge,' recalls Large, 'a quick set-up and we were ready to hit the bar – no draught beer so it was Newcastle Brown, by the neck. You could get some kind of bacon or sausage butty, which did for dinner. In winter, the hall was heated by industrial gas blowers, until the crowd arrived, when on a good night two or three hundred hot and hungry kids generated their own heat. We loved it, loved several of those hot female kids, got tanked on three or four Browns then went on and just did it.'[16]

Another of the Island brotherhood of bands were the Birds, featuring Ronnie Wood, youngest brother of Art of the Artwoods. (Middle brother Ted was also a musician.[17]) As well as harbouring a future Rolling Stone, the Birds were notable for a publicity stunt dreamed up by their manager Leo de Clerck, owner of Hounslow's Zambezi Club. In August 1965, American group the Byrds, whose 'Mr Tambourine Man' had just spent two weeks at number one in the British charts, landed at London Airport (now Heathrow) to begin a thirteen-date British tour. They were met on arrival by their British namesakes and their manager, who delivered the Californians with seven writs, including an injunction to stop them using the name and another for damages for loss of earnings. The antic at least got the Birds a never to be repeated appearance on the cover of *Melody Maker*. Otherwise, they were another constantly gigging R&B outfit plying a modest trade in provincial clubs and halls up and down the motorways of Britain. 'We were the biggest thing since sliced bread in Salisbury,' Ronnie Wood told his biographer Terry Rawlings.[18]

Wood saw the Island as a musical boot camp as much as a gig. 'You'd go and see John Mayall and Screaming Lord Sutch would be standing next to you. It was always like that, lots of double takes and who you could bump into. There was a lot of learning going on in those days.'[19] Ex-Yardbird Top Topham agrees, recalling the inspirational musicians he saw at the Island: 'Keith West's Tomorrow, who had Steve Howe from Yes on guitar; the Butterfield Blues Band with Mike Bloomfield on guitar and Howlin' Wolf's rhythm section; and Savoy Brown who had a very good guitarist called Martin Stone.'[20] One of the most memorable performances Topham saw, he says, was due to his friend, Eric Clapton being late for a gig with John Mayall: 'So Robin Trower – later of Procol Harum – got up on stage until Eric arrived. That sort of thing happened all the time at Eel Pie.' Some lucky Eelpilanders remember being present one Wednesday night in May 1964 when Jeff Beck was joined in an onstage jam session by Jimmy Page, Bill Wyman and Ian Stewart. 'We all liked the same thing,' says Topham. 'You'd see people, share a new guitar lick. It was very much like you were part of a real community. You didn't necessarily know them that well, but you had a shared interest.'

The acts everyone most wanted to see, though, were the original Black American bluesmen. Arthur Chisnall managed to bring a number of them to the Island. Celebrated harpist Little Walter appeared, as did guitar legend Buddy Guy (who performed with Rod Stewart and the Soul Agents), and pianists Champion Jack Dupree and Memphis Slim. Several Eelpilanders recall the spectacle of one-man-band Jesse Fuller, who performed with an instrument of his own invention: a large six-string bass viol that he played with his foot via a system of pedals and levers. With his other foot Fuller operated a hi-hat cymbal. He also wore a harness to hold a harmonica and a kazoo, and played a twelve-string guitar and sang. When Howlin' Wolf visited, Stones bassist Bill Wyman was in the audience and was invited to get up and join the band onstage. The great John Lee Hooker played in June 1967 but, for reasons unknown, he only completed half a set – this is according to a handwritten note on Chisnall's contract which indicates that Hooker's was fee slashed from £75 to £50.

Artists' interactions with Chisnall tended to be minimal. Agents or managers made the bookings and sorted out things like the guest list. But Derek Griffiths remembers him as a generous man who voluntarily raised the band's fee from £40 per gig to £60 which, he says, compared favourably to other club venues. Adjusted for inflation, £60 in the mid Sixties works out to about £1,200 today, which is good money.

For most bands, Eel Pie Island was a good gig: it had character, it was somewhere fellow musicians hung out and it was financially worthwhile. But if the Island was fun to play as an artist, it was arguably even more special to be a member of the Eelpiland crowd.

CHAPTER 8

A HEADLONG RUSH TO HEDONISM

Boys, girls, fags, pills and Newcastle Brown – the mid Sixties heyday of Island life

SINCE THE FIRST SPLUTTERING GAGGIA had arrived in Soho in 1953, the sound of the espresso machine had become synonymous with youth, music and anything that got up the noses of the older generation. By the early 1960s, Richmond had several coffee bars of its own, but the most popular by far was L'Auberge, on the corner of Hill Rise and Ormond Road, on the lower slopes of Richmond Hill. 'The routine was to start out at L'Auberge in the early evening,' recalls Eric Clapton in his 2007 autobiography, 'have a couple of coffees, and then wander over the bridge to Eel Pie.'

L'Auberge was opened in 1956 by the Hill family, who sold it on to a young Italian couple, Andy and Maria. At one end, the café was about five feet above pavement level, and out front was a terrace

FACING: By 1964, jazz featured only on Saturdays on the Island; the other nights, Sundays and Wednesdays, were now R&B and blues, with different dances and dress.

commanding the approach road to Richmond Bridge and the river.[1] Inside, the wall facing onto Ormond Road had big windows, with high-counter seating – this was the 'fish bowl', looking onto the neighbouring Odeon cinema and down the high street. Many of those who used L'Auberge were into the beatnik scene, and there were chess players, guitar pickers and a legendary jukebox filled with R&B. Coffee came in cafetières or frothy in glass cups, and beside burgers and chicken curry, there was exotic fare like spaghetti bolognese and cheesecake. Andy could be persuaded to advance hard-up regulars a plate of food on the promise that the debt would be cleared on payday. Better yet, the place kept Soho hours, staying open after the pubs closed.

Christine Boulton, a regular in the late Sixties, remembers long summer days at L'Auberge, 'sitting in the sun on the raised patio smoking dope, dropping acid and watching life drift on a haze of hash smoke and incense.' Around the same time, Annie Sanchez was a nineteen-year-old French au pair whose host family lived up the hill: 'I was told not to go to L'Auberge because it had a bad reputation but, of course, I went and loved it. I spent my days off there, only able to afford a cup of coffee, but they'd feed me for nothing and I was in awe of the culture there.' It was, depending on your point of view, the coolest of hangouts or a public nuisance. Richmond schoolgirl Angie Page remembers a vicar stopping her on Ormond Road and warning her away from the coffee bar at the end of the street.

L'Auberge was also a hub of information: if someone was looking for a job or a place to stay, it was a good place to ask around. Work was easy to come by in Richmond at this time: there were plenty of places that hired by the week or even the day. L'Auberge was also where you found out what bands were playing and picked up word of parties to gatecrash. 'What would happen,' remembers Yardbirds drummer Jim McCarty, 'is that someone would find out the address of a party and come closing time everybody would bowl round to this poor guy's house; invariably his parents would be away. It was always outrageous; they got pissed, the kitchen would get wrecked, food would be slung everywhere.'

'L'Auberge was where we all hung out,' says fellow Yardbird Chris Dreja. 'As a down-and-out student or musician, you could make that coffee last four hours. All of us – Eric, myself, other players – started to drift there.' Clapton would turn up with his Washburn acoustic and his long thumbnails and show off the riffs he'd lifted, but he wasn't even considered the best guitarist there. That was generally agreed by L'Auberge regulars to be Johnny Vanstone, who played a fingerpicking style on twelve-string guitar. He gave lessons to Donovan and sold him his first guitar, but he never took his own talent seriously. The closest he came to appearing on a recording was when Donovan thanked him in one of his album's sleevenotes for 'every little blade of grass', a nod to Vanstone's other notable role as one of Richmond's best-known drug dealers – he wore a pea coat with a torn lining that let him stash pills in the sleeves.

The route from L'Auberge to the Island began with a walk over Richmond Bridge then a five-minute bus ride or, on balmy evenings, a meander along the river, past the grounds of Marble Hill House and Orleans House, along the high-walled lane between York House and its gardens with tableaux of naked nymphs, and up Twickenham Embankment to cross the arcing footbridge over the river. At the far side waited an old woman in a sentry box-like kiosk, which in winter was warmed by a blazing brazier. Whatever the weather, she was always swathed in heavy coats topped by a headscarf. She wore fingerless mittens and 'had warts all over her fingers', claimed island regular John Stephens.[2] Her name was Rose, or Rosie. There was a rumour she was the mother of the Eel Pie Island Hotel's owner

Local kids sometimes amused themselves by jumping into the Thames from the Eel Pie Island bridge. One summer evening in the mid 1960s, one boy upped the ante by saying he would do it while on fire. He spritzed his shirt with lighter fuel, set it aflame and leaped. Before the leap, one of the group ran home and grabbed a camera and shot this photograph.

Michael Snapper. She collected the toll of a few pence, which went to Snapper. In summer, some clubbers were mad enough to strip to their underwear and swim over to the island to avoid paying.

'It was the thing of going over the water,' says local author Judy Astley, who first visited the Island as a schoolgirl, 'like you were going to another country. Then you went along this long windy path in the dark. I think there was one lamp. There was a "somewhere else" feel about it.'[3] For former Eelpiland passport holder Barry Munday, the appeal was all about the gratification of base teenage desires: 'It was like going to someone's house, a big house, for a party. You had live music, beer and girls. You're young. You can't ask for more than that.'[4] As you followed the path through the trees, music could be heard ahead. 'You'd walk faster,' says Sandy Bradshaw. 'You'd run. You couldn't get there quick enough.'[5]

The path led down the side of the building and around to the riverside frontage, where a short flight of steps led up to the ballroom entrance. There was a modest admission to be paid, negotiated or avoided. 'On Wednesday nights we never had enough because we'd spent our money at the weekend,' says Margaret Willatts.[6] 'The guy at the door would say, "How much have you got?" We'd tell him and he'd say, "Okay, go on in then".' One dodge was that one person would pay, have their wrist stamped, go in and quickly back out, breathe on the stamp to make the ink damp and press it against their friend's wrist. One stamp could stretch to three people.

Once in, clubbers descended into the ballroom. The aroma that rose up to meet them was redolent of armpits, stale beer and cigarettes, Brylcreem, wood rot and a whiff of dank river that emanated from below the floorboards. In the winter, there would also be a lingering smell of gas from the two big burners, like jet engines on wheels, that were run for twenty minutes before the audience began to arrive. Once the hall began to fill, the crowd

The interior of the ballroom in the mid 1960s, viewed from the back; above the stage, with its mural, is the small room where the musicians hung out between sets.

generated enough heat that the place quickly became stifling. By this time, the mural that decorated the back of the stage had been joined by cartoons and caricatures that covered the walls – many of the regulars were art students, after all. Windows were cracked, weeds pushed through gaps in the walls, ivy crept in through the ceiling. But few clubbers noticed because it was generally dark by the time they turned up and the place was feebly lit. The main source of light and activity, at least until the band came on, was the long bar, famed for serving bottles of Newcastle ales – Brown and Amber – which were largely unknown elsewhere in London. The only gripes from clubbers might have been about the toilets. The cubicle doors had no locks and there were holes in the floors, but these at least helped to drain the overflow from the frequently blocked urinals. When the tide was up, the toilets would flood. If the queue was too long, men would simply go outside and relieve themselves into the river.

Bob Wagner was a student at Twickenham Art School who was spending so much time on the Island that he and a friend thought they might as well have jobs there. They became pot-boys, collecting glasses three nights a week; Saturdays were the hardest shifts because jazz fans were the biggest drinkers. The boys also came in on Saturday afternoons to clean, which meant sweeping the cigarette ends, scrunched-up fag packets and broken glass into the many holes in the floor. 'There wasn't a lot of cleaning went on,' recalls Wagner. 'And nobody ever did any maintenance.' He remembers hearing that a girl had gone to the toilet, pulled the chain and the cistern had fallen on her head.

By the mid Sixties the music was changing but the type of people drawn to the Island remained largely the same. 'Most of us had read Jack Kerouac's *On the Road*,' says former Eelpilander Ray Everitt.[7] 'The mainstream was listening to "Like a rubber ball I'll come bouncing back to you...". That was the shit that was going on and we weren't into that.' Not every Eelpilander was an arty middle-class drop-out, but the prevailing spirit was one of creative rebellion. There was still no advertising of Eelpiland and the club maintained its membership by word of mouth, building a network of like-minded young people. 'I was a sixteen-year-old boy, just left school, and my hobby was doing as little as possible and looking for girls, which is why I went to the Island,' remembers Phil Eves.[8] 'I lived in Teddington but I used to go to Richmond because it was a bit more glamorous. One night, coming back with a friend we thought we'd get off the bus and nip over to Eel Pie Island. We found this was more the bohemian side of things, and that seemed to be more my style, and the girls on the Island were more exotic and interesting. I'd go over to the Island whenever I could after that.' Judy Astley was drawn to the Island by the sense of belonging she felt there:

'You'd see people from school, people from parties, people you'd been at the Crown with on Friday nights. You could go on your own because you'd know people when you got there. It was somewhere you felt comfortable in your own skin mixing with people who liked the same music that you did.'

Eelpilanders habitually faced – or even courted – parental disapproval. 'I was sixteen in 1964,' says Margaret Willatts.[9] 'I heard about Eel Pie Island from older girls at my school. I went with a group of friends for the first time. Lots of the other girls' parents had forbidden them from going to the Island. That was quite common because it had a bad reputation. So a lot of the girls didn't tell their parents they were going. My parents were quite liberal, so that was okay. The first couple I saw in the grounds were a man and lady in flowing garments, very eccentrically dressed, with hats on and long Victorian clothes, and she had a Siamese cat wrapped round her neck on a lead, and as soon as I saw them I thought, "I think they're right about this place".'

'I think the first time I heard about Eel Pie Island was probably my mother discussing it with the neighbours,' says Judy Astley. 'They were saying it was a den of vice and that whatever happened Judith must never go there. Of course, once somebody has said that, you want to go.' When Jan Eves' parents heard she'd been to the Island they banned her from going again. She used to tell her parents she was going out to see friends then change from her 'respectable' clothes into her Island gear, which she kept hidden in a bag behind a postbox.

As musical styles changed, so did what Eelpilanders wore, but the overall look was always bohemian. 'You couldn't possibly have gone there looking smart, you would have been so out of place,' says Wendy Edmonds, who was another who'd undergo a metamorphosis between house and Island in a bid to keep her parents in the dark.

Some Eelpilanders wore vintage chic to the Island, but most dressed down in jeans and sweaters. It was not a place to wear smart clothes.

'At that time ordinary people didn't wear jeans,' says Heather 'Fluff' White. 'So if you spotted someone in the distance with a duffel coat and jeans, you knew they were one of yours.' Among the art-school scruffs there were the peacocks, decked out in full-on thrift shop glam. 'One girl,' says Gill Ross, 'wore a full-length pink leather coat and had blonde hair down to her waist. People wore Victoriana, velvet coat and ruffled shirts. Girls would buy things like 1920s beaded dresses and make clothes out of furnishing material.' Gill Green used to wear her mum's dressing gown: 'My mum had a fabulous 1920's crêpe dressing gown that I chopped up. It makes me horrified when I think about it now but we wanted miniskirts.'

Her friend Maureen Kent wore an old black frockcoat: 'Somebody had given me this thing and the lining was coming off, but I was absolutely delighted and it was my pride and joy. I used to put safety pins all the way down and that was really cool.'

Subi Swift wore Biba, but then she was from Kensington. She met a boy from Isleworth who introduced her to the Richmond scene and the Island. 'It hit me like a storm,' she says. 'Seedy, noisy, dark, naughty. Everything you wanted at sixteen. All your dreams come true in one place.' Her boyfriend was part of Arthur Chisnall's inner circle and through him she got a job in the cloakroom, which was a little hatch next to the stage – 'A glorified broom cupboard, really.' Swift wasn't paid but she was allowed to keep the fees for the coats, so made decent money in the winter. Because the hatch faced the side of the stage, she couldn't see the bands very well – 'I knew everybody's profile but I had no idea what they looked like from the front' – but she could hear them, and it was a great spot for people-watching. 'Nobody there was straight. There was nobody in a tweed skirt and a polo neck jumper. They were all in long flowing clothes, long flowing skirts. Lovely. The clothes and music were really important.'

Although locals considered the Island their own, the audience came from across London, and even further afield. 'There were lots of people coming from Windsor, Ashford and Feltham,' says Gill Ross. 'Some of the friends I made were people I met on the train.' Future Genesis guitarist Steve Hackett lived in Pimlico but had friends in Richmond who told him about the Island and after a first visit he became a regular. 'I was only sixteen but that didn't stop me,' he says. 'In those days it was a tube to Richmond from Sloane Square then it was a bus. It was a bit of a hike but I loved it. Sometimes I ended up walking all the way back home in the middle of the night.'

There was no distance between the bands and the audience, and over the years many who were in the audience stepped up to the stage and made their names.

One consequence of the spreading renown was that there was often no longer room to dance. 'I mean sometimes,' says Gill Green, 'you were jammed in so tightly and the sweat would be pouring down the walls. The floor would be so sticky you could hardly lift your feet.' Since the early days, Heather White had gone to the Island to jive but now she avoided Sundays because they were always too busy, and stuck to the less crowded Saturday jazz sessions.

Drinkers could escape to a second bar, which was in the hotel proper and open to the general public – in other words, you could use this bar without having to pay to get into the ballroom. It was notable for the footprints on the ceiling, an Eel Pie tradition created by turning someone upside down and hoisting them up feet first. In summer, people bought beers at the hotel bar and drank them on

159

the grass outside, overlooking the river. You could still hear the band inside. There were often people with guitars, jamming or busking. After finishing up, revellers were given to pitching their mugs into the river. According to pot-boy Bob Wagner, one spring when the Richmond and Teddington locks were closed and the stretch of Thames between was reduced to a trickle, he was sent into the mud to collect the glasses, from which he then had to scrub off the green slime and return them clean to the bar.

The undergrowth around the hotel offered plenty of concealment for couples. 'People were always getting off with people,' says Judy Astley. 'It was the music, the atmosphere. You just felt very relaxed.' There are Eelpilanders who will claim nothing of the sort went on – the same folk who will tell you there were no drugs on the Island – but they are contradicted by the testimonies of so many others. 'It wasn't unusual to see couples copulating by the river bank, smoking reefers or indulging in some sort of horseplay in the woods,' says Don Hughes, a Mod who spent his teenage years hanging around west London clubs. He says he never saw anything like Eel Pie Island anywhere else.[10]

For the majority of Eelpilanders, though, the hedonism and socialising paled behind the opportunity to see some of the planet's most celebrated musicians, working their magic in an environment that was both intimate and gratifyingly wild. 'I used to go specifically to see guitarists,' says Steve Hackett. 'I just missed the era of the Stones playing there and Jeff Beck. But John Mayall was still very much in full flow and he was the presiding deity as far as I was concerned. He had the young Peter Green, who was stunning, and who I learned a lot from. I also got to see [American blues harmonica player] Paul Butterfield, with Mike Bloomfield on guitar. That was terrific because ten years before I played guitar I was a harmonica player. [Butterfield] had that sound of distortion and vibrato that made it sound like a cross between a guitar and a trumpet.' Island regular Brian Ranken remembers turning up one night with a friend to see venerable American one-man blues band Jesse Fuller. They managed to position themselves right up against the stage. At some point the friend managed to pour a glass of beer over himself and Ranken later discovered he'd done it on purpose to disguise the fact he'd wet himself rather than lose his place at the front. Margaret Willatts has special memories of Georgie Fame: 'He was a regular and he was really good. Me and my friends used to sit on the stage right at his feet and he used to keep winking at us.'

Encounters with the Island's headliners weren't only confined to the stage. Andrea Hiorns remembers seeing Brian Jones and Bill Wyman in the crowd one night. 'I nerved myself up to go and ask for their autographs. This was not a cool thing to do but I had to do it. I had nothing to write on so I tore open an empty Embassy cigarette pack and they signed their names on the inside.' On other occasions it was Hiorns who was the subject of attention, particularly when she dressed in her fox fur, herringbone jacket, Anello & Davide shoes and cloche hat: 'Eric Clapton came over and asked if I'd go away for the weekend with him. I was flattered but held myself in more self-esteem. "No thanks, I'm not a groupie." I said the same to Rod Stewart when he came up and put his arm round me and asked me on a date.'

As the Sixties progressed, R&B remained popular but more acts were ditching the old Chuck Berry and Bo Diddley riffs for something much harder. When Eric Clapton played the Island during the first half of 1966 it was as part of blues guru John Mayall's outfit; when he returned in August he was hammering cranked-up, heavy-riffing rock with Ginger Baker and Jack Bruce in the power-trio Cream. The following year psychedelia arrived via groups like Tomorrow, featuring future Yes guitarist Steve Howe. They would

Decrepit and unsanitary as it was, Eelpiland always felt safe and it was a place that girls were happy to visit on their own or in groups.

have been peddling their recent single 'My White Bicycle'. 'The most startling were Pink Floyd,' remembers Judy Astley. 'I think in my diary I wrote, "Well, that was different". It was all bubble lights everywhere.' They played the Island three or four times in 1967, first as 'The' Pink Floyd, then as just Pink Floyd. This was the Syd Barrett era and sets would have included the recent trippy singles 'Arnold Layne' and 'See Emily Play', as well as free-form freak-outs like 'Astronomy Domine' and 'Interstellar Overdrive'.

By 1967, Pink Floyd were being touted as one of the most exciting groups in the country, so when a German crew arrived in Britain to make a zeitgeisty documentary about Swinging London, they set their cameras up at the UFO club on Tottenham Court Road to catch the band in pursuit of improvisational nirvana. *Die Jungen Nachtwandler* (*The Young Nightgoers*) also featured the Who in performance at the Marquee, along with footage of Jimi Hendrix and the King's Road in Chelsea, and two segments shot at Eel Pie Island. The filmmakers had Arthur Chisnall talking about his club's social-working agenda.[11] They knew about Chisnall because in the previous twelve months two clubs had launched in West Berlin modelled on Eelpiland. Seven Eelpilanders had designed clothes to present to an official study group from West Berlin. All this was being done with the backing of the Berlin Senate, the equivalent of the Greater London Council. 'One finds it hard to imagine,' commented *The Putney and Roehampton Herald*, 'the Education Committee of the GLC, and of Richmond upon Thames Council for that matter, eager to have more than one Eel Pie Island.'[12]

At around the same time *Die Jungen Nachtwandler* was screened in Germany, Odeons and Gaumonts around the UK were showing a British-made film about Eel Pie Island. *Look at Life* was a series of documentary shorts that ran before the main feature in cinemas. In April 1967, audiences eagerly awaiting David Niven in Bond spoof *Casino Royale* were first transported to Eelpiland. The short film follows clubbers over the bridge and shows them paying the toll and having their wrists stamped before entering the 'anteroom to paradise'. 'Or,' the narrator asks, 'is it hell?' For much of its brief running time, the film focuses on clubbers who'd had their lives turned by Chisnall. Jack Lambert is interviewed and shown leading a children's adventure playground in Camden, where many of the kids, according to the narrator, come from poverty and broken homes, and 'where the margin between a deprived child and a depraved child is frighteningly narrow.'

A less charitable view of the island was presented on the BBC's *Twenty-four Hours* current affairs programme, which accused the club of 'encouraging drugs, under-age drinking and sexual promiscuity'. Responding to the allegations, the Reverend Derek

Landreth, Vicar of Richmond, told *The Richmond and Twickenham Times*, 'I think it would be miraculous where you have any collection of youngsters today to find that none of them were taking drugs.' He added, 'You get drugs everywhere: in local authority youth clubs, cinemas and coffee bars – but you don't close them all down.'[13]

Chisnall had maintained good relations with local authorities. They were generally on his side, not least because it made sense to keep live music and its excitable crowds isolated on the Island. So, when a local woman complained to the council about drunken revellers using her garden as a 'last-minute lavatory' and the disturbance caused by the toll collector shouting after people who'd dodged payment, a valuation panel approved a cut in her rates and that was the end of the matter.[14] Similarly, Chisnall went out of his way to be accommodating to the police – who, in fact, were not allowed onto the hotel grounds without permission or a warrant because it was private property. In warmer weather, they would cruise by on their patrol boats and flash their searchlights over the bushes. According to Downliners Sect guitarist Don Craine, they also stationed plain-clothes officers on Twickenham Embankment, by the foot of the bridge to monitor the Island's comings and goings. 'They'd be trying to look casual but were totally out of place. You'd walk past them and say, "Good evening officer," and they'd always reply. They were sure something subversive was going on but it was just kids. They were getting drunk, popping a few pills. The odd one got pregnant, but that was it.'

In light of the fuss stirred by the BBC report, the local authorities began to keep a closer eye on the Island. On 3 June 1967, a Saturday night, Chisnall was approached by two officers who asked if they could look around and talk to a few of the club members. Chisnall gave the go-ahead and then watched in dismay as the police questioned three young girls all of whom failed to present evidence of club membership. For this breach of licensing regulations, Chisnall was ordered to shut down the club. The last act to play Eelpiland were the Heart and Souls on Wednesday 6 September.

'I was there on the day it was closed,' says Wendy Edmonds. 'I can remember walking up to the bridge and there was a barrier across and it said, "Lost licence. Hotel closed". Everyone was devastated. This was our music, our time, our Island.'

In October, Chisnall was up before the magistrate at Feltham Court. During the proceedings, the club was described (not inaccurately) as 'dirty, almost devoid of furniture, dimly lit and with a foul atmosphere'. The police officers described how of the five double doors that acted as fire exits, only one was in use. The others were so overgrown they couldn't be opened. The defence highlighted Chisnall's work on behalf of vulnerable young people and presented two letters of support. This was taken into account and the result was a token £10 fine, with five guineas costs.

That wasn't the end of it. In order to reopen, the club had to secure a new and proper music and dancing licence. This wasn't straightforward, as Chisnall was not the licensee. That was publican Jack Marrs, who managed the hotel or, more precisely, the only functioning elements of the hotel, which were its two bars, on behalf of landlord Michael Snapper. Chisnall managed to get the two men's verbal agreement to obtain a new licence and went ahead with the application. The council responded that it would issue the licence but only on condition that necessary works be carried out in the ballroom, including a new floor, stage, cloakroom and lobby, and new fire doors, electrics and ventilation. The estimated cost of the work was in the region of £2,000. Snapper had no interest in putting up the money and Chisnall certainly couldn't afford it. Eelpiland remained closed.

CHAPTER 9

THE SHAPE OF THINGS

A coalition of indignant club administrators and nimbyish residents colludes to snuff out live music in Richmond

BY THE TIME JEFF BECK TOOK HIS PLACE IN THE YARDBIRDS, in March 1965, the group was rarely to be seen at the Crawdaddy. The Beck line-up only played the Richmond rugby clubhouse three times. By now, they were almost permanently on the road, crammed into Bill Relf's van on a six-night-a-week schedule of ABC, Gaumont, Majestic, Odeon... Swindon to Southsea to Oldham by way of Bromley. In June, they opened two shows for the Beatles at the Palais des Sports in Paris and in September embarked on a brief and not entirely successful first tour of the United States, where they were prevented from playing to paying audiences because they had the wrong kind of visas.

The 'birds might have flown but the Crawdaddy club remained

FACING: The Yardbirds, with Jeff Beck (left), about to go on stage as Friday night headliners at the 1965 National Jazz and Blues Festival in Richmond.

167

a going concern. By now, Giorgio Gomelsky and Hamish Grimes had a roster of groups, some of which they also managed, and none of which – unless you were there at the time – you will ever have heard of.

The act Gomelsky promoted to succeed the Yardbirds was Sussex-based Gary Farr and the T-Bones. Formed in February 1964, the group was fronted by the blond-haired son of former British boxing champion Tommy Farr. The group had contacted Hamish Grimes, and after he and Gomelsky went down to see them perform at the Starlight Rooms in Brighton, they were put on the books. Gomelsky paired them with the Yardbirds at the Star in Croydon, bumping them up to headliners when the Yardbirds moved on. He also secured them a residency at the Marquee, and got them onto the bill at the National Jazz & Blues Festivals in 1964 and 1965. They must have been a decent live act because they racked up ninety-two appearances at the Marquee; the club took fifty percent of the door, so if a band didn't pull in the punters, they weren't rebooked. This didn't translate into record sales, because none of the three singles and an EP the T-Bones released bothered the charts.[1] If the T-Bones are remembered at all now, it is because for a short spell, in late 1965, the band's line-up included keyboard player Keith Emerson, future cape-wearing purveyor of pomp and bombast as one third of supergroup Emerson Lake & Palmer.

The Authentics were from Bedford, and comprised Mick O'Neill on vocals, brothers John and Berne Williams on guitar and bass, and Stewart Collins on drums. They were spotted by Hamish Grimes playing the Scene in London's West End and signed as support to the Yardbirds at the Marquee. They played at the Croydon Crawdaddy on Wednesdays and/or Saturdays, alternating with the T-Bones. Taking the money on the door was seventeen-year-old Julie Driscoll. She had approached Giorgio Gomelsky having heard he was looking

Some fans lamented the loss of Eric Clapton but following his departure the Yardbirds had hit after hit, reaching an audience far beyond blues and R&B purists.

for a girl singer to record and in the short term he employed her at the Crawdaddy and around his Soho Square office – which was a room in the offices of the National Jazz Federation, from which Barbara Pendleton still hadn't been able to winkle him out. When Gomelsky found Driscoll a song – Inez and Charlie Foxx's 'Don't Do It No More' – he asked John Williams to write a B side. 'I recall that I spent a day with Julie at Giorgio's flat in Lexham Gardens, to practise the song,' he says. Williams played on both tracks, along with organist Brian Auger. The Authentics occasionally appeared at the Richmond Crawdaddy and played the National Jazz & Blues Festival in 1964, when Mick O'Neill also sang with the Yardbirds as a replacement for the hospitalised Keith Relf.

Jimmy Page was another friend of the Authentics: he introduced the band to American singer-songwriter Jackie DeShannon, whose 'Needles and Pins' and 'When You Walk in the Room' were hits for the Searchers. She offered the band one of her songs ('Without

You'), which they recorded, with Page producing and playing on the track. But according to Berne Williams, Gomelsky buried the track because he was more interested in DeShannon writing for the Yardbirds.[2] John Williams never trusted Gomelsky and in 1965 the Authentics unhitched themselves from his management and took up with promoter Ricki Farr, brother of Gary Farr of the T-Bones.[3]

Another band in the Gomelsky stable were the Grebbels, who not only played the Richmond Crawdaddy, they got together at the club. 'My friends Roy and Peter Acres had gone over to the Crawdaddy,' recalls Peter Moody. 'They told me they'd seen a great band there [the Yardbirds], so next time I joined them. It blew me away, the whole atmosphere of the place. One Sunday they had a different guitarist and we asked Bill Relf, Keith's father, who was the band's roadie, who he was, and he told us Roger Pearce. Roy got talking to Roger about joining our band, so we met up and had a session.'

Pearce was an old friend of Keith Relf who had performed with him in the duo the Dreamers. He filled in on lead guitar for the Yardbirds on the odd occasion that Clapton was unavailable. In February 1964, Pearce began rehearsing with Roy Acres (second guitar), Peter Moody (bass) and Peter Acres (drums), along with Tony Carter, another Crawdaddy club regular, on vocals. They practised at the South Western Hotel, where the Yardbirds rehearsed – and the Stones before them. Relf took Gomelsky along to a rehearsal and the Georgian agreed that the group could open for the Yardbirds at the Crawdaddy. It was Relf who suggested the name the Grebbels after small cartoon characters that an art school friend used to doodle, which he described as a cross between gremlins and rebels.

'Our first engagement was Sunday 26 April 1964,' says Moody. 'We opened, then the Yardbirds did two sets. By June, we still did the opening set but then we also did the interval. When the Yardbirds were on, especially during their last set, I always watched them.

Especially Eric. I still believe, for me, he was at his finest around then, at the end of 1964.' Moody recalls a set the Grebbels did backing Sonny Boy Williamson at the Crawdaddy. 'One night, I was in the dressing room and the Yardbirds had just finished their set, so Eric and I are sat there chatting. Sonny Boy walked in and Eric was sat there with his guitar. Sonny said, "I'll show you how to play guitar!" He sits right next to Eric and says, "You play the notes, I'll play the strings." Eric was like a schoolboy. Eric knew [Sonny Boy] was the real McCoy, we all did. We'd never met a proper bluesman up close before.'

Moody says the Grebbels were 'gutted' when the T-Bones got the job as the new headliners, replacing the Yardbirds at the Crawdaddy.

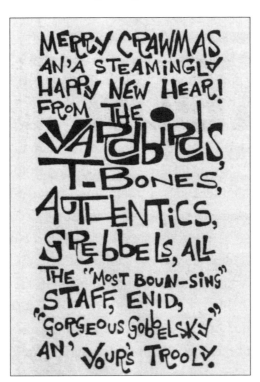

A Crawdaddy ad lettered in Hamish Grimes' distinctive hand. Enid was the girlfriend of Giorgio Gomelsky, aka the 'Gorgeous Gobelsky'.

'We had a great following by then but we never got to be the band of the night.' The Grebbels split soon after, playing their last gig in early February 1965. A single, recorded at Olympic Studios near Marble Arch and produced by Gomelsky, was never released. Moody and Pearce joined the Surbiton-born drummer John Dummer to form the John Dummer Blues Band.

Other Crawdaddy occasionals included Ian McLagan's Muleskinners, the Brian Auger Trinity and the Ingoes, which is a terrible name but an improvement on the Grave Diggers, the name vocalist and rhythm guitarist Brian Godding and bass-player Brian Belshaw dreamt up when they first got together in 1962. As the Ingoes (the name comes from the Chuck Berry instrumental, 'Ingo') they stalked Gomelsky until he caved in and took them under his managerial wing. He thought they were raw but showed promise and packed them off for a club residency in Dortmund for a few weeks to polish their act. On their return, the Ingoes became regulars at the Crawdaddy clubs and the Marquee.

Gomelsky came up with the idea of an exchange scheme, whereby the Alan Price R&B Combo, who were big on the scene in their native Newcastle, and the Yardbirds would change places and play one another's gigs. By the time the Geordie outfit came south they'd become the Animals. Some sources credit Gomelsky with the change of name but most histories of the band say it was Graham Bond's idea. He was the front man with the Graham Bond Organisation, who had played the Club A Go-Go in Newcastle, where the Alan Price R&B Combo were the house band. They'd impressed Bond, and he suggested they should try their luck in London and put them in touch with Gomelsky. The Animals played the Richmond Crawdaddy, squeezed between gigs at the Ricky Tick clubs in Windsor and Guildford. They were so well received in the south that in early 1964 they decided to move down permanently.

Eel Pie Island also plays a part in the Animals' story. In 2018, John Steel, the group's drummer, gave an interview to a South Australian news website in which he said that when the band played the Island in January 1964, in the audience that night were Peter Grant, who was a booker for the Don Arden Agency (and would later become the manager of Led Zeppelin), and producer Mickie Most. As a result of that gig, Grant booked the group onto a package tour of the UK with Chuck Berry and Carl Perkins, and Most became the band's agent.

Starting in September 1964, Gomelsky added Friday night sessions to the Crawdaddy calendar, with the Grebbels as the resident band. They were joined on several occasions by the Moody Blues, billed on posters as 'Birmingham's answer to the Yardbirds', in town to promote their new single 'Go Now'. Other Fridays, guests included visiting American blues artists Little Walter, Sugar Pie Desanto and Jimmy Reed.

A few months into 1965, finding new bands to play became the least of the club's concerns. There were the unhappy letter writers of Richmond to contend with. The Athletic Association Grounds' committee had been receiving complaints from residents living nearby, objecting to the bad language used by club-goers and the noise of revving scooters. One had written directly to the club's landlord, the Crown Commissioners. 'We've got our lease to think of,' a spokesman for the Association told *The Richmond and Twickenham Times*.[4] 'This is Crown land and the Crown Commissioners don't care for this sort of thing.' Speaking to the local press, Hamish Grimes acknowledged there had been some issues and that they'd had to purge the club of 'a few morons' fed on 'too much margarine' who spoilt it for the decent kids.[5] 'What people don't realise,' said Grimes, 'is that, while it may not be the kind of publicity Richmond wants, this club put the place on the map in America. It is still making a name for the town.' But was Richmond interested in acquiring renown in America? Apparently not, and certainly not at the expense of offending the Crown. The Athletic Association committee decreed that the Crawdaddy had to go. On Sunday 25 July 1965, Gomelsky and Grimes's club hosted its last gig at the rugby ground.

There is some irony here, because only twelve days later, over the weekend of 6–8 August, 33,000 ravers from all over the UK, with their long hair, doss bags and stashes of gear, descended on Richmond Athletic Association Grounds for the 5th National Jazz & Blues Festival. By now the balance of artists had swung emphatically away from jazz to R&B. There was some modern jazz on the Saturday afternoon, represented by Ronnie Scott and Dick Morrissey, and trad jazz on Sunday afternoon, including Ken Colyer and Chris Barber, who was featuring for the fifth year in a row. Kenny Ball was advertised but never made it. Otherwise, the rest of the line-up was all British blues and R&B bands – no guest American artists this time around. The weekend was recorded for both radio and TV.

Friday night was billed as 'Ready, Steady, Richmond' because it was being broadcast live on Radio Luxembourg's *Ready, Steady, Radio* show. The whole thing was also being filmed for US pop show *Shindig!*, which ran festival highlights over two programmes, compered by lounge lizard DJ Jimmy O'Neill, whose enthusiastic introductions perfectly backed up Hamish Grimes' claims that music was making Richmond's name across the Atlantic: 'Howdy hi Shindiggers! I'm Jimmy O'Neill and tonight *Shindig!* is proud to bring you the fantastically exciting Richmond Jazz Festival. Now we came all the way over here because this is where it all began, the greatest sounds and music, and the greatest groups you'll be hearing next year in the States.'

The festival's Friday line-up was stellar: the Moody Blues, the Who and the Yardbirds. At this time, the former were less moody and more bluesy: the Mellotrons, flutes and strings of 'Nights in White Satin' were still a couple of years away and this was a hard-edged, sharp blue-suited outfit showcasing tracks from debut LP *The Magnificent Moodies*, released just two weeks previously, including recent hit 'Go Now'. Next act the Who were something else. They were already leaving R&B behind and even performed their own songs. While their set began with Motown covers, they also played the self-penned 'I Can't Explain', 'Anyway, Anyhow, Anywhere' and an as-yet unrecorded track called 'My Generation'. 'I just remember the utter madness and excitement,' says Simon Goode, a local schoolboy at the time. 'Not only was the music fantastic, but it was the performance. The windmill guitar antics. And Keith Moon, you'd never seen anything like it. It was a crescendo of destruction.' Although when Roger Daltrey skipped across the stage, kicking out the front stage lights as he went, Barbara Pendleton was so annoyed she deducted damages from the band's fee.

The Yardbirds were probably the only group that had a chance of following such an act. Not only were they playing to a home crowd but 'For Your Love' had reached No.3 in the charts just a few weeks earlier inspiring nationwide 'birdmania. Keith Relf took to the stage with an appreciative, 'It's so nice to be back in Richmond!' 'We all knew Jeff Beck,' says Brentford girl Andrea Hiorns, 'and by the time they came on we were all standing on our chairs. I sat on [my boyfriend's] shoulders and waved at Jeff. He waved back and so did Sam [Paul Samwell-Smith] who waved his maracas above his head.' Having just seen Keith Moon firing on all toms, Jim McCarty set about thrashing his drums into submission, while new boy Beck roared through revved up versions of 'Guitar Boogie' and 'Here 'Tis'. The Yardbirds set triggered some of the only bad behaviour of the

The 5th National Jazz and Blues Festival was a success on all counts – even the weather was brilliant. Even so, it would be the last time it would be held in Richmond.

weekend when a section of the crowd broke through barriers to rush the stage and had to be restrained by security guards.

A line-up of British blues bands on Saturday night was led by the Graham Bond Organisation (featuring Graham Bond, Ginger Baker, Jack Bruce, Dick Heckstall-Smith and John McLaughlin), followed by Georgie Fame and the Blue Flames, Gary Farr and the T-Bones, with Manfred Mann wrapping up the evening. On Sunday, the queue waiting to get into the grounds stretched for a mile down the A316 Twickenham Road. Acts that day included Steampacket, with Long John Baldry, Rod Stewart and Julie Driscoll. Among the numbers they performed was the Holland-Dozier-Holland classic 'Can I Get a Witness', which Baldry dedicated to beatnik-hating

Sergeant Probyn of Richmond police station. 'All the Richmond tribe cheered,' remembers Andrea Hiorns.

Steampacket were followed by Spencer Davis, with Steve Winwood, who took to the stage to screams – not for the group, though, but in response to the fast-spreading news that the Beatles had been spotted. Not all of them, but John Lennon and George Harrison, with partners Cynthia Lennon and Pattie Boyd. Publicity officer Audrey Barber (sister of Chris Barber) steered them to a marquee where she ordered up scotch and cokes. Eric Burdon had invited them down to see his group, the Animals, who were the festival closers. Security erected barriers around the Beatles' table to keep the crowds back but before long they had to be whisked away to a smaller, more private tent. Soon that was surrounded and the Lennon-Harrison party made a getaway before things got out of hand. Animals drummer John Steel told a reporter, 'Sometimes I feel really sorry for them in spite of their success. They never get a moment's peace.'[6]

Newcastle's the Animals provided the high-energy climax to the weekend. The crowd was supplemented by approximately 500 Animals fans who'd been outside the main gates having failed to get in but who now burst into the grounds. One fan who'd paid to get in was Alan Sherriff, who fifty years later would be addressing the Richmond Local History Society. A native Tynesider, he'd travelled down especially for the festival, attracted by the rarity of an open-air concert. He'd seen *Jazz on a Summer's Day*, the 1959 film of the previous year's Newport Jazz Festival and thought it looked idyllic. Richmond wasn't Rhode Island, but the experience, he says, was equally blissful. 'I do remember that the weather was glorious,' he says. 'It was great being in a big crowd of people who all seemed to be moving to the same beat. I was very interested in clothes in those days and I'd go up and ask people where they got their shirt or jacket from, and they'd happily tell you.' For the second half of the Animals' set they were joined onstage by a seven-piece brass section of trumpets and saxes. For the very last number the stage was crowded by some of the evening's other artists – 'The whole thing ended up,' says Sherriff, 'like the last night at the Proms, with the crowd singing along.'

What nobody in the crowd could have known at the time was that this weekend marked the end of an era. The fifth NJF festival was a farewell to the short-lived phenomenon that was British R&B. The Beatles and the Who had led the way, and from here on the majority of artists would write their own material, creating new forms of music no longer so imitative of old New Orleans or the blues of Chicago. R&B and the blues would still have their fans, but they would be rapidly overtaken by a new wave of British sounds.

It was also a farewell to Richmond for the festival. Organiser Harold Pendleton was quoted in the local press saying that the 1965 festival was the best ever, musically, financially and for the blisteringly good weather, but not everybody was so cock-a-hoop. 'The Richmond Jazz Festival may have been a screaming success for Mr Pendleton but for me and several other people I have spoken to it was a pain in the neck' – the local letter writers had gone into overdrive. 'May I respectfully suggest that the next one be held on Salisbury Plain?' added TA Goldney of Bicester Road on the letters pages of *The Richmond and Twickenham Times*. 'These dirty, filthy, useless work-shy, cadging, lay-abouts bring nothing but a bad smell to Richmond.'[7]

Since the first festival there had been friction with local residents, the inevitable result of a green and pleasant middle-class oasis being invaded by hordes of young people with little respect for aerated lawns and a well-tied Windsor knot. There were concerns about drug use, predictably stoked by the local press, which prior to the

1964 festival was reporting that Richmond was set to become a centre for the distribution and sale of hemp, heroin, cocaine and amphetamines.[8] But the major flashpoint was fans sleeping rough around town. In previous years, the organisers had provided a large marquee on the site for those with nowhere better to spend the night but, in 1965, the local council had asked Pendleton to stop doing this. The result was more rough sleepers, with some even occupying the grassy centre of Richmond Circus traffic island. There were also bodies sprawled on the rolling hummocks of the exclusive Royal-Mid Surrey Golf Course (which happened to be adjacent to the Athletic Association Grounds) and this despoliation of the greens was more than the town could bear. Harold Pendleton responded to the festival's critics in the press, pointing out that the nearest campsite was in Croydon and asking for help developing better accommodation arrangements going forward.[9] Self-appointed Richmond guardian TA Goldney responded, 'If they must build something for these useless articles, may I suggest a few sulphur baths and a delousing station.'

The upshot was, in the words of a local newspaper headline, 'Jazz Festival Told: Get Out'. The Richmond Athletic Association, the paper reported, had reached a decision not to allow the festival back again because it was felt 'undesirable types' were being attracted to the town. Pendleton asked the council if they would consider alternative sites, for instance, Twickenham Stadium. Residents of Twickenham immediately made clear their feelings on this: 'The residents of Richmond upon Thames, during the past five years, have shown considerable leniency and understanding of this modern trend of music, and we feel that this is an ideal opportunity to have this event transferred to outside the borough boundaries.'[10] They got their wish. This was not the end of the jazz and blues festival, but it was the last time it was held in or anywhere close to Richmond.

Meanwhile, for Giorgio Gomelsky the Crawdaddy closure was unfortunate but he had his hands full with the Yardbirds. Just a few weeks after the Richmond festival he was in America with the group for their first visit. Trouble with work permits meant they could not play to the public, but Gomelsky organised some valuable promo appearances and pressed $600 into the hands of Sam Phillips, discoverer of Elvis Presley, to get the band an unscheduled session at the Sun Studio in Memphis, Tennessee. They were back in the States in December, for a tour that saw them crisscross the country, including two stints in Chicago, where they got to catch Muddy Waters and Howlin' Wolf, and where they recorded at the legendary Chess Studios. Out of this session came the extraordinary 'Shapes of Things', the first single written by members of the group (McCarty, Relf and Samwell-Smith) and a track arguably unlike like anything else heard before – rock journalist Mick Wall described it as sounding like a marching army of robots, while music historians cite it as possibly the first truly psychedelic record. They could even release a track based on Gregorian chanting – 'Still I'm Sad', the oddest rock record of 1965, with Gomelsky singing the bass parts – and it would chart. This was Gomelsky's dream, a group prepared to experiment and treat music-making as an adventure – unlike the Rolling Stones, who Gomelsky derided for having sold themselves to the highest bidder. He must have been devastated when in April 1966 the Yardbirds sacked him.

For some time, the band had been expressing frustration at what they saw as a lack of publicity and lack of recognition.[11] They complained in the press about not having a UK tour set up on their return from America. They blamed a manager about whom they were feeling increasingly ambivalent. 'He was encouraging of creativity and going out on a limb,' says Paul Samwell-Smith, 'but he shouldn't really have had so much to do with the business and finances.' Put simply, the members of the Yardbirds weren't making as much money as they felt they should be given their non-stop tour schedule and hit records. The 1983 *Yardbirds* book, on which Chris Dreja and Jim McCarty collaborated with author John Platt, reproduces Dreja's pay stub for the week ending 12 October 1965, showing his net pay was just £247 from a £527 gross amount. McCarty never believed Gomelsky was deliberately withholding money from the band, simply that he was hopeless with finances. Samwell-Smith is more critical. 'He wasn't good as a manager. The number of gigs we did that were so far apart. We had to sit in the van and travel for hours. It wasn't good organisation. Then he took the publishing on a B-side of ours, which was definitely dodgy behaviour. He was slightly crazy, slightly out of control, slightly mad, slightly dodgy. Dodgy is a good word for Giorgio.'

The Yardbirds quickly found a new manager in Simon Napier-Bell, a failed musician turned music editor who'd worked on the score for recent hit film *What's New Pussycat?* and who'd just written the lyrics for Dusty Springfield's 'You Don't Have to Say you Love Me' (he would later manage Marc Bolan and Wham! among others). And Giorgio? 'I should never have been a manager: I needed someone to manage me,' he said.[12] He regrouped in Soho, in offices not far from Harold Pendleton, who was absorbed in running the Marquee club and finding an alternative site for his festival. In the long run, being booted out of Richmond was no big deal for either of them.

UND:° Please phone 892—4677 and ask for
Ian — (cash reward).

MARCH	18th.	MIKE ABSALOM	8 8
MARCH	25th.	TERRY MASTERSON	7
APRIL	1st.	SCOTTY ~~DEREK BRIMSTONE~~ £8 £10
APRIL	8th.	JOHN TOWNSEND + KEITH CLARK ~~ALAN ROBINSON~~ £7„10o gua
APRIL	15th.	COMEALLYE
APRIL	22nd.	CLIFF AUNGIER £12 + ex.
APRIL	29th.	RALPH McTELL

£8 guarantee

MAY	6th.	WIZZ JONES £10
MAY	13th.	JOHN MARTYN £10 „10o guarante
MAY	20th.	C.A.Y.
MAY	27th	TERRY GOULD £10
JUNE	3rd.	AL STEWART
JUNE	10th	DAVE WAITE + MARIAN SEGAL
JUNE	17th	JOE STEAD £8 guara
JUNE	~~23rd~~ 24th	C.A.Y.
JULY	1st	RALPH McTELL + MACK £10 gua
JULY	8th	
JULY	15th	SHIRLEY COLLINS £12„10o gu
JULY	22nd	JOHN MARTYN 12 gus
JULY	29th	AL STEWART £20
AUG.	5th.	DAVE TRAVIS £12
AUG.	12th.	CAY.
AUG.	19th.	RON GEESIN £10 guar
AUG.	26th.	JeK
SEPT.	2nd.	DAVE WAITE MARIAN SEGAL ~~Ralph McTell~~ R Wheeler
SEPT.	9nd.	RALPH McTell £10
SEPT.	16	DORRIS HENDERSO
SEPT.	23	✓ JOHN MARTYN £14
SEPT.	30	C.A.Y.
Oct	7	DEREK + BRIMSTONE
Oct.	14	JOHN + JAMES £8
Oct.	21	✓ AL STEWART £20
Oct.	28	✓ Dave Waite + Marian Sagal f
Nov.	4	DAVE + TONI £15 ARTHUR

CHAPTER 10

LIVE AT THE HANGING LAMP

A crypt on Richmond Hill welcomes young folk with acoustic guitars, as well as the occasional fiddle, penny whistle and crumhorn

DESPITE THE LOSS OF EELPILAND, the Crawdaddy and the jazz and blues festivals, music hadn't entirely vanished from beside the Thames. The Palm Court Hotel, by Richmond Bridge, continued to host modern jazz two or three nights a week, as it had since 1963. Bookings were made by double-bassist Ed Faultless, who also fronted his own trio, and who continued to bring in scene stalwarts like Art Theman, Dick Heckstall-Smith and Dick Morrissey, promoting their shows with ads in *Melody Maker*. There was more jazz at the Madingley Club, a members-only drinking den in a large old riverside house on Willoughby Road in East Twickenham; at one time the Brian Rutland Band was the house band.[1] There were impromptu sessions at the Imperial, a late-

FACING: A page from a notebook belonging to Ian Shircore, who booked the acts for the Hanging Lamp. 18 March was the club's 1968 opening date.

Victorian pub in central Richmond, which had made its name in 1965 as the home of the jug and washboard movement. Like the skifflers of a few years earlier, jugbands played a junk shop array of instruments, but with the notable addition of a jug played with buzzed lips to give a sort of trombone sound. The resulting music sat somewhere between blues, jazz and end-of-the-pier novelty act. For reasons now forgotten, the centre of the British jugband phenomenon was Richmond, and specifically the Imperial, home to both the Kaiser Bill Jugband and the Jericho Jugband.[2] The latter was led by Anthony 'Duster' Bennett, a blues guitarist and harmonica player from Ham, who played with Top Topham and Peter Green, and later joined John Mayall's Bluesbreakers. Green called him the 'best harp player in Britain'. Bennett recorded a clutch of albums (his track 'Jumping at Shadows' was covered by both Fleetwood Mac and Gary Moore), before late one night in 1976, after performing with Memphis Slim, he fell asleep at the wheel and was killed when his van hit a truck. Before it closed, the jugband craze made it over to Eelpiland, where jazz outfit the Original Downtown Syncopators added teapot, biscuit tin and kazoo to become Spencer's Washboard Kings. There was also folk.

Britain's folk revival took off in a big way after skiffle's bubble burst, and its devotees split roughly in two directions: beat groups and folkies. Supported by a trickle of expat Americans, including Bob Dylan, who spent time in London in 1962–63, and Paul Simon, who made several trips to England in '64 and '65, a generation of would-be singer-songwriters came together in back rooms across the country. In London, the folk heartland was Soho, with Bunjies, off Charing Cross Road, and Les Cousins, on Greek Street, as the tent poles of the capital's *rus in urbe* music scene. Something was definitely blowing in the wind out west, too, not least in a string of clubs along the Thames, from the Half Moon in Putney, through

Richmond and Twickenham to Kingston and beyond. If Soho had a folk club on every corner, then this stretch of the Thames corridor boasted a folk night in almost every other pub.

The Richmond Folk Club had been gathering at the Richmond Community Centre on Sheen Road since the early 1960s.[3] The club was led by Glaswegian folk singer Alex Campbell, aided by 'Big Theo' Johnson. Johnson had limited musical ability, but Campbell was a terrific performer, good with audiences, who signed off performances with the Lead Belly standard 'Goodnight, Irene'. When Campbell moved on and the club folded, Johnson launched the Open Folk and Blues Club at the Crown, a pub on the main road midway between Richmond and Twickenham. Johnson, who once served on a factory whaling ship in the Antarctic, was more hustler than musician – a 'big guy on a small moped', beetling around town, making things happen. For a time he ran Bunjies in Soho and was a key figure in other clubs, including the Crypt at St Martin-in-the-Fields on Trafalgar Square. When an unknown Paul Simon pitched up in London in 1964, Johnson arranged a gig for him at the Labour Rooms in Richmond, a basement in a house on Church Road, which was owned by the Richmond Labour Party and for a brief period hosted small folk gatherings.[4] Johnson lived in a first-floor flat at 400 Richmond Road, on the Twickenham side of Richmond Bridge, not far from the Crown. It was an open house for friends and acquaintances, who were welcome to claim one of the mattresses scattered about the place. 'He would tell people, "Take the tube to Richmond, then walk over the bridge and ring the bell at the house with the blue door on the left side of the street", recalls Bridget St John, one of the musicians who occasionally flopped there. Regular acts at Johnson's folk nights at the Crown included singer Beverley Kutner (soon to become Beverley Martyn), twelve-string guitarist Johnny Joyce and singer-songwriter Michael 'Mac' McGann, who together played as the Levee Breakers. Other performers included Bert Jansch, John Renbourn and American expat Jackson C Frank, who at the time was more highly regarded than Paul Simon, but who would die destitute and homeless. After Johnson, the club at the Crown was run by the charismatic Johnny Silvo, born to an African-American soldier father and Irish mother, who taught himself guitar while in the army, joined the Mike Peters Florida Jazz Band (Eel Pie Island regulars) and when trad dropped out of fashion switched to folk.

Neighbouring Kingston also had an active folk scene, centred around the Folk Barge (formerly the Jazz Boat), another club run by Theo Johnson. Small and dark with tightly packed bench seating, it operated three nights a week. Anyone willing to play a floor spot got in free. Kingston Art School student Sandy Denny made her first public appearance here in 1965, the same year Paul Simon played the Barge. When a young singer-songwriter named John Martyn arrived down in London from his native Glasgow in April 1967, he became a Folk Barge regular (and a lodger at Johnson's flat). There was also the Strawberry Hill Folk Club based at St Mary's College, a teacher training institution in Twickenham. One of the students involved in the club was a keen guitarist from South Shields, Frank McConnell. During his last weeks at the college, he was asked if he'd meet Father Brian Maxwell of East Sheen, a priest who wanted to open a folk club for the young people of his parish and who wasn't sure how to go about it. McConnell suggested a first step would be finding an unusual venue, a place with some character. Father Maxwell came back with the crypt of St Elizabeth of Portugal on the Vineyard, on Richmond Hill.

There have been two actual vineyards in Richmond. One is mentioned in manorial records of 1445, and is described as being close to the riverside; the other existed in the early eighteenth century on the lower slopes of Richmond Hill. One of them – historians are not sure which – gave its name to the present street called the Vineyard, which presumably was the old path to the grapes. These days it's distinguished by three historic groups of almshouses, as well as seventeenth-century Clarence House – associated with both Bernardo O'Higgins, general, statesman and liberator of Chile, and Brian Blessed, *Z Cars* police constable, Roman emperor and ally of Flash Gordon, who lived there from 1967 to 1976 – and the Grade II-listed St Elizabeth of Portugal Catholic church, built in 1824. The crypt of this historic structure turned out to be a stark and chilly space with a clutter of stone pillars blocking sight lines and a ceiling so low that it posed a serious risk to anyone of above average height. 'It was filthy, this place,' says McConnell. 'It was damp. It was smelly. It was awful and we loved it.'

McConnell had been joined by three others who were up for the idea of running a music club. Verity Stephens was a schoolgirl from East Sheen who had a sweet voice, a good guitar style and idolised Joan Baez. Ian Shircore was Verity's boyfriend. The third collaborator, Will Creavin, had left Dublin to join the army as a musician (he played the penny whistle and mandolin) and found himself saddled with a tuba at the Royal Military School of Music, at Kneller Hall in Whitton, near Twickenham. Among the junk piled in the church crypt they found a small black lamp that held a single candle, which they rescued and hung on the wall, and on 18 March 1968, the Hanging Lamp opened to the public.

The club operated one night a week, on Mondays. McConnell was the resident act, supported by Stephens and Creavin, whose playing was bolstered his charisma and gnomish charm.[5] Shircore used his wiles to persuade guest artists to play for the pennies on offer. The opening night featured Mike Absalom, a singer-songwriter with a skewed sense of humour (his 1969 album would be called *Save the Last Gherkin for Me).* Those who followed included Wizz Jones, who Bert Jansch once called 'the most underrated guitarist ever', and Shirley Collins, one of the foremost voices of the English folk revival. Apart from the billed guests, there would be floor spots, giving audience members the opportunity to step up. Many were dabblers, others were auditioning for a regular slot. 'Our little folk club became the *X Factor* of its day,' says Shircore.

McConnell and Shircore met Ralph McTell, whose first album was released in early 1968, and booked him for £2 to do a gig at the Lamp. The following year McTell put out his second album, *Spiral Staircase*, which opened with the song 'Streets of London', and soon after he was selling out the Royal Albert Hall. They also booked a hippie-ish duo called the Sallyangie, fronted by twenty-two-year-old singer Sally Oldfield, backed by her fifteen-year-old brother Mike on guitar. They were promoting their whimsical debut album *Children of the Sun*. It sunk without a trace. Mike did better with his own solo album four years later – *Tubular Bells*. Another regular was Irish comedian and folk singer Noel Murphy, who was married to Shircore's best friend. In 1968, Murphy began performing with a seventeen-year-old Scottish banjo and mandolin player named Davey Johnstone, who Shircore remembers playing at the Lamp 'squatting shyly on a stool next to Noel, hidden behind a cascade of blond hair'. Johnstone was a bit of a prodigy, dazzling audiences by tearing into traditional reels at a speed that made his fingers a blur. After two years with Murphy he became a session musician, playing on, among other recordings, Elton John's 1971 album *Madman Across the Water*. He subsequently joined John's band as guitarist and musical director, a position he still held as this book was being written, over 3,000 live shows later.

Al Stewart, who was already a well-established name on the scene having appeared regularly at Bunjies and Les Cousins,

Scottish singer-songwriter Al Stewart performing at the club – that is the titular hanging lamp on the wall beside him.

became another Lamp regular. His gigs coincided with the release of his 1969 album *Love Chronicles*, notable for its eighteen-minute autobiographical title track, in which Stewart describes all his girlfriends from school days to present, and earns notoriety for using the word 'fucking' – a first for a major label release. Father Richard, priest at St Elizabeth's, was mortified when Stewart performed the song in unexpurgated form in his church. According to McConnell, whenever Stewart turned up at the club he always had a different pretty girl on his arm but never a guitar; instead, he'd borrow McConnell's and then complain about its poor strings all night.

One night, an unknown named Pete Atkin did a floor spot that so impressed Shircore he immediately invited him back as a headline act. Shircore was surprised to discover Atkin had a bodyguard, 'a chunky, heavyset man with small dangerous-looking eyes'. It turned out he was the lyricist and his name was Clive James.

Leo O'Kelly of Irish progressive folksters Tír na nÓg, who in a long and ongoing career have played support for groups including Jethro Tull, Procol Harum and the Who, remembers the Hanging Lamp being one of their first gigs when they were new to London. They did a floor spot and were invited back. O'Kelly remembers the gig being advertised in *Melody Maker*, which pleased him, and arriving to see a queue snaking around the corner and down the hill. 'The fantastic thing about it was someone like Ralph McTell would be playing the Festival Hall one night and the Hanging Lamp the next,' says O'Kelly. The club was also, on occasion, graced by the presence of Ewan MacColl, the undisputed godfather of the British folk scene and composer of much-covered classics 'Dirty Old Town' and 'The First Time Ever I Saw Your Face'.

Somewhat perversely, the man who handled bookings never liked folk music: 'I wasn't interested in finger-in-ear, Aran sweater stuff,' says Shircore. 'A lot of the people who I was interested in had fuck all to do with folk, they were just songwriters.' McConnell remembers Shircore turning up at his flat with the first James Taylor album, released in December 1968 on the Beatles' Apple label, which the two of them listened to avidly. Both agreed, this was it, this was what they were looking for. 'It was a guitar aficionados club to some extent,' says Shircore.

It was Frank McConnell who first saw John Martyn. It was when McConnell was involved with the Strawberry Hill Folk Club; one night they had booked Scottish folkie Hamish Imlach, who turned up with a young man and said, 'Give him a decent spot. He's good'. They did and were blown away – so much so, they gave him a booking of his own later that week. 'I met lots of whizz guitarists,' says McConnell, 'but most of them were well up themselves. John was not. He just wanted to play and experiment and explore. He was walking off into space from where the rest of us were.'[6] At McConnell's urging, Shircore went to see Martyn perform at the Folk Barge and immediately booked him for the Hanging Lamp. His first appearance was at only the club's third session, in April 1968, and he would come back regularly over the next four years.

Shircore's new girlfriend, Pat, was one of three girls sharing a flat across the street from St Elizabeth's. It had the attraction of a small roof terrace. On some nights, a small crowd would head over after the club closed to continue the music. McConnell remembers being there and jamming with Martyn. 'I could follow what he was playing melodically and harmonically, but had no idea where his hands would be flying to next. Even though the music was beautifully logical in its development, I couldn't always work out how he was producing it. Sometimes his turns in the middle of a piece were unexpected and it would take to the end of the phrase to realise that you'd continued straight down the road and he'd turned left when you weren't watching.'[7]

By 1972, Martyn was already a youthful veteran of five albums and had established himself as one of the brightest of the new generation of folk-influenced singer-songwriters. With his 1971 album *Bless the Weather*, he had moved away from what he scornfully described as the 'dingly-dangly-dell' and begun blurring the boundaries between folk, blues and jazz, veering off into uncategorisable territories of his own making. Shircore recalls how baffled audiences were when Martyn first turned up at the Lamp with his board of electronic gizmos. He'd kick off the evening with intimate acoustic recitals, including the lullaby-like title track of *Bless the Weather* and 'May You Never' (which will appear on his next album, 1973's *Solid Air*), one of the most beautiful songs of love – or loyalty – ever written. He'd end his first sets by cajoling the audience into a singalong

Folk Forum

FRIDAY cont.

AT THE SUGAWN KITCHEN.
Duke of Wellington, Balls Pond Road, N1.
CALLINAN-FLYNN
Adm 20p.

CAPRICORN, Albany, opposite Great Portland Street tube, W.1. 8 pm.

FINBAR & EDDIE

FUREY

CITY POLY FOLK

KEITH CHRISTMAS
ANNE BRIGGS

at SU Hall, 84 Moorgate, EC2, London Wall ent. 8 pm. 30p.

DIZ DISLEY, Three Tuns, High Street, Watford.

FOLK PLUS, Crooked Billet, Penge.
SINGERS NIGHT
Residents: **WILD OATS,** 693 4263.

GENERAL HAVELOCK, High St, Ilford.

TIGHT LIKE THAT

HERGA CEILIDH with Oak. Hugh Rippon at Whittington, Pinner.

GUILDFORD, Star, Quarry St.
DECLAN AFFLEY
from **AUSTRALIA**

ORGAN INN FOLK CLUB, London Road, Ewell.

E. J. FIRKINBOLE

Residents **MOSAIC.**

PUTNEY HALF MOON
LOWER RICHMOND ROAD

NOEL MURPHY

SEVENOAKS FOLK CLUB, 47 Bradbourne Vale Road (A25).
DAVE TRAVIS
Residents: **DAVE LEWRY** and friends. Floor singers welcome. — 0732 53803.

STARTING GATE

WOOD GREEN (opposite Wood

SATURDAY

ANGLERS, TEDDINGTON

DAVE LAMBERT

AT COUSINS, 49 Greek St., 7.30 pm.

JOHN MARTYN

FOLK CELLAR

8 pm. Cecil Sharp House, 2 Regents Park Road, Camden Town
CLIVE WOOLF
Residents: Kevin Sheils and Brian Grayson.

LONDON CO-OP presents the Singers Clubs, Union Tavern, Kings Cross Road, WC1. 7.45 pm.
GABE SULLIVAN, JOHN FAULK-NER, SANDRA KERR. Members 30p. Non-members 35p.

PEELERS REOPENS

At the **ADAMS ARMS, CONWAY STREET, W.1,** opposite main entrance, GPO tower. Nearest station Warren Street, also near Great Portland Street, Goodge Street, Tottenham Court Road stations. Only appearance in London.

PLANXTY

PLUS FROGMORTON

TROUBADOUR, 265 Old Brompton Road. 10.30 pm.
CLIFF AUNGIER

SUNDAY

BLYTHE HILL, Tavern Folk Club, Stanstead Road, S.E.23, 8 pm.
FINBAR AND EDDIE FUREY

BOUNDS GREEN FC, Springfield Park Tavern, Bounds Green, N.11.

McCALMANS

PLUS FROGMORTON

CAMDEN TOWN. The York & Albany, Parkway Canary Flatfoot.

MONDAY cont.

HANGING LAMP

The Crypt, St Elizabeth's, The Vineyard, **RICHMOND,** 8 pm.

JOHN MARTYN

ORPINGTONFOLK, Royal Oak, Green Street Green, Callinan-Flynn.

TABBY'S FOLK
OPP EALING BDY TUBE W5.
KEITH
CHRISTMAS

LIC BAR — 8 pm START

TUESDAY

AT CATFORD RISING SUN.
SINGERS NIGHT BLUNDER-BORE.

CHELSEA FOLK, The Stanhope, Gloucester Road (opposite Underground). **OPEN 7.15 PM.**
ELLIOTT-BLOSSE
Celia O'Neale

DOWN RIVER, Crooked Billet, Walthamstow.

KEITH
CHRISTMAS

7.30 BETTER COME EARLY.

INTERNATIONAL FOLK CLUB, Half Moon Tavern, Herne Hill, SE24, 8 pm.

RODNEY
and
RAGGY FARMER

MARIAN SEGAL

OVAL HOUSE FESTIVAL
10 pm. Adm free (Festival membership 5p). 54 Kennington Oval, SE11. 2 mins Oval tube.

POETRY & MUSIC, Sydney Carter and Jeremy Taylor. Queen's Park Library, W10. Tuesday, May 9, 7.30. Free.

THE WHITE HORSE, ISLINGTON, Liverpool and Theberton Street, N.1.

AL MATTHEWS

(EX-RICHIE HAVENS SIDEMAN)
Residents: Doodlang'lldoo Band

The folk listings page of *Melody Maker* for the week that someone snuck recording equipment into the Hanging Lamp and captured John Martyn's performance.

Martyn's *Live at the Hanging Lamp* album, which
appeared forty-one years after the concert took place
(and four years after Martyn's death).

version of 'Singin' in the Rain'. For the second half of the evening, he
would plug in and fly off into sonic experimentations in delay, echo
and repetition, his guitar squalling and unleashing pulsing waves
that reverberated off the close stone walls and ceiling. 'He would
play for twelve minutes with all these sounds building up,' recalls
Shircore. 'People were very unsure. Nobody shouted "Judas" but
it was a bit like a Dylan-going-electric experience.' What Shircore
doesn't remember is anybody recording any of Martyn's Richmond
shows. Someone obviously did, because in 2013 an album titled
Live at the Hanging Lamp appeared as a bonus disc in a deluxe John
Martyn box-set. The tapes had apparently been sitting on a shelf
for forty years before being rediscovered, mastered and released for
public consumption. It's clear the club management didn't know the
show was being recorded because all the way through the show Irish
jigs play faintly in the background, possibly from a radio. Shircore

was definitely there because his is the first and last voice heard on the album, introducing Martyn and telling the audience at the end, 'Come back next week for Windfall.' Who?

There were times the club's talent-spotting antenna went on the blink. Karina Gabner was a teenager of maybe fourteen or fifteen when she got into trouble at her Catholic convent school in Sheen. Her mother spoke to Father Maxwell and confided her worries that her daughter seemed to lack any sort of direction. He asked, 'Does she like folk music?' Which is how Gabner ended up making coffee at the Hanging Lamp – being in a church basement meant there was no alcohol. She remembers a night when John Martyn brought along a young man he introduced as Nick Drake, who said he'd like to play a floor spot. There were too many names on the list that night and he was told to try again the following week. Come the end of the evening, Gabner remembers, 'John Martyn had buggered off and Nick had nowhere to stay, so I took him home with me.' The walk to her family home on Sheen Road, she says, was about a mile and Drake stayed silent the whole way. 'The next morning my mum woke me and said, "There's a chap on the sofa fast asleep. Who is it?" And I said, "Oh, it's a bloke from the folk club mum".' Gabner remembers that he was eventually given a floor spot, but the club never booked him.

Another miss came to light when Elvis Costello published his autobiography. In 1959, the family of five-year-old Declan MacManus (as Elvis was then) moved to Beaulieu Close, off Cambridge Park on the Twickenham side of Richmond Bridge. They were there for more than ten years. For a time, someone connected with the Yardbirds lived on the next street over; Costello remembers there was often a battered white van parked there with messages scrawled in the grime: 'I Love Jeff' and 'I Love Keith'. In his early teens, MacManus owned a jumbo acoustic guitar, bought on weekly instalments, and used to go to the Hanging Lamp to see how it should be played by watching guitarists like Davey Johnstone and Welsh finger-picking wizard John James. In the summer of 1970, at the age of sixteen, he felt confident enough to put his name down for a floor spot. The song he performed on his public debut, 'Winter', was the first he had written. 'It was in the cheery key of E minor,' Costello recalls in his book. He also remembers that when he looked up at the audience, there was Ewan MacColl, the grand old man of British folk, with his head bowed, asleep. 'The church crypt was a good place to fail quietly,' he writes.

Just down the road from the Hanging Lamp was another important part of the local music scene – also with Elvis Costello associations: Potter's Music Shop. At the foot of Richmond Hill, at 18 Hill Rise, a few doors from L'Auberge, Potter's sold both records and instruments, mainly acoustic guitars. You could try out the former in listening booths and the latter up the stairs in the backroom. Lilian Alda, Costello's mum, worked at Potter's. It is here her son bought his first guitar. 'The owner, Gerry Southard,' writes Costello, 'was a hulking, bearded man who gave the impression of being hard to impress but who stocked records that couldn't be found elsewhere, whether they were jazz, blues, folk, ballads or classical recordings.'[8] Costello says that one afternoon he saw Fleetwood Mac founder Peter Green browsing the blues albums in Potter's, 'looking like a hippie Jesus in a rugby shirt', and another time he arrived to hear that Mick Jagger had just been in. Paul Samwell-Smith remembers that he and fellow Yardbird Keith Relf used to buy blues records there: 'It's where I bought my first Jimmy Reed album'. There was also a downstairs workshop where highly regarded luthier and designer of 12-string guitars Johnny Joyce worked. Joyce also performed with the likes of Davy Graham, Bert Jansch, John Renbourn, Paul Simon, Al Stewart and the Strawbs.

A few doors from Potter's, at 10 Hill Rise, was another retailer intimately tied up with local youth culture. The Ivy Shop was opened by an East Ender named John Simons in the summer of 1965. He wanted to offer British businessmen the sort of clothing worn by their smart American counterparts, who sported Ivy League college looks. As it turned out, the demand came not from middle-aged Surrey stockbrokers but from working-class kids looking to dress as sharply as their idols Paul Newman and Steve McQueen. Whether Simons was aware of it or not when he chose the location, the Palm Court Hotel, which was just down the street from his shop, was the big hangout for Richmond Mods, who were occasionally joined there by scooter gangs from other parts of southwest London. The Ivy Shop was one of the key suppliers outside the West End for three-button mohair suits, Lion of Troy Oxford cotton button-down shirts, Crombie overcoats and wing-tip brogues. It was Simons and the Ivy that popularised the Harrington jacket. This was a smart golf jacket with elasticated waist and cuffs, and a tartan lining that was often worn by Rodney Harrington, a character played by Ryan O'Neal in US drama *Peyton Place*. When Simons displayed the jackets in his window he added a handwritten note saying 'The Rodney Harrington jacket', later shortening it to 'Harrington'. The name was adopted by manufacturers the world over. Simons subsequently opened shops in Soho, Chelsea and Covent Garden, but he kept the Richmond original going until 1995.

Shircore and McConnell, for their part, also experimented with expanding the activities of Hanging Lamp. There was a series of gigs at the Institute of Contemporary Arts in central London that featured Frank McConnell playing the first half and Al Stewart, John Martyn or Ralph McTell headlining. There were also some unsuccessful gigs at the larger venue of the Richmond Community Centre; the second of these, they discovered too late, fell on the same night as a gig at the Athletics Association Ground by visiting American blues-rockers Canned Heat. 'For something like fifteen years I owed Ralph McTell his guaranteed minimum fee of £35 because we only had a handful of people show up,' remembers Shircore.

Meanwhile, the regular club continued to nurture new artists. Shircore recalls a bunch of young slightly weird guys turning up, a four-person line-up of lute, recorder, bassoon and one guitar, a couple of whom doubled up on archaic, J-shaped crumhorns. 'They were sensational. This was not folk music. It was medieval stuff,' he says. 'We said get a name, get a forty-five-minute minimum set together and we'll have you back in five or six weeks.' They came back as Gryphon, playing music that had a foot in both the folk and progressive rock worlds. 'We were invited back many times and always had a great reception,' says guitarist Graeme Taylor of the band's Hanging Lamp gigs. 'It really did feel like the place to be at the time – so long as you were careful of your head.' Gryphon would go on to release five albums of their hybrid medieval rock. Legend has it that at a lunchtime concert at London's Victoria and Albert Museum, they were pursued through the corridors by schoolgirl fans after a rousing performance of first album highlight 'Sir Gavin Grimbold'. Similarly eclectic were Gas Works, a duo from Lancashire whose romantic ballads were enlivened by a music hall sensibility and drily witty introductory monologues. They managed to surpass even Gryphon in the odd instrument stakes with their playing of a phonofiddle – it resembles a viola neck fitted with an ear trumpet and the sound it makes has been described as like a mosquito with a sore throat. They weren't a total novelty act and their songs were good enough that Tony Visconti, producer of David Bowie and T-Rex, worked with them on their self-titled first album.

Remarkably, St Elizabeth's was not the only church gig on the Vineyard. Literally next door is another house of worship. Younger

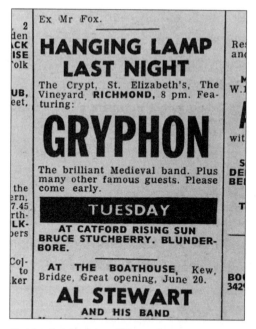

Ex Mr Fox.

HANGING LAMP
LAST NIGHT

The Crypt, St. Elizabeth's, The Vineyard. **RICHMOND**, 8 pm. Featuring:

GRYPHON

The brilliant Medieval band. Plus many other famous guests. Please come early.

TUESDAY

AT CATFORD RISING SUN
BRUCE STUCHBERRY. BLUNDERBORE.

AT THE BOATHOUSE, Kew, Bridge, Great opening, June 20.

AL STEWART
AND HIS BAND

On Monday 19 June 1972, the Hanging Lamp opened its doors for the last time. The act on that final night was medieval folk-rock band Gryphon.

than its Catholic neighbour by seven years, the Protestant Vineyard Church has notable political connections: Lady Stansgate, mother of the Labour MP Tony Benn, was a parishioner in the 1940s, followed by local resident and two-time British prime minister Harold Wilson in the 1960s. In early 1972, the church was frequented by a future PM, not as a parishioner but as part of a short-lived stint in the music business. Tony Blair had left school and decided to take a gap year before going to Oxford.[9] He moved out of the family home in Durham and relocated to London, where he wound up renting a room on Cassilis Road in St Margarets, over the river from Richmond, in a house owned by a man named Norman Burt. Blair and a friend, Alan Collenette, fancied themselves as rock promoters and Burt, who was a deacon of the Vineyard Church, which had a basement youth club (where Keith Relf's early band the

Dreamers played a handful of gigs), arranged for them to use the space. The pair ran music nights with live bands, notably a group of Westminster public school old boys who called themselves Jaded. Tony, with shoulder-length hair, tight shirts and flared jeans, took the money at the door and operated the 'Spacematic DISCO with LIGHTS' (as advertised on the hand-drawn flyers). He sometimes indulged his exhibitionist side by joining Jaded to perform Rolling Stones numbers 'Brown Sugar' and 'Honky Tonk Women'. After six months of putting on discos and bands at the Vineyard, capacity 150, Blair and Collenette felt ready to step up. They booked the Alexandra Hall in Kensington, capacity 2,000. Nobody showed up. Anyway, it was time for Blair to head to Oxford.

That same year, 1972, there was a fire at Frank McConnell's Twickenham flat, from which just about the only thing to survive was his guitar. Soon afterwards, he and his family moved out of the area. Some months earlier, Ian Shircore had begun writing a music column for *The Richmond Herald* and that had now evolved into a full-time position. The club had become an obstacle for both of them and in June that year they took the decision to snuff out the Lamp.[10]

CHAPTER 11

COLONEL BAREFOOT'S ROCK GARDEN

Music returns to the Island, louder, heavier and trippier than before, with a side order of trouble

BY 1967, R&B WAS HISTORY. The blues had burst into psychedelic bloom, trousers had flared, skirts had shortened, hair went uncut, girls had kaleidoscope eyes. If any part of London was primed to provide the perfect setting for a summer of love, then Richmond was it. It was one of the few places in which to find a sophisticated urban centre set beside a *Wind in the Willows* riverbank, with meadows, woods, weirs, medieval mounds and underground grottoes. Youth lolled on the grass in the shade of trees, under skies abuzz with birds and bees, drifting off to the sound of oars splashing in the water and the strains of a gently strummed guitar. It was the place for LSD-fuelled excursions down the rabbit hole, for spiritual journeys of self-discovery, or for indulging in

FACING: Eel Pie Island began hosting gigs again in 1968 but the atmosphere and music were very different to the old Eelpiland days – heavier in every sense.

whimsical 'back to the garden' pastoralism. 'I mean, Richmond was magic,' says Teddington-raised Tony Thorne, an author, linguist and lexicographer specialising in slang. 'It was beautiful. You'd go up to the Terrace Gardens and sit and smoke dope, and meditate and play guitars. You'd go up into the park and just wander around, and see these groups of freaks communing.'

Tom Newman, who in 1973 co-produced Mike Oldfield's *Tubular Bells*, grew up on a repurposed World War II landing craft moored near Richmond Lock. 'Boats were the cheapest way of living,' he recalls. 'They were moored all the way down to Brentford, all ex-war department, a lot of them had been to Dunkirk. Hundreds of us lived on houseboats. The whole thing was a very bohemian situation.' Tony Thorne remembers one evening walking from Twickenham to Richmond in the company of some French friends. 'It was dusk and it was a really warm evening and we were passing the hippies in their houseboats who greeted us as we walked by on the towpath. These French friends of mine, who had been all over the world on the hippie trail but had never been to Richmond before, said how fabulous it was and that it was just like India.'

Richmond had a well-worn hippie trail of its own, leading not to Kandahar or Varanasi, but Cornwall. The town was the starting point for annual summer expeditions down to St Ives. Since 1963, when singer-songwriter Donovan spent a summer in the Cornish seaside resort celebrated for its artistic heritage, it had become a warm-weather haven for beatniks, then hippies. Plans were laid at L'Auberge and rucksack-totting parties assembled on the terrace before setting off for the A316, signboards in hand. Twickenham resident Alan Winter was among them. 'The exodus started one afternoon at L'Auberge and we all had little bets on who would get there first. Nobby Clark and I decided we would hitchhike and the girls we were with would go separately. Our theory was they were more likely to get a lift as two girls. We were right. They were down there in about seven hours, and it took Nobby and me about two-and-a-half days.' Once down in Cornwall, the Aubergeniks slept on the beach, beneath hedgerows, in derelict cottages and in an old World War II pillbox. Everyone used the bathroom facilities at one of two pubs, the Lifeboat Inn or the Sloop: 'The landlord would let us as long as we spent some money,' says Winter. 'People found various ways of surviving. Someone would follow the milkman and nick some milk. Someone else would find a field and dig up some potatoes. It was extremely basic.' Although St Ives attracted dossers from all over the country, Winter remembers there being a sizeable contingent from around the Richmond and Twickenham scene. 'We seemed to know everybody we met there. They were the same people that we saw back home at gigs.'

Richmond developed its own small countercultural scene. There was the Parade Gallery on Paradise Road, which hosted both exhibitions and happenings; the people behind the gallery also put out the *Richmond Area Free Press*, a local version of the recently launched *Time Out*. One of London's hippest music boutiques, One Stop Records of South Molton Street (just off Oxford Street), chose to open its second branch at 2 the Square in Richmond. There was also a far less legitimate form of commerce that thrived locally, which was the selling of drugs. At this time, there was no part of London where mind-altering substances weren't being smoked or ingested in quantity, but drugs were so prevalent around the area that in 1967, Richmond police station instructed two police constables to dedicate half their hours to narcotics-related activity. One of those officers was Oliver Harries, popularly known as Dudley, who came to Richmond having grown up in a small town in Wales, where drugs were something you got from the chemist. 'You could stop anybody with long hair in Richmond and they'd have some cannabis,' recalls Harries. He says that L'Auberge was a notorious venue for buying and selling, despite the owners supposedly advertising a no-drugs policy. Henry Boxer, who was using heroin while still at school, remembers people were dealing all day in the Fishbowl. 'I was sixteen or seventeen, going in there scoring amphetamines, heroin, LSD, methedrine… Any drug I wanted, I could pop in there of an afternoon and I'd be able to get it.' Richmond-based Boxer remembers it as an extraordinary time. 'I never looked at myself as a junkie, just someone who was having a great time and experiencing the Sixties. There was a spirituality at the time and we thought it was all going to change everyone's lives.'

Around the end of summer 1968, notices appeared advertising gigs once more at the Richmond Athletic Association Grounds. Initially, they were promoted by Middle Earth, the psychedelic club based in Covent Garden. The first group to perform at the rugby clubhouse under this arrangement was Pink Floyd, on 4 September. Since they last played in these parts, at Eel Pie Island the previous summer, they had jettisoned their lead singer and main songwriter Syd Barrett. His increasingly erratic behaviour, which has generally been attributed to excessive drug use, led to the rest of the band simply deciding not to pick him up one time when they were heading off to a gig down in Southampton (Barrett was living in a flat on Richmond Hill at the time)[1]. They were promoting their second album, *A Saucerful of Secrets*, recorded with new guitarist Dave Gilmour, which had been released in the UK at the end of June – and which features a rear cover shot of the band in Richmond Park. Local music fan Alan Winter was at one of the gigs and he remembers Pink Floyd turning up in a Transit van and bassist Roger Waters asking fans for help carrying in a huge gong. The sightlines, he says, were generally terrible because there was no longer any sort of stage and the band just set up on the floor at one end of the room.

It wasn't such a problem in the case of Pink Floyd, he says, because the audience was thin. Winter says that he and his friends spent most of the gig in anticipation of some serious gong banging but nobody laid a hammer on it until the very last number. Despite the low turnout, the group was booked again for November.

Between Pink Floyd's two appearances were gigs by the Aynsley Dunbar Retaliation, which was a vehicle for drummer Dunbar after his stints in John Mayall's Bluesbreakers and the Jeff Beck Group, and American blues-rockers Canned Heat, who were in the UK to capitalise on their wheezy recent chart hit 'On the Road Again'. There were also gigs by Blossom Toes, Free, the Nice and an early Fleetwood Mac, led by Peter Green – they played the week after Chicken Shack, who featured on keyboards and vocals Christine Perfect, soon to become a member of Fleetwood Mac.

When Pink Floyd returned, the box ad in *Melody Maker* was headed 'Crawdaddy', in lettering almost as big as that of the band. Two gigs the previous week at the rugby clubhouse were also advertised as Crawdaddy events. At this point, Giorgio Gomelsky had his own record label with a roster of talent and swanky offices in the West End, so it is unlikely he had anything to do with these events. Instead, the agency behind the gigs seems to have been the Student Union at Isleworth Polytechnic, which was a couple of miles away on the other side of the Thames. The union's events had outgrown the campus bar and they must have come to an agreement with the Athletic Grounds' committee to hire the clubhouse.

Despite being announced for 29 November 1968, the newly formed Led Zeppelin ('Formerly Yardbirds', notes the advert) were a no-show. Alan Winter clearly remembers turning up for this gig only to find a handwritten notice on the door saying it had been cancelled. Otherwise, the gigs continued into 1969 with Yes, featuring Jon Anderson, Peter Banks, Chris Squire, Tony Kaye and

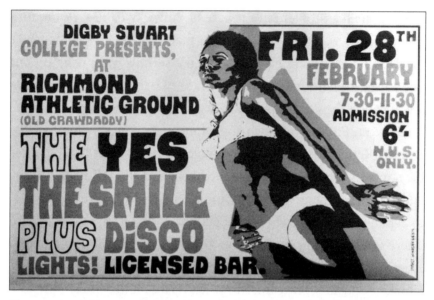

The promoter of this event, featuring Yes and half of the future Queen, was an all-girls teacher training college in Roehampton, now part of Roehampton University.

Bill Bruford. The support act for Yes, in only the group's second-ever professional gig, was Smile, a three-piece that included Brian May and Roger Taylor, soon to link up with Farrokh 'Freddie' Bulsara and become Queen. Even without Page and co, that's not a bad run of gigs for a local rugby club bar.

The Crawdaddy name was also briefly attached to another local venue. This was a wreck of an old hotel on an island in the Thames – not Eel Pie Island, but another one six miles upriver at Hampton. Tagg's Island is named for a family that ran a successful boat-building business there in the nineteenth century. They built a hotel in 1870 which, like the Eel Pie Island Hotel, also became a popular destination for boaters up from London. However, after the family patriarch Thomas Tagg died in 1897, the business went into decline. Enter Fred Karno. Born Frederick John Westcott in 1866, he was a former acrobat who performed first in circuses, then in the music halls of Victorian England. He combined his athletic feats with a repertoire of physical comedy routines, one of which was supposedly the original custard-pie-in-the-face gag. His mind was obviously as agile as his body, because he became one of the greatest of music hall impresarios. He also converted a row of houses in Camberwell, in south London, into a 'Fun Factory', a combined writers' workshop, prop department and talent school. Graduates included Charlie Chaplin and Stan Laurel. Karno discovered Tagg's Island in 1904 and began spending summers there, lodging on his custom-made houseboat, the *Astoria*, which was said to have cost him around £7,000, an enormous sum at the time. Eight years later he bought the island, including its existing hotel, which he had demolished and replaced with a new property designed by renowned theatre architect Frank Matcham (responsible for London's Hippodrome, Hackney Empire, Coliseum, Palladium and Richmond Theatre, among others). Christened the 'Karsino', it was advertised as the most luxurious hotel of the day – how many hotels could boast a Palm Court Concert Pavilion with a reversible stage, so that when the weather was fine audiences could watch performances from seating on the lawn? What Karno hadn't foreseen was that very soon nobody would be interested in the stage whichever way you looked at it – music hall was torpedoed by cinema and by 1925 Karno was bankrupt. In the following decades, the hotel changed hands several times and by the Sixties it was derelict and decaying. In its final years, the only part functioning was the old pavilion, which was used as a sometime music venue, operating intermittently from around 1965 to 1968. Some of the concerts were promoted under the banner of the 'New Crawdaddy'. Given that some of the dates overlap with the period when Gomelsky and Grimes were running their Crawdaddy clubs at Richmond, Croydon and Finsbury Park, it's possible that they might have had a hand in this island venture, but it's more likely that it was an opportunistic appropriation of the name. Acts known to have played Tagg's Island around this time include Chris Farlowe, Georgie Fame, the Shotgun Express featuring Rod Stewart and Mick Fleetwood, Led Zeppelin and Pink Floyd.

The former Karsino was demolished in 1971 following a fire. Karno's houseboat, the *Astoria*, survives and is still moored close by Tagg's Island. Appropriately, since 1986 it has served as a floating recording studio owned by Pink Floyd guitarist Dave Gilmour. Parts of each of the last three Floyd studio albums, *A Momentary Lapse of Reason* (1987), *The Division Bell* (1994) and *The Endless River* (2014), were recorded on the boat.

Back downriver, in spring 1968, over six months after the courts shut down the Eelpiland club, the hotel's drinks licence was still being withheld. Since the closure, Arthur Chisnall had been trying to raise money and petitioning his influential friends for support. It was no longer about putting on concerts for the kids – he now wanted to buy the lease on the entire hotel. He was still providing shelter for twelve 'crisis cases' at his house in Strawberry Hill, four or five of whom were on the Home Office drug register and a handful more who were in need of psychiatric support. His aim was to use the hotel to expand this work. However, around the same time, in his attempts to convince the court to allow the hotel to resume selling alcohol, owner Michael Snapper told a licensing hearing at Feltham Court that he wouldn't have Chisnall back on the Island because, 'He got the place a really bad name.'[2] He also blamed lessee Jack Marrs for what he called 'the disgusting state' of the hotel. What Snapper wanted to do, he told the court, was to turn the hotel into a youth centre with boating, water-skiing and horse-riding.[3] The fantasy was exploded by police officers who'd been sent to inspect the hotel and reported back that the place remained in a deplorable condition. Snapper's repairs amounted to little more than new paint being applied on top of rotting woodwork. 'The general effect,' said the officers, 'was one of covering up instead of putting right the structural defects.'[4]

Despite the continued lack of a licence (and of necessary building repairs), in summer 1968 the Eel Pie Island Hotel began hosting live music again, but without a bar. Arthur Chisnall was no longer involved and the music was now organised by Southbank Artistes, which was a company connected with West End-based promoter and booker John Sherry. While the venue had been dormant for less than a year, the music scene was radically changed. There had been hints the previous summer, in the last months of the Arthur Chisnall era, with early appearances by Pink Floyd and Tomorrow, but since then the rest of the field had been playing catch-up. The Ingoes, for example, had been a house band at the Crawdaddy, banging out Wilson Pickett, and Martha Reeves and the Vandellas covers; in August 1968 they were performing at the Island as the Blossom Toes, playing songs about 'Mrs Murphy's Budgerigar'. Similarly, Ealing outfit the Tomcats, who not long ago entertained Eelpilanders by aping Bo Diddley and Chuck Berry, were back as Indian-inspired, reverb-drenched psych-rockers July. Keith Emerson and Lee Jackson, both Crawdaddy regulars as members of solid R&B outfit Gary Farr and the T-Bones, were now half of the Nice, whose signature piece was an over-the-top rock arrangement of Leonard Bernstein's 'America'. Local author Judy Astley saw them at the Island that August and remembers Emerson doing his signature trick of jamming a dagger into his keyboard to hold the note then jumping off the stage – only on this occasion he was prevented from getting back up by a steward who didn't realise he was part of the band. When the Moody Blues last played in these parts, they were promoting soulful hit single 'Go Now' – at the Island in September 1968 they were pioneering prog-rockers riding high on 'Nights in White Satin'.

Local boy Dave Dadswell, who was around seventeen at the time, was present at many of the gigs mentioned above. He remembers the ballroom being in a terrible state, 'just an empty shell of a building'. Most of the sprung wooden floor, he says, was gone and the audience now stood on the bare concrete on which the old floor had been laid. But the music was magnificent, says Dadswell. He remembers Joe Cocker, in particular, 'sang his arse off' to compete with support act Terry Reid, who a few days later was due to be opening for Cream on their farewell tour of America, playing to arenas filled with 15,000 fans.

Although they were a west London group and gigged locally, Arthur Chisnall never booked the Who. It wasn't so much the band as their fans – Chisnall feared an invasion of scooter-riding Mods roaring over the bridge to invade the Island. In September 1968, the Who's Pete Townshend and wife moved into a house on Twickenham Embankment right across from the Island. At the time, the guitarist and chief songwriter was working on material for a new album about a deaf, dumb and blind kid who sure played a mean pinball. The Island probably seemed like a convenient, low-key gig to try out some of the new material and the Who made their one and only appearance there on Wednesday 30 October. Twickenham resident Alan Winter was there: 'I remember Pete Townshend saying, "For you locals who have seen me burning the midnight oil with the lights on over the road where I live, I'm working on this new thing, which I call a rock opera. I'm going to play a little bit of it and I want you to tell us what you think."' At the end of the piece – early versions of music that would end up on the album *Tommy* – Winter, who was down near the front, shouted, 'Stick to your three-minute singles, mate'.

For reasons unknown, live music on the Island was suspended from mid November 1968, resuming at the end of January the following year with the gigs now promoted under the banner of

Founded in 1967, Release was (and still is) a charity
providing legal advice and representation for people
charged with the possession of drugs.

'Peach Filled Blossom Presents'. This lasted just a few weeks and
then the ballroom fell silent again for several months. The only
music to be heard there came from a local band called Hickory,
who were allowed to use the room as a rehearsal space because the
drummer's parents knew Michael Snapper; they were members of
something called the Converted Cruiser Club (now the Richmond
Yacht Club) which, from the late Fifties, rented a plot on the Island
just south of the hotel. They built a clubhouse there, where the
members regularly put on shows. As a young boy, still in short
pants, Hickory's drummer – Chiswick-born, Hounslow-raised Phil
Collins – gave his first public performances at the clubhouse, which
means the future Genesis frontman can legitimately claim to have

211

played Eel Pie Island before the Rolling Stones, Rod Stewart or the Who. Collins remains a patron of the yacht club and his photograph still hangs prominently in the clubhouse his dad helped build.

In summer 1969, Twickenham resident Grenville Sheringham persuaded Snapper to let him use the empty ballroom for his twenty-first birthday party. A new group calling itself Hawkwind Zoo (they would soon drop the Zoo part of the name) heard about the party and asked if they could provide the music. Group founder Dave Brock was a former Eelpiland regular and had always wanted to play the Island. In fact, the party ended up with two bands, the second being west London hard rock outfit Stray, whose claim to fame was that they were managed for a time by Charlie Kray, brother of twins Ronnie and Reggie.

Sheringham ran the Richmond Arts Workshop, which took its inspiration from the Drury Lane Arts Lab, established in central London by expat American Jim Haynes in 1967.[5] The original Arts Lab laid down a template for a short-lived but influential nationwide mushrooming of small-scale enthusiastic ragbag arts collectives. An October 1969 issue of counterculture newspaper *International Times* devotes most of a page to listing the addresses and activities of Haynes' protégés: leading the list is 'BECKENHAM ARTS LAB: contact David Bowie at 460 6489' – imagine, back then you could phone David and tell him in person what you thought of his recent hit, 'Space Oddity'. Also in there is 'HOUNSLOW ARTS LAB: c/o Dave Cousins [of the Strawbs], 9 Tennyson Rd, Hounslow' and 'RICHMOND ARTS WORKSHOP/EEL PIE ISLAND PROJECT: contact Grenville Sheringham, Flat 2, 188 Sheen Rd, Richmond, Surrey (tel 940 7974).'

When Sheringham founded the Richmond Arts Workshop, it met every Tuesday evening in the crypt at St Elizabeth's Church on the Vineyard. There, in the summer of 1969, the collective worked on an original production titled 'Confusion: the Mind in Conflict', described as a punchbowl of music, dancing, poetry and singing, with a folding screen separating the 'sober from the psychedelic'. 'For example, on one side we have classical ballet and on the other flashing lights,' Sheringham told a local newspaper.[6] After holding his birthday party there, he came to the conclusion that the Eel Pie Island Hotel offered greater possibilities for the Workshop's mind-expanding offerings.

'Because the place had been closed down by the fire brigade and police, Snapper agreed that we could open it for a trial, rent free for a month or two,' remembers Sheringham. *The Richmond and Twickenham Times* sent along a reporter who joined Workshop members in trooping round the hotel's three floors to view the dusty cobwebbed rooms.[7] Sheringham told the journalist he intended to move in ten people as soon as possible to make the hotel rooms habitable and ready the place for opening. The plan was to raise revenue from letting rooms, and by running a coffee bar and weekly dances. 'If we can establish in the next few years an arts centre for the whole of the borough,' the paper quotes Sheringham as saying, 'the council should take notice and step in, perhaps buying the property as an arts centre.'

They held their first Friday dance on 3 October 1969 with Mighty Baby, a hard-edged psychedelic-prog outfit. They were followed in subsequent weeks by the return of both Hawkwind Zoo and Stray. However, the project had barely even begun before *The Richmond and Twickenham Times* was proclaiming 'Arts Workshop Bails Out From Island'. The newspaper reported that the Arts Workshop had been asked by Snapper to share the ballroom with another party who wanted to use it for music on Friday and Sunday nights, and the Workshop refused. The upshot was that Sheringham and his Workshop withdrew.

The 'other party' who now took over the ballroom was a bombastic charmer by the name of Caldwell Smythe. He was born and brought up in Glasgow, where his father ran a driving school. In 1964, the family moved down to Sussex and the nineteen-year-old Caldwell landed a job at a sports car dealership in Chiswick. As if being tall and good-looking with easy access to fast cars wasn't enough, he could also sing. He fronted Wandsworth band the Cloud before stepping up to the Riot Squad, a pop group in which a lot of people saw promise – they were managed first by impresario Larry Page, then by Joe Meek, and their line up at one time featured Mitch Mitchell (who would go on to drum for Jimi Hendrix) and, briefly, David Bowie. Ultimately, Riot Squad failed to deliver. None of their singles charted and by the time Smythe joined they were close to being a cabaret band, performing in face paint and hats. One press release described them as 'the funniest group in showbusiness'.

After a year of heavy touring, rounded off with a month in Germany, Smythe quit and began looking for something else to do. In autumn 1969, he became aware of the hotel on Eel Pie Island, and the fact that it was, to all appearances, sitting empty. He had experience booking bands from a brief spell working for a West End agency. 'So I went down to see Snapper in Kingston, and I said I'm really interested in doing a deal with you on the Island,' says Smythe. Almost fifty years later, Smythe can't remember how much Snapper wanted in rent, but he must have been willing to pay more than the impoverished Arts Workshop.

'I knew all the agents,' says Smythe – who used the name Marc Newton when booking bands (because, he says, he was fed up of people calling him Cromwell Smith). 'I'd ring up and ask, "Who've you got in my price range?" And they'd say, "Well, we've got Free who'll do two-fifty." Or they would do door deals – seventy quid plus seventy-five percent of the door.'

For the first time, gigs on the Island were regularly advertised: Smythe paid for boxed ads every week in *Melody Maker* which, although small, stood out among the full page of listings by virtue of being rotated ninety degrees – which was clever. He produced flyers and plastered southwest London with posters. 'I was going out on my own with a big bucket of wallpaper paste and a floor brush. Nobody else would do it. They thought they might get arrested.' The music was on Friday and Saturday, with two bands each night. 'We would get the big band over [the bridge] first, get them set up, let them soundcheck. Then we'd get the small band over. Some of them wheeled their stuff but generally we'd use a minivan, which I bought specially. It cost thirty quid. It fitted over the bridge and went all the way to the hotel and through the double doors into the ballroom. We'd turn it round inside, unload all the stuff and then let the roadies get on with it.'

The headline act would be on the main stage, while the support act would set up on a small platform Smythe had constructed at the back of the hall. This second stage was close by the door into the hall, which was also the way to the toilets. 'I used to sit and play twelve-string guitar,' remembers Anthony Phillips, who in spring 1970 was lead guitarist with a pre-Phil Collins Genesis for their two Island appearances. 'I was on the far right of the stage and the twelve-string has a long neck, so every time someone wanted to go to the loo I would have to swing my guitar out of the way.' He felt it wasn't their sort of audience: 'We were doing a lot of textural stuff on twelve-strings and that wasn't what people had come for.'

What people came for, as they always had, was a good time, involving a simple formula of music, dancing and booze. Under the new management, gigs at Eel Pie were now promoted under the banner of 'Colonel Barefoot's Rock Garden'. The choice of name hints at the sort of groups that were now being booked – those from

215

The well-coiffed Caldwell Smythe (left) and his Jaguar. The other guy is Alan Birch, lead guitarist in Thunderzone, a band managed by Smythe.

the heavier, proggier, trippier end of the spectrum. So Islanders were treated to the likes of Deep Purple, the eccentric Van Der Graaf Generator (with a saxophonist who blew two instruments at the same time), the Edgar Broughton Band (notorious for the disorder that often accompanied their live shows) and Black Sabbath, who appeared promoting their eponymous debut album.

Unlike the Chisnall era, there were no residencies and most gigs were one-offs. One notable exception to this rule was blues band Shades, who Smythe put on regularly because they were willing to allow him to sing. 'They were kind of like my own personal stereo,' he says. Blues-rockers Free appeared a couple of times. Two members of the group, guitarist Paul Kossoff and drummer Simon

216

Kirke, had previously played the Island in one of the ever-changing line-ups of circuit stalwarts Black Cat Bones. Before joining Free, Kirke lived with a cousin in Twickenham and was part of the crowd at L'Auberge: 'It was a great place,' he says, 'very bohemian… furtive hash smoking on the patio overlooking Richmond Bridge.' He worked for a spell at Ellis's wine merchant's on Water Lane in Richmond (now the site of a Curzon cinema). 'It didn't pay very much but you could drink four bottles of beer a day while you were there,' remembers Alan Winter, who worked at Ellis's with Kirke. It was one of several places where anyone short of cash could just turn up at eight in the morning and pick up a day's work. Kew Gardens, where casual labourers were always needed to pick up litter was another option. According to Winter, it was a L'Auberge regular who helped bring about the formation of Free. Her name was Saffron and her dad was Alexis Korner. She introduced Kirke and Kossoff to dad and he, in turn, put them together with fifteen-year-old bassist Andy Fraser and gave the band its name.

The first time Free played the Island, in February 1970, listening from a distance was Pete Townshend. The Who guitarist was interviewed at his Twickenham Embankment home not long after for US rock journal *Rolling Stone* and he told the reporter, 'Free were on the other night. I opened the double frame windows and listened and they sounded good.' They played the Island again in June – their new single 'All Right Now' had spent two weeks climbing the charts and was just about to break into the Top 10, so you imagine the place must have been rammed.[8]

The biggest hit with the local crowd, Smythe says, was Mott the Hoople, who played in April 1970. 'I arrived and the bridge was already packed with people. I spoke to my guy and said, "What's all this about?" and he said they've come to see the band. This is six o'clock and the band's not on until nine.' He remembers they had a lot of kit and it took four trips to get it all across the bridge. Fire regulations allowed for 250 people in the hall but Smythe reckons he packed in about 625 that night. At this point the band had released one indifferently received album and were still two years away from their defining hit 'All the Young Dudes', but their reputation as an exciting, rambunctious, riotous live act clearly preceded them.

If the headliner warranted it, they might be accompanied by a groovy light show. For a couple of months in 1969, this was provided by an outfit called Aural Plasma; later effects were provided by Jeff Dexter, whose regular gig was light and sound at Middle Earth, where he also DJ'd alongside John Peel. 'You would just stand there in the middle of the floor watching all the light bubbles go around the ceiling, walls and floor,' remembers Alan Winter. 'A lot of us already had pretty disoriented brains when we were over there.' Because the premises no longer had an alcohol licence any disorientation had nothing to do with drink – until Smythe believed he'd come up with a solution. 'I hit on this great idea of giving out free booze,' he says. 'I checked out the law and you can give away free alcohol provided you don't incorporate the cost of it into the entrance fee.' Smythe put up the entrance fee up and then waited two or three months before he began advertising free 'Colonel Barefoot's killer punch' on his flyers and posters. The punch was a mix of cider and cheap cooking brandy mixed in a big drum, specifically formulated, says Smythe, to get punters pissed quickly.

The Colonel's potent mix of rough booze and hard rock was effective. 'It was the most extraordinary thing that had ever happened to me,' says Tony James, a Hampton Grammar schoolboy who lived within walking distance of the Island. He'd bought and loved the Black Sabbath debut album, and then a friend mentioned they were playing at the Island. 'I went to see them and I was so blown away because I had obviously never seen a live group before. It was the

COLONEL BAREFOOT'S ROCK GARDEN EEL PIE ISLAND TWICKENHAM

JUNE

FRIDAYS	SATURDAYS
5 Wild Angels Alma Mater plus Metropolitan Grease Force	**6** Edgar Broughton Little Free Rock and Ginger Johnsons African Drummers
12 DEEP PURPLE and THUNDERZONE plus BLACK VELVET	**13** GYPSY plus SEMPER VIVUM plus JUNCTION
19 FREE plus RAPTURE	**20** Steve Miller Delivery and BONE
26 THE AMAZING "Shades" plus TINY CLANGER	**27** East of Eden plus BLOOD SON

FREE COLONEL BAREFOOT KILLER PUNCH
VERY CHEAP HOT SNACKS
SOFT DRINKS FAGS ETC.
INCREDIBLE LIGHT SHOW BY AURAL PLASMA
FREAKY SOUNDS - INCENSE
DOORS OPEN 7.30 p.m.

300 yards from Twickenham Station   Buses: 27, 33, 90, 90b, 110, 203, 267, 281

Unlike Arthur Chisnall, who never advertised Eelpiland events, Caldwell Smythe ran ads in *Melody Maker*, pasted up posters and distributed flyers, like this one, from June 1970.

loudest thing I'd ever heard in my life. It was incredible… Suddenly I was going to see rock groups and having long hair. That was really the start of everything.'[9] Five years later James was playing in a band called London SS, along with Brian James (later of the Damned) and Mick Jones (future member of the Clash); the following year, 1976, he co-founded punk outfit Generation X with Billy Idol.

Clubbers who knew the Island from the Arthur Chisnall days were less enamoured. 'Went to the Island but didn't have a good time. The place is changing, the magic is dying. The music is getting worse and all the cool people don't go there anymore,' long-time Eelpilander Andrea Hiorns confided to her journal. Speak with anybody who was a regular at the island in its R&B heyday and you hear the same thing repeated: 'It was a very friendly atmosphere and it felt very safe,' Eelpilander John Stephens told an interviewer in 2013.[10] 'It felt very safe, it was almost like going to a youth club,' remembers Judy Astley. That was no longer the case. 'There were a few problems on the door every now and again, as there would be at any dance hall, people trying to get in without paying,' says Smythe. People inside would open the emergency exits to let friends in, so Smythe chained the doors. The sort of rock bands he was booking attracted a less peaceable crowd which, ultimately, included local groups of Hell's Angels. 'They frightened people. I tried to dissuade them but they were quite a nasty bunch.' The drug use had changed, too, from a convivial joint to hallucinogens, like LSD. Some of the dealers lived in the hotel itself, which since 1969 housed a growing hippie commune, some of whom got by on selling drugs to the clubbers who poured in for the weekend dances. As the hotel had no electricity, the resident hippies made a hole in the wall separating the ballroom and hotel, and helped themselves to power.

In August, and again in October, the ballroom received visits from the police. They asked to see membership books, which couldn't be produced, and noted that the ticket office was a 'disused lavatory with the bowl stuffed with rubbish'. The police were present when the lights fused and candles were deployed to illuminate the wooden ballroom – where only one of the exit doors could be opened, the others being chained closed. Summonses followed. 'What, with the Hell's Angels, and the police and fire department trying to close me down and the hippies nicking the power, I just thought I've had enough of all this', remembers Caldwell Smythe.

On Saturday 21 November 1970, the ballroom hosted the band Quintessence. A product of west London's Ladbroke Grove scene, their mash-up of acid rock and hymnal Indian chants made them a hugely popular live act, and they'd been snapped up by Island Records. One writer would later describe them as the 'last great hurrah of the Sixties' – they also proved to be the last great hurrah of live music at the Eel Pie Island Hotel. Their performance that night brought to an end fourteen years of live music that had begun back in 1956 with Ken Colyer and His Jazzmen.

CHAPTER 12

SEX, DRUGS AND HEAD LICE

As the music ends, the Eel Pie Island Hotel is transformed into Europe's biggest doss house

HE MAY HAVE BEEN SHUT OUT OF THE EEL PIE ISLAND HOTEL, but Arthur Chisnall was still to have a hand in how events there were to play out. Among the strays once drawn to Eelpiland was a self-proclaimed anarchist named Clifford Harper, who through the club got to know its bearded Prince of Pan. In 1969, Harper was on the lookout for lodgings for himself and his group of disruptors. Maybe it was pure benevolence or perhaps it was mischief, but Harper's old friend Arthur pointed the anarchists in the direction of the Island's empty hotel. With this suggestion, Chisnall set in motion the final act in the building's story.

Clifford Harper was born in Chiswick, west London, in 1949, and brought up in Twickenham. He told an interviewer in 2007

FACING: Residents of the Eel Pie Island Hotel celebrate at one of several weddings that took place in 1969/70, generally in order to secure one of the partners a UK residency.

223

that he first heard the word 'anarchy' as a young teenager and was 'hooked straight away'.[1] He was, he says, a 'little rebel and trouble-maker' for as long as he could remember, expelled from school at thirteen and facing two years' probation at fourteen. He regarded the middle-class world around him as something that had to go and saw anarchy as its replacement. In the mid Sixties he was living in Richmond, which he'd later credit with having a special place in the history of English counterculture, with its 'large bedsit population up on Richmond Hill, a couple of local art colleges, lots of drugs, good music and an anarchist group right in the middle of it'.[2]

Some of this anarchist group, Harper included, decamped north to live out their ideals in an old farmhouse in Cumberland. After the misplaced urbanites barely survived a harsh winter in one of England's most rugged counties, they returned to London. Harper ended up crashing in a house on Richmond Hill that was owned by a friend of Chisnall's. It's around this time that Arthur would have directed Harper toward the hotel. He went along with some compatriots to take a look. This was late summer 1969. Harper remembers an athletic girl named Sally McLean climbed in through a small window and opened the door for the rest of the group.[3] They immediately took up residence, establishing the Eel Pie Island Commune. Their stay would last for just over eighteen months and in that time numbers at the hotel would reach well over one hundred, with people drawn not just from London, or England, but from around the world. The hotel would become renowned as the largest doss house in Europe and would rapidly descend into a self-devouring free-for-all.

Harper initially imagined the hotel as an incubator for an arts-led rebellion. He was an admirer of New York's experimental Living Theatre, whose members shared digs and created plays together, generally with some sort of anarchist or pacifist message. They performed these out on the streets, and in other non-traditional venues, such as prisons. When the group visited London in summer 1969, they settled in for a month-long residency at what was then a hub for alternative happenings, Camden's Roundhouse. Harper claimed to have seen every performance. He thought he and his fellow communards might follow Living Theatre's example and use their Island base as a launchpad for intellectually provocative raids on mainstream society. What he didn't foresee was the great number of people who'd flock to an empty hotel on an island in the Thames once word got out, nor how quickly he and the other commune founders would become marginalised. Almost from day one, a stream of dropouts began turning up at the hotel, drawn there for all sorts of reasons but with one thing in common: a desire to pursue their own thing and not be told what to do, including by Harper. 'People didn't want to know,' says Harper, 'so I just let it go the way it wanted to go.'[4]

Chris Whitehouse (also known as Weed) had been of no fixed abode since the Thames riverboat he was dossing on, the *China Tea Steam Navigation Co*, caught fire.[5] Through someone he knew from L'Auberge, he was offered the job of secretary to the Richmond Arts Workshop, which was then negotiating with Michael Snapper for use of the hotel. The understanding was that along with the job came a place to stay. Harper and friends would already have been in residence and one wonders how Snapper and Sheringham were planning to deal with them as they discussed terms and rent. In the meantime, rather than the hotel, Whitehouse moved into the small room above the stage in the ballroom, which had served as the green room in Eelpiland days. The way Whitehouse remembers it, it was the Arts Workshop who brought in Caldwell Smythe to help run some money-raising dances for them. He recalls the towering Smythe turning up in shades and with two large Alsatians on leads.

Policemen observe the hippie squatters at 144 Piccadilly. The scale and location of the squat led to a media-organised moral panic.

When Smythe gazumped the arts crew and they left, he inherited Whitehouse with the fixtures and fittings. He ran the cloakroom for Smythe and cleaned up after the gigs. 'He was effective,' Whitehouse says of Smythe. 'It was a bit of a job getting that place going again. He did what needed to be done and he put on some good music.' It can't have been the cosiest of accommodations for Whitehouse – a cavernous, creaky, unheated, decrepit old ballroom, deserted except for two nights a week when it was invaded by hordes of loud, sweaty rock fans. But Whitehouse says he enjoyed seeing the bands for free and he wasn't often on his own, as there were usually one or two others crashing with him. Still, after about three months, he joined the growing community in the hotel.

In June 1969, American Chris Faiers, a member of an evolving hippie colony in Miami's Coconut Grove, received his draft notice – the US was still at war in Vietnam – and promptly dodged it by catching a flight to Europe. He made his way to London, where he had a cousin living not far from Richmond. One Saturday, he joined a gang from L'Auberge heading for Hyde Park and a free gig headlined by the Edgar Broughton Band. Afterwards, Faiers and one or two others took a walk over to 144 Piccadilly, headline news that week because it was being squatted by members of the radical London Street Commune.[6] Large numbers of young people were rolling up in the capital lured by the myth of 'Swinging London' and many of them had nowhere to stay – the Street Commune came together to highlight the issue. 144 Piccadilly was a sixty-room mansion overlooking Green Park and famously the residence of Lord Palmerston when he became prime minister in 1855. Doorways were barricaded against the police and access was via a makeshift drawbridge from a window. Faiers and his friends were recognised as part of the tribe and invited in. The sightseeing visit turned into an overnight stay. According to Faiers, the pervasive paranoia over impending police action made for an uncomfortable vibe and he left the next day, missing by a few hours the inevitable raid, during which around a hundred squatters were arrested.

When his cousin kicked him out, Faiers bummed around, sleeping rough, hitchhiking to see Bob Dylan at the Isle of Wight, dossing on floors back in Richmond, until he heard about the commune on the Island. He headed down, walked through the front door and found Clifford Harper: 'Cliff was a big bear of a man… He had long, straw-like brown hair and an unkempt beard. With his granny glasses he looked like a professor gone bad.'[7] Faiers was taken with the set-up, particularly Harper and his girlfriend's large room, which was furnished with an easel and layout table (Harper was an artist), and a large mattress heaped with quilts and blankets. It was, Faiers thought, very artsy, very cosy and very bohemian. Harper invited Faiers to pick out a room for himself.

Faiers says that there was only a small group of occupants when he first arrived – accompanied by an American friend, named California Jon, and two girls they knew from L'Auberge. Everyone lived on the two upper floors, which is where the bedrooms were. The best opened onto a long first-floor verandah, which overlooked the river and the fields of Ham Lands. Some of the residents made an effort to beautify their personal spaces: sixteen-year-old Angie Page, who'd just left home and moved straight into the hotel with her boyfriend, painted the walls of their room purple and festooned the place with ostrich feathers stolen from Biba. The residents shared a single functioning bathroom with bathtub, and one small kitchen area, although it had no facilities beyond a small Calor Gas stove. The ground floor had a series of large rooms that had been the hotel's bar, lounges and dining rooms. Despite holes in the floor caused by rot, these rooms were used as communal spaces and to accommodate the single-night dossers. There was also a cellar and some broken-down outbuildings.

Over the following months, people came and went, but mostly came. Numbers were augmented by 'weekend hippies', who appeared on a Friday to hang out and get stoned, returning home Sunday night in readiness for the working week. There were others who lived in the hotel but would slip away every now and again to their parents' homes for a bath, to use the washing machine and have a decent meal. According to Faiers, most evenings were spent smoking hash while somebody strummed a guitar. There was always somebody strumming a guitar. And there were always drugs. Drugs were the reason many were at the hotel. Not just hash but a lot of LSD, mescaline and speed. A teenage Mark Pickthall was one of the many drawn to the hotel by such substances. While there, he and a friend, Peter Crisp, organised a communal trip. They bought acid from a dealer in Richmond: 'The guy opened up this big American fridge and it was filled with dropper bottles of acid,' says Pickthall. The following evening, a few people created a large mandala on the hotel lawn from fruit, food and guitars, and everyone took their place around it. Crisp recalls that the debut album by Renaissance was playing as Pickthall squeezed a drop onto each person's tongue.

The hotel also had resident heroin users. Heroin was not illegal at this time. It came in pill form and registered addicts could get it at a local chemist on receipt of a prescription. To be registered, all a person had to do was buy a pill on the black market, take it, then go to the doctor and confess to being an addict. A blood test would confirm the reality of this and the doctor would write a prescription. Otherwise, it was straightforward enough to buy both prescriptions or pills at a number of locations, including Piccadilly Circus. The hotel's youngest resident, fifteen-year-old Gary Cowan, better known as Little Brother (he'd run away from home to join his big brother on the Island only to find big brother was in prison), owned a motorbike and made money by taxiing the junkies around to pick up their fix.

Friday and Saturday nights, the grounds of the hotel were regularly invaded by hundreds of partygoers, there for Colonel Barefoot's rock gigs. With severely limited access to alcohol, a better option for getting off their heads was to visit the hotel next door and buy some hash from the residents. Among the gig-goers were gaggles of schoolgirls, viewed as choice prey by some of the commune members. 'I thought I was Henry Miller and this here was the Tropic of Twickenham,' recalls one.[8] In May 1970, police searching for a missing twenty-two-year-old French au pair found her at the 'hippie hotel' in a room with three boys and a floor scattered with smoked joints. Parents who worried about what their daughters were getting up to on the Island around this time were entirely justified in their concerns.

Other than one notable raid in November 1969, the police tended to leave the hotel alone. It was too easy to see them coming and there was plenty of time to hide the evidence. There were attempts to infiltrate: on one occasion four undercover offices wearing wigs visited the Island but they were rumbled and chased off. Oliver Harries of Richmond police station believes that at one point Twickenham police had an informant inside the hotel but, if this was so, it didn't lead to any major busts. And it seems not to have reduced the drug use.

Towards the end of summer 1970, the Hog Farm came to visit. An ad hoc collective founded in California in 1966, the Hog Farmers lived on a mountaintop rent-free in exchange for looking after forty pigs. They acquired an old school bus and used it to travel around spreading the message of a more sharing and egalitarian society. In 1969, they served as the disarmingly polite security at Woodstock, under the moniker of the 'Please Force' – as in 'Please, would you not do that, sir'. During the festival, the hog leader, Hugh Romney, who soon after adopted the name Wavy Gravy, acted as master of ceremonies, introducing the bands on stage. The following year, the Hog Farmers bussed around the United States, setting up stages for rock bands, running food kitchens and performing. In summer 1970, the Hog circus decided to drive its fleet of what was now five buses all the way to India – and they dropped in on Eel Pie Island en route. They erected their tepees on the hotel's front lawn beside the Thames and hung around for a few weeks. During this time, some of the group performed shows, under the name Stoneground, at the Roundhouse in Camden. Someone who worked at the venue at the time remembers the group's prodigious drug intake – they employed a kid to sit above the stage during their sets, rolling joints as fast as he could and throwing them down for the band to pick up and smoke.[9] At Eel Pie Island the permanent residents were similarly in awe of their visitors. 'They were massive, man,' recalls Gary Cowan. 'Guys with beards halfway down their chests and hair halfway down their backs. Six-foot-two tall and muscly.' The Hog Farmers tended to be older than the hotel residents, most of whom were still in their teens or barely into their twenties, and a lot more worldly – there were a number of Vietnam vets among them. What they did not have, however, was knowledge of the Thames tides. One night the river rose high, flooding the lawn and the visitors had to snatch up their gear and retreat into the hotel.

Before their departure, the Hog Farmers went shopping and made a goodbye present of a busload of food. Stacked floor to ceiling it filled most of a corridor in the hotel. 'It was a nightmare,' says Gary Cowan. 'Word got out and every scallywag, dosser and junkie for twenty miles turned up to get their hands on it. There were people stuffing suitcases and knapsacks and carrier bags, and carting it away over the bridge. It was like a feeding frenzy of sharks.' When the Farmers left, they also took some people from the commune with them, including at least one hotel dweller's wife.[10]

Another occasional visitor was Twickenham Embankment resident Pete Townshend. Mark Pickthall and Peter Crisp were two of those who befriended the musician, and he lent them a four-track tape machine, handed over with the sage advice, 'Don't get high before recording.' Gavin Kilty, another commune member, told rock writer Richie Unterberger, 'Me and Peter Crisp would go over to his house across the river and he'd allow us to play his guitars. We were clearly pestering him because one day we came over in "high" spirits and he refused to let us in.' [11] Other members of the commune took to knocking on Townshend's door asking for food. The Who man cracked when he received a visit in the early hours of one morning – he grabbed a hammer and, in his own words, 'nearly killed the fucker.'[12]

His experience with the commune fed into the lyrics for the Who's 1971 single 'Won't Get Fooled Again'. That August Townshend told the *New Musical Express* that the song was written 'at a time when I was getting barraged by people at the Eel Pie commune. They live opposite me, and there was like a love affair going on between them and me... At one point there was an amazing scene where the commune was really working, but then the acid started flowing and I found myself at the end of some psychotic conversations and I just thought, "Oh fuck it." I don't really want to be talking to people about things flying around in space.'

Other musicians were sometimes drawn into the hotel's orbit, notably Fleetwood Mac founder Peter Green. He was persuaded to play a benefit gig on the lawn in front of the hotel on midsummer's eve in 1970. He performed a solo set by candlelight to no more than about one hundred people. The idea was to raise money for the commune but everyone was too stoned to remember to pass the bucket round and, besides, why spoil a beautiful evening? Gary Cowan says that on his sixteenth birthday he was serenaded by a makeshift band made up of Roger Daltrey on penny whistle, Pete Townshend on guitar, Cat Stevens on drums and Steve Hillage on guitar, all in a room at the hotel.

Another occasional feature of hotel life were the weddings. Mark Pickthall remembers there being at least three, although there may have been more. These were unions of expediency made to secure one of the partners the legal right to reside in the UK. They were also good excuses for a party. There was plenty of coupling going on that didn't lead to matrimony but did result in pregnancies. Mostly the mothers had the sense to leave the hotel before the birth.

Clifford Harper continued to espouse class revolution from the top of the hotel. On one side of the property, which faced the Thames Launches boat-building yard, he daubed 'Why work?' in

Hotel residents assembled around a fruit mandala (with a bowl of reefers) at one of the commune's occasional alfresco acid parties.

big red letters. On the front of the building he wrote out the radical anti-capitalist poem by Christopher Logue 'Know Thy Enemy' – 'He does not care who lives in the room at the top / provided he owns the building'. But Harper and the original communal activists had long become a negligible presence in the hotel as ever more newcomers streamed into the building and dossed down wherever they could drop a mattress. Chris Whitehouse remembers there being a particular spike in numbers in the wake of the Phun City free festival held at Worthing at the end of July 1970.

Harper told an interviewer that by the end of that summer the hotel had one hundred people. Others put it at more like 130, or even

150. Bodies now filled not just the upper two floors of bedrooms, but also the ground floor, which resembled a refugee camp, with rooms divided by carpets and blankets hung in hopeless attempts at privacy. Even that was preferable to the basement, where the least fortunate dwelt, hidden away from daylight – the 'cellar people' they were called. And there were those who had taken up residence in the hotel's ruined outbuildings, patching up missing walls and roofs with cardboard and driftwood.

No one had any money. There was a local bakery that employed casual labour, where some of the residents worked night shifts, returning in the morning with bags of loaves and rolls. Chris Faiers and a friend gardened at Twickenham Cemetery. Some sold drugs to the weekend visitors. Other shoplifted (not always successfully – *The Richmond Herald* reported on 'unemployed of Eel Pie Island Hotel', who was arrested three times in one month for the theft of groceries from shops before being remanded in custody for psychiatric and medical evaluation). Then again, there were few expenses. When Clifford Harper and friends first occupied the hotel, they actually gave Michael Snapper a small rent of around £20 a week, and paid rates and utility bills. But when the person collecting contributions disappeared with the money, all payments stopped. 'Nobody was motivated by money,' says Angie Page. 'That was one of the last things anybody thought about. You'd always be looked after.'

'It's like street drinkers,' says Chris Whitehouse, 'there's always one person who finds enough money to buy the drink for the day.' What he remembers people wanting more than money was cigarettes. 'If you were a visitor you'd probably be asked for cigarettes a dozen times. Everybody wanted tobacco to mix with the hash.'

As the numbers increased the altruism diminished. 'It became quite a strange place,' says Whitehouse. 'There were a lot of people who didn't know each other, a lot of people were there for different reasons. Most of them were good people but there were some you didn't want to be around.' Factions and splinter groups formed. Beyond the odd event, such as the Peter Green gig and a couple of come-all-ye dinners out on the lawn (one of which went disastrously wrong when someone tossed foraged belladonna into the salad), there was now little that was communal about life in the hotel.

Speaking today with former residents, attitudes to their time at the hotel are mixed. Loretta Leu, her partner Felix and their two children, aged one and two-and-a-half, resided at the hotel from September 1969 to January 1970. 'We lived, made food, played music, painted – on paper and walls – admired the swans and the ducks on the river, smoked weed and took LSD when anybody had some. Everything was magic, colourful and joyous.' Except when the outside world intruded. In November 1969 there was a farcical drugs bust when thirty-three policemen with dogs poured into the hotel and failed to find anything more than a small piece of hash in one room. When they tried to pin it on one resident, everybody in the hotel claimed ownership, *Spartacus*-style, and the police gave up. 'So they decided to take our two little kids by force instead,' says Leu. A WPC doctor who was part of the raid claimed the kids were in need of care and attention.[13] 'They were both perfectly healthy and not in need of saving from anything, except the authorities.' Leu managed to get them back the following day, albeit placed into her mother's custody. A month later she won a court case to regain full custody herself. The episode persuaded her to take her family and relocate to the Balearic Islands.

'We bubbled with the naivety that only the Sixties had, declaring no rules, no restrictions of any kind,' Gavin Kilty has written.[14] 'I remember once we removed all doors because they were barriers, until the cold forced us to hang them again.' For Canadian Chris Faiers, the hotel was a sexual playground. He was a good-looking guy who, other residents remember, always had a couple of pretty girls in his room. His memoir, *Eel Pie Dharma*, relates a whole series of horny encounters with fellow residents and with girls who visited the island for the music – 'They would come in packs, and many of them were gorgeous young English roses of fifteen or sixteen.'

Others, who were there maybe more out of desperation than choice, are more ambivalent. 'It had its good moments,' says Gary Cowan, 'but it was pretty desperate and sordid for me.' Faiers blames the effects of too much LSD. 'Acid had a freeing effect on most people for the first few trips, but for those with mental problems, the acid quickly worsened their state. It had a similar effect on group dynamics. The effects of a strong hallucinatory trip were so overwhelming that some people looked for leadership at any cost to free them from the confusion. A few of the Eel Piers were only too happy to assume the mantle of acid guru.' Peter Crisp, who was led to the hotel through a chance encounter with a beautiful girl carrying a wicker basket of joints at the 1969 Isle of Wight Festival, arrived in a state of euphoria and exited in a straitjacket. 'I was having a ball. In love, learning guitar and practising in a dark closet-sized room to become the world's greatest idiot dancer.' He and a handful of fellow acid freaks would roam the neighbourhood, off their heads, 'putting on little plays on buses and trains, and spelling out mystical parables with the shapes of our bodies.' When he stole some women's clothing from a shop in Twickenham and went back the next day to exchange them, wearing a dress, with a shaved head, and covered in blue ink, he was arrested, jailed for thirty days and then transferred to an asylum.

Clifford Harper blamed the speed freaks, who he believed constituted a major destructive force and who he characterises as 'lightweight criminals'. Mark Pickthall had his guitar stolen by another hotel resident and his attempt to claim it back got him a broken nose. 'It was time to go,' says Pickthall. 'It was entropy. Things fall apart.' Increasingly, there were worse things happening at the hotel than broken noses. Chris Whitehouse witnessed homophobic bullying, an elderly alcoholic getting badly beaten up in an unprovoked attack and the gang-rape of a sixteen-year-old girl.

By the winter of 1970–71, there was no longer any gas or electricity – Caldwell Smythe had quit putting on gigs in November and since then there was no power to steal from the ballroom. In desperation the residents began tearing up the hotel's floorboards and partition walls to burn for heat. 'It dawned on me it was getting ridiculous when one night I saw the banisters go from the stairs,' says Harper.[15] 'That was OK, but when I saw the stairs themselves going, I thought, how the fuck are we going to get to the first floor?'

It was about this time that the Hell's Angels got involved. By some accounts, they had been around since summer, not in the hotel itself but hanging out in the grounds, drinking and harassing passing boaters.[16] In October 1970, they invaded the hotel. Some remember it as a clash between gangs, with a local chapter of Angels holing up inside the hotel and fortifying it to repel an assault by rivals from Windsor. Others say it was a raid by a bunch of bikers called Freewheelers Wessex, who were there specifically to intimidate the hotel residents into leaving. 'They turned up, they shot a dog and they beat one bloke up,' says Gary Cowan. Either way, the end result was the same: there was some sort of pitched battle, possibly involving the throwing of petrol bombs, and the hotel was completely smashed up.

At this point, you wonder what the hotel's owner, Michael Snapper, was doing about all this. The residents had long since stopped paying rent, which had always been nominal anyway, and now the place was being ripped apart by a combination of freezing junkies and warring bikers. This, it seems, was fine with Snapper who, after repeatedly failing to have the hotel's drinks licence renewed, had decided the best course of action was to get rid of the place and sell the land for redevelopment. This is not conjecture: Snapper is quoted as saying as much – 'because of local politics... I am letting my hotel and land go' – in an article in *The Times* of 11 February 1970. The more structurally unsound the property and the more horror the hotel hippies evoked in the borough, the more likely the local council was to agree to Snapper's scheme. Already in 1969, a developer called Contemporary Homes of Wembley was seeking planning permission for the demolition of the Eel Pie Island Hotel and its replacement with forty-one houses, a block of six flats and a restaurant, plus a new road bridge connecting the island to Twickenham Embankment. The company was reported to be offering Snapper £60,000 for the site. The application was withdrawn in March 1970 following opposition from local residents, supported by Greater London Council member for Richmond Toby Jessel.

In January 1971, Snapper came back with a new proposal.[17] This was presented to a public meeting on the future of Eel Pie Island, sponsored by the River Thames Society and held at the council offices in York House in Twickenham. There, Snapper told an audience of over 200 people that the court's continued refusal to renew his drinks licence had left him no choice but to find another use for the hotel. He also revealed that the borough's Social Services Committee had issued a demolition order for the hotel on the grounds that it was 'unfit for human habitation'. The hippies he had allowed to live at the hotel, he said, had brought the demolition order on themselves. He claimed they had taken over the hotel in good condition. 'If they hadn't ruined the place all this wouldn't have been necessary,' he said. Clifford Harper, who was at the meeting with a few of the other residents, confronted Snapper. He told the audience that the hotel was already a slum when they moved in. He further claimed that it was Snapper who had invited in the Hell's Angels, who had wrecked the place.

Snapper preferred to keep the focus on the model he had brought along of his proposed redevelopment of the site with twenty new homes. Following the meeting, he posted a notice in the hotel kitchen ordering the residents to be out by the end of the month. He also turned off the water, until he was served notice by Richmond Council instructing him to turn it back on. Not that the Council supported the hippies. It was doing what it could to see them off the Island, but using the force of the law. According to a piece in the *International Times*, between mid-January and the end of February, there were no fewer than five police raids targeting the communards. These culminated in an action on 26 February, when plain-clothes officers swooped on the Cabbage Patch in Twickenham, a pub frequented by hotel dwellers; twenty-three people were arrested, including every Eel Pie Islander present.

Numbers in the hotel had fallen by this stage to no more than about twenty or so of the hardiest and most desperate. Clifford Harper quit in February.[18] As an indication of how unhealthy had become, he was admitted straight into hospital with TB and remained there for three months. A fanciful portrait of the hotel in its twilight exists in an article that ran in the 4 February 1971 edition of *Rolling Stone* magazine. It starts, 'A sign outside the red front door of the Eel Pie Hotel advises visitors: "Policemen and others bringing bad scenes wait at the door". 'Red front door' makes it sound like a Cotswold retreat – as do descriptions of the hotel as a 'clean' place where 'communal meals of rice, vegetables, bread and fruit were served on a huge round table', and mention of a craft room 'just a few feet from the Thames' where 'members of the commune made leather clothing and other articles to be sold'. This suspect idyll is invoked to contrast against the current state of the smashed apart building, and tales of skinheads and Hell's Angels and violence and theft – and the fact that the RSPCA has just been and taken away the hotel's last few skinny chickens because they weren't being looked after properly. In the article we meet Davina, a short, dark-haired London girl in a Lebanese dress, who is dossing at the hotel but preparing to move on, as is Malcolm, her man, and Mick and his Swedish girlfriend Gunn. 'Even Brian, a squat, curly-haired part-time junkie, who has been living in the hotel's beer cellar for the last four months, is leaving… As he walks away from the hotel, all his belongings in a small backpack and a blue laundry bag, Brian looks back at the big white building and says with disgust, "This used to be a really good scene. Now look at it."'

In mid-March the last of the residents gave in and moved out. Demolition began almost immediately. On the morning of Tuesday 30 March 1971, somebody called the fire service. The Eel Pie Island Hotel was ablaze. Curiously, fire crews from Twickenham station were already out on call tackling a fire at the Casino Hotel on Tagg's Island. Replacement fire engines came from Kingston, Hayes and Sunbury. They were hampered by parked cars in Water Lane that blocked access to Twickenham Embankment. It also transpired that water supplies to the Island were turned off because of works to the main. Firemen had to run hoses over the bridge. By the time they were able to start tackling the fire, all three floors had collapsed into the flames. All the firefighters could do was work to prevent the blaze spreading to the boatyard next door and to nearby houses. In the aftermath, a police spokesman said the fire was caused when a bonfire lit by demolition workers to burn rubbish got out of hand.

More than fifty years later, many former Eelpilanders and hotel residents remain convinced that Michael Snapper was behind the burning of the hotel, that he paid someone to torch the property.

This makes no sense. The hotel was already empty and there were workers on site in the process of tearing it down. It is strange that two old hotels on Thames islands, just a few miles apart, should suffer fires on the same morning, but there is no evidence that this was anything other than coincidental. Coincidental and also symbolic: where Eelpiland had once existed as a place in which young people could enjoy themselves away from closed-minded mainstream society, embracing the spirit of Sixties idealism, the flames marked the end of an era and the turning point into the solipsism of the Seventies.

CHAPTER 13

THE END OF THE RAINBOW

The new Richmond scene of partying rock stars and squatters, and further true adventures of Arthur, Giorgio and Harold

WHERE LONG-HAIRED YOUTH WITH GUITARS were once the scourge of the local gentry, by the Seventies they were the local gentry. A number of graduates of the Crawdaddy and Eel Pie Island stages were now raking in the money and, what's more, had accountants urging them to spend, spend, spend in order to minimise the amounts payable to Her Majesty's taxmen. Richmond and adjacent stretches of the Thames were well provisioned with suitably extravagant hilltop and riverside homes, secluded enough to ensure privacy but close enough to the studios, clubs and dealers of central London.

Former Bird Ronnie Wood, now a member of the Faces, used the money made co-writing the likes of 'Stay With Me' and 'Gasoline

FACING: A stunning 1968 poster for a trio of acts all managed by Giorgio Gomelsky and signed to Marmalade, the label he founded after being sacked by the Yardbirds.

Alley' with fellow Eelpilander Rod Stewart to buy a twenty-room Georgian mansion called the Wick, at the top of Richmond Hill. Purchased from actor Sir John Mills and writer wife Mary Hayley Bell in 1971, he reckoned it the 'most beautiful house in the world'.[1] Except he couldn't quite stretch to the asking price of £140,000, so fellow Face Ronnie Lane chipped in and for his share got the three-bedroom cottage at the bottom of the steeply sloping garden. Lane parked his mobile recording studio, an Airstream caravan, next to the cottage, while Wood converted the basement of the house into a musical playpen. It's where Wood recorded his first two solo albums: *I've Got My Own Album to Do* in 1974 and *Now Look* in 1975. In the process he turned the former home of Sir John and, before him, 18th-century portraitist Joshua Reynolds, into an open-all-hours clubhouse for the new rock aristocracy. Some of those dropping by to play included Keith Richards, Mick Jagger, George Harrison, Rod Stewart, Ian McLagan, Mick Taylor (Stones guitarist), Kenney Jones (Faces drummer) and Bobby Womack. One jam session at the Wick with Wood, Jagger, Kenney Jones on drums, a session player called Willie Weeks on bass and David Bowie on backing vocals resulted in a rough demo of future Stones hit single 'It's Only Rock'n'Roll (But I Like It)'. In January 1973, when Pete Townshend organised a comeback gig for Eric Clapton, who was just emerging from a long period of heroin-induced inactivity, the rehearsals for the concert (which would feature Clapton, Townshend, Wood and Steve Winwood) took place at the Wick. At other times, various members of Monty Python or actor John Hurt would turn up for marathon snooker sessions at the bar of the neighbouring Petersham Hotel. 'Day would turn into night and another day, and by then more friends would show up, and before any of us knew it we'd been up for four days drinking, getting stoned and making music,' recalls Wood.[2] Amazingly, no one died and Wood's friendship with Richards and

244

Uxbridge boy Ronnie Wood and wife Krissy in the garden of the Wick, the house on top of Richmond Hill bought with the proceeds of his co-writing credits.

Jagger came in useful when in December 1974 the Rolling Stones were looking for a new guitarist to replace Mick Taylor.

Before then, in 1973, a disillusioned Ronnie Lane walked away from the Faces. He was reportedly unhappy with the way singer Rod Stewart's solo success was overshadowing the group. He put physical distance between himself and his former band by moving out of the Wick, retreating to a farm on the Welsh borders. The finest legacy of Lane's time spent at the Wick is the standout track on the Faces' second album, 1971's *Long Player*, called 'Richmond'. With Lane on acoustic guitar and Ronnie Wood on slide, it's a country-blues lament offering homesick thoughts from America. By this time, Wood was flush enough to buy back the garden cottage. This may or may not have been a good move, when one night Keith Richards came to visit and stayed for five months, making the cottage his own. Even after he moved out, he remained a frequent house guest. His regular presence at the Wick provided an excuse for a badly mistimed raid by the Drug Squad, with a police posse kicking in a two-hundred-year-old door to find Wood and Richards were off in Europe, and only Woods' wife and a girlfriend were at home.

Twenty-odd years on, in 1996, when Ronnie Wood came to sell the Wick in order to pay a vertiginous tax bill, the buyer was Pete Townshend. He'd lived in the borough since 1967, when, as a newlywed, he and his then wife, Karen Astley, settled at No.2 Twickenham Embankment, across from Eel Pie Island. The house wasn't chosen because of any particular love for the Island – far from it. He told interviewer Peter Watts in 2011, 'I have very little affection for the Island. I simply lived opposite the place for years. I don't much like the little shacks and sheds on it. However, I know people who live and work there, and I like them very much, and understand why they like living there.' Later, the Townshends moved half a mile downriver to Twickenham Riverside, then around the corner to Chapel House, on Montpelier Row, overlooking Marble Hill House and park. From 1973, Townshend had a small, 25ft boat called *Babajan* moored on the Island that he used to commute to the Who's studio in Battersea, while recording *Quadrophenia*. Later, he upgraded to a 55ft commuter boat, *Zephyr*, made to order by Bill Sims, an Eel Pie Island boatbuilder. Sims also sold Townshend a two-storey riverfront property close by Richmond Lock called the Boathouse, which he converted into the Meher Baba Oceanic

Centre. This was intended as a meeting place and lodgings for the followers of Indian spiritual guru Meher Baba, whose teachings had helped Townshend deal with his alcohol problems. The centre also incorporated Eel Pie Studios, a recording facility used by Townshend and the Who, and also run as a commercial venture: in 1982 Pink Floyd recorded parts of *The Final Cut* here; the following year a now-solo Roger Waters was back working on *The Pros and Cons of Hitchhiking*. A-ha recorded their debut album *Hunting High and Low* (1984–85) here, including hit single 'Take On Me'. In 1989, part of the building was taken over by indie band Cocteau Twins and renamed September Sound Studios.

Further cementing his presence in the area, in October 1978 the intellectually curious and well-read Townshend opened a bookshop in central Richmond, on King Street, just off the Green. Called Magic Bus (after the Who song of the same name), its stock reflected Townshend's own tastes and those of the people working there, including manager Peter Hogan, also a follower of Meher Baba. In addition to the standard array of fiction, the shop was strong on music, mysticism, spiritualism, health-conscious cookbooks, holistic medicine, and books by and about Baba. 'The shop was a real magnet where people would come and hangout,' says Hogan. 'We attracted anybody young and interesting. Elvis Costello was a regular.' (After time spent in Liverpool, Costello had moved back to the area and was now living in nearby Whitton.) Hogan remembers a signing at the shop for northern poet John Cooper Clarke at which Costello was one of only two people to turn up.[3]

Beyond the Seventies, more rock aristocracy took up residence. Bruce Welch of the Shadows, Fleetwood Mac founder Peter Green, Greg Lake of King Crimson and ELP, and Thin Lizzy's Phil Lynott all settled in or around Richmond. Some years after offloading the Wick, Ronnie Wood returned for a spell to live on the Green, while

In the late 1970s, Pete Townshend (left) entered the bookselling business, launching the Magic Bus bookshop in Richmond, which was managed by Peter Hogan (right).

his new boss, Mick Jagger, bought Grade II-listed Downe House on Richmond Hill, the one-time residence of playwright Richard Brinsley Sheridan, where he lived with wife Jerry Hall until they separated, at which point Jagger moved into a flat next door.

On occasion, bands passed through the doors at the clubhouse at the Athletics Association Grounds, although not necessarily to perform for the paying public: in August 1972 prog rockers King Crimson used the place to write and rehearse tracks for their fifth album, *Larks' Tongues in Aspic* (which would be released the following March). Otherwise, there was no longer any local music scene to speak of.

The seeds planted by the Eel Pie communal project, on the other hand, took root. The year after the hotel burned down, some of the former residents opened up a squat on Grosvenor Road in central Twickenham, right behind the local police station. Most of the street's properties were empty pending redevelopment and in a short time all bar two were occupied by squatters. Over the course of the next three years the squatting population expanded to 112 adults and sixteen children, occupying eighteen houses in five streets. A derelict warehouse on the corner of the Grosvenor Road was cleaned out, fitted up and opened as an arts centre with music, fringe theatre, exhibitions, and a Punch and Judy show. It all lasted until 1976, when Bovis, owners of the site, were granted a possession order to evict the squatters and begin redevelopment.

There is an excellent documentary-drama written about the events surrounding Grosvenor Road by Islington-born playwright James Saunders (1925–2004), whose *Next Time I'll Sing to You* played in the West End with a cast that included Michael Caine and won the 1963 Evening Standard Award for Most Promising Playwright. Called *Squat*, his Grosvenor Road play premiered at the Orange Tree theatre in Richmond in August 1976 and has rarely – if ever – been performed since. You can find the transcript online. Instead, the community's most lasting legacy is a piece of graffiti. The first house to be opened up on Grosvenor Road was No.7, which from then on served as a social and operational centre used by the whole street. In the kitchen, as part of the accumulated nonsensical dialogue and messaging scrawled on the wall, someone wrote 'CATS LIKE PLAIN CRISPS'. The gnomic statement started appearing on walls and streets signs around Twickenham and, most prominently, at a major roundabout in Richmond. After that, it took on a life of its own – it appeared on flags and banners at festivals and, in the mid 1980s, an all-girl group on the Isle of Wight used it as their name.

It is no surprise that social-working Arthur Chisnall should pop up in connection with Grosvenor Road. After his connection with

'CATS LIKE PLAIN CRISPS' was first scrawled on a wall in a Grosvenor Road squat, then reproduced, possibly by the same happily deranged person, elsewhere in London.

Eel Pie Island was severed in 1967, he continued his idiosyncratic social working. He was a founder member and leader of the Twickenham Community Services Group, which formed in 1972. One of the group's first projects was to renovate a 'professionally wrecked' house on Grosvenor Road. The developer, Bovis, had deliberately ripped up the floorboards to make sure no one could occupy the house while they went about buying up the surrounding properties. Chisnall thought this verged on the criminal and wanted to make sure the houses could be used by the homeless until Bovis was ready to start work. The plan was that once volunteers had made the property liveable it would be handed over to the charity Shelter who would find a deserving tenant. When the time came, squatters got into the property first and refused to vacate.[4]

Around the same time, Chisnall also became involved with BIT, which was a free-information service that grew out of the *International Times* counterculture newspaper. If someone was looking for somewhere to crash rent-free or to join a Buddhist commune, build their own yurt, seek help for LSD-induced psychosis or cycle overland to India, they could drop by the BIT offices in Kensington Park Road in west London (open every day of the year from 10am to 10pm) or call the twenty-four-hour phone line, and one of the BIT volunteers might be able to provide assistance. The service was barely and erratically funded by proceeds from the sale of BIT travel guides to Asia and Africa, along with occasional handouts from rock stars – notably Paul McCartney and Pete Townshend. Chisnall, who knew BIT founder John 'Hoppy' Hopkins, helped the organisation secure funding from the Gulbenkian Foundation, and shared the contacts and experience he'd gained in over a decade of running Eelpiland. In a similar fashion, he was also loosely involved with Release, the agency that provided legal advice for people charged with the possession of drugs, as well as with *Spare Rib*, the feminist magazine launched in 1972.

In 1974, Chisnall was one of three authors contributing to *Unattached Youth*, the book version of a report originally commissioned by the Joseph Rowntree Memorial Trust dealing with the crisis of identity among young people. The quasi-academic, jargon-filled text explored why it was it that many young people were choosing to drop out and indulge in teenage revolution and delinquency. It offered the examples of the BIT Information Service, Arts Labs and Eel Pie Island Jazz Club as ways of engaging with this disaffected generation.

Meanwhile, Chisnall continued to run 31 Waldegrave Gardens as a halfway house. 'It was an absolute shambles,' remembers his girlfriend of the time, Auriol Hall (also one of the authors of *Unattached Youth*). 'Full of people, extremely dirty and lost.' The kitchen sink was always blocked and rooms were knee-deep in newspapers and junk – Chisnall was a hoarder, forever hauling broken and discarded bits out of skips and carrying them home. The place smelled appalling but, as well as being tone deaf, Arthur had no sense of smell, so it didn't bother him.

And what of the other two characters who were key to the transformation of Richmond into a pioneering Sixties music hub? When the National Jazz & Blues Festival was given the boot, Harold Pendleton moved it to Royal Windsor Racecourse. It was held there for two years, until the festival's new sound system landed Pendleton in serious trouble. This is a story worth telling because it's another example of just how much the jazz-loving accountant from Southport contributed to the development of the UK rock scene – in this case, by making it a whole lot louder.

Until now, bands generally played through a couple of 100-watt speakers. This was loud enough for indoor venues but the sound tended to get lost in a field. Pendleton was approached by audio engineer Charlie Watkins, who offered to build him a 1,000-watt system. Increasing the wattage by a factor of ten does not equate to ten times the volume, but it would be at least twice as loud as anything heard before. The system was ready in time for Windsor in 1967. For most of the festival Watkins held back on the volume, building the power up slowly: 500 watts, 600 watts... Then on Saturday night, bill-toppers the Crazy World of Arthur Brown took to the stage. When the group performed their big hit 'Fire' and Brown launched into a banshee screech of 'Burn! Burn! Burn!', Watkins whacked the system up to full. 'I can hear that scream now! It was amazing! No one had ever heard a sound like it!'[5] he told an interviewer. The group was still playing when Watkins felt a hand on his shoulder and a voice said, 'I must ask you to accompany me to the police station, sir'.

The show was allowed to continue – cancelling it would have resulted in thirty or forty thousand pissed-off music fans

By the time of its seventh edition, the former Richmond Jazz Festival – now relcoated to Windsor – had fully got its freak on.

rampaging round Windsor – but an irate local council decided to seek an injunction banning the festival from the town in future. Pendleton decided to fight and for his legal representation he engaged the formidable barrister Quintin Hogg, Lord Hailsham of St Marylebone, a former Conservative Party chairman.[6] 'You've never seen so many people in a magistrates court because he was an absolute star,' remembers Barbara Pendleton. 'He wiped the floor with them so they had to give us the licence.' But the win didn't matter when the owners of the racecourse, eager to stay on the right side of the council, told Pendleton he couldn't use their ground anymore. The festival moved to Kempton Park Racecourse in Sunbury in 1968 where, after just one year, Pendleton was told never to come back. It found a home at Plumpton Race Track, just north of Brighton, in 1969 and 1970, before being moved on again. The festival landed in Reading in 1971 and has remained there ever since (it is now known simply as the Reading Festival). Harold Pendleton ran it for another twenty-one years, before selling out his interest in 1992. Along the way, many of the aspects that almost every major international festival has since adopted as standard – from multiple stages to the ubiquitous wristbands, originally imported from a hospital supplier in America, and flushing portable toilets – were pioneered at Reading.

Harold Pendleton's other musical venture, the Marquee, also did rather well. It flourished as a central London stronghold of the R&B scene, hosting residencies from the Yardbirds, Manfred Mann, the Who, Long John Baldry, the T-Bones and Rod Stewart, among others. The Rolling Stones, who played their first gig together at the Marquee on Oxford Street, returned to the club in 1971 – and resumed their feud with Harold. It was 26 March, a month before the release of *Sticky Fingers*, at the tail end of a nine-city UK tour. This was a small club performance staged for filming in front of a small invited audience. Before starting, Keith Richards wanted the large Marquee logo on the back wall of the stage covered up. Pendleton said no, and Richards tried to take his head off with a swing of his guitar.

'He didn't think they were the best R&B band in the world, but he wasn't anti-Rolling Stones,' says Harold's son, Nick, who spent his childhood hanging around the Marquee and later followed his parents into the business. When it came to booking acts, Harold wasn't one to let personal taste get in the way of making money. Entering the Seventies, the Marquee played host to bands in just about every musical genre, welcoming AC/DC, Black Sabbath, David Bowie, Dire Straits, Fleetwood Mac, Genesis, Elton John, King Crimson, Led Zeppelin, Motörhead, Queen, Roxy Music, Simon and Garfunkel, and Stevie Wonder. Later, the club embraced punk and new wave with gigs by Adam and the Ants, Bauhaus, the Boomtown Rats, the Cure, the Jam, Japan, Joy Division, the Police, the Pretenders, REM, the Sex Pistols (one appearance only, after which they were banned), Simple Minds, U2, Ultravox and the Undertones.

Pop Svengali Simon Napier-Bell considered the Marquee to have been the basis for the 1960s rock invasion of America and the 1970s boom in stadium rock – and he is not alone in this. The venue was the starting point for so many major British groups – and a first toehold in the UK for international acts – that *Melody Maker* was moved to call it 'the most important venue in the history of pop music'. Napier-Bell once asked Pendleton how he had been so adept at picking the best new groups. 'It was the coat-check girl,' Harold replied. 'She told me who to book and I booked them.'[7] It's a cute story, but the truth is Pendleton employed a succession of extremely savvy club managers and he left the booking to them.

And Giorgio Gomelsky, last heard of being dumped by the Yardbirds for financial incompetence? Tireless and charming hustler that he was, Gomelsky immediately bounced back with his own PR and artist management firm, Paragon, and his own record label, Marmalade. He had somehow secured the backing of major

Giorgio Gomelsky (left) oversees a recording session with the Chris Barber Band of a Paul McCartney tune, with the Beatle playing keyboards, alongside Brian Auger.

record labels Polydor and Deutsche Grammophon, who provided magnificent offices on Stratford Place, just off Oxford Street in central London, and a lavish expense account that Gomelsky worked to the full – he bought himself a Ferrari Superamerica convertible. 'Giorgio's office was at the end of a corridor, with a lovely view out of the window,' recalls Jim Cregan of Paragon-managed outfit Blossom Toes, who dropped by once a week for his salary. 'He had a big desk and behind the desk was a collection of mirrors of all shapes and sizes, which was really annoying because as you walked in you wouldn't really look at Giorgio, you were too busy checking that your hair was right and that you hadn't got any spinach between your teeth. It was really arty but annoying.'

Marmalade launched in August 1966 with a shameless bit of back-scratchery called 'We Love the Pirates' – as in pirate radio stations – written and performed by a bunch of studio musicians under the name the Roaring 60s. Otherwise, label artists included Crawdaddy alumni Julie Driscoll, Brian Auger, Gary Farr and Blossom Toes, but also jazz guitarist John McLaughlin, who would release his first album, *Extrapolation* (1969), with Gomelsky before moving to the States and recording with Miles Davis and founding cosmic jazz-fusionists Mahavishnu Orchestra. Gomelsky recorded old friends the Chris Barber Band, including one lively session at Chappell Studios on Bond Street – handily, just around the corner from Gomelsky's office – where they cut a version of an old instrumental Paul McCartney had written for the Beatles called 'Catwalk'. For this jazzy strutting version it was renamed 'Cat Call' and McCartney played on the session, along with Brian Auger. Part way through, you hear Gomelsky's shouted instruction to the musicians, 'Please play slower'.

Gomelsky also recorded a handful of demos with rising Canterbury jazz-rockers Soft Machine, although these remained unreleased for several years because of a dispute over studio costs. The label's big hope were Blossom Toes, previously the R&B band the Ingoes, but now totally converted to flower power. He installed the group in a communal house in Fulham that became infamous as a non-stop swinging party pad attracting the likes of Eric Clapton, Eric Burdon and Captain Beefheart. 'People kept turning up all the time, and that's fun, but we're all human,' main songwriter Brian Godding told an interviewer in 2014.[8] 'Even at that age you can't stay awake for a month, or a year! You've got to go to bed, but when you go up to your bedroom there's about eight people in there copulating... You kind of think, fuck this! "Mum, can I come home?"' Gomelsky got the band a showcase at the Saville Theatre, which at the time was being run by Beatles manager Brian Epstein. 'He had us all wear kaftans and it looked like I was wearing my mother's curtains,' says guitarist Jim Cregan. When the band released its whimsical and wigged-out debut album, *We Are Ever So Clean*, in 1967, one contemporary review called it 'Giorgio Gomelsky's Lonely Hearts Club Band'. Except while sales of the Beatles' album are totted up in millions, buyers of the Blossom Toes' debut could have squeezed into a Mini. A second album ditched the English whimsy for heavyweight riffs but did no better. Frustrated by their manager's manipulations, the band split.

Marmalade's only certified commercial success was Brian Auger and Julie Driscoll's version of the Bob Dylan-penned 'This Wheel's on Fire', which made the UK Top 10. Driscoll was the darling of the music press: *Melody Maker* labelled her the 'Face of '68' and its readers voted her 'Top Female Singer in Britain' that year. In 1969, Gomelsky was grooming another of his wilfully eccentric acts, who went by the excruciating name of Frabjoy and the Runcible Spoon. Marmalade released one single by them ('I'm Beside Myself' b/w 'Animal Song') but plans for an album were thwarted when, after two years of seeing no return on their investment, Polydor pulled the plug on the whole Marmalade/Paragon enterprise. Frabjoy and the Runcible Spoon, who were Lol Creme and Kevin Godley, would team up with another songwriting pair, Graham Gouldman and Eric Stewart, and eventually be launched on Jonathan King's UK Records label as 10cc. By that time Gomelsky had quit London for France, telling an interviewer he'd had enough of the 'perfidious Albions'.[9]

While in Britain, Gomelsky had already worked with two of France's biggest stars, co-producing albums for Johnny Hallyday (*La generation perdue*, 1966) and Serge Gainsbourg (*Initials BB*, 1968), both of whom had crossed the Channel to tap into the Swinging London sound.[10] But soon after arriving in Paris, Gomelsky attended a concert by exploratory rock band Magma and completely fell for them. They produced cosmic soundscapes, with lyrics sung in a made-up language called Kobaïan – bandleader and composer Christian Vander claimed not to write the music and words, but to channel them. Gomelsky became Magma's manager and produced a couple of their early albums, including, in 1973, their first UK release, the apocalyptic *Mekanik Destructiv Kommandoh* (its fans include both the Sex Pistols' John Lydon and 1980s snooker champ Steve Davis). Building the band's fanbase by touring was hampered by France's lack of a nationwide network of music venues, so Gomelsky created his own. He strung together a circuit of youth centres, mostly associated with local socialist and communist parties, and, alongside Magma, signed up a clutch of other art-rock bands to play them, including England's Henry Cow, and Germany's Can and Amon Duul II. Gomelsky also worked with Gong (founded by Soft Machine's Daevid Allen, now resident in France), producing their third studio album, *Flying Teapot*, and getting them a deal with Richard Branson's fledgling Virgin Records. There were sessions with Greek electronic composer Vangelis – music from which later appeared on two albums, *Hypothesis* and *The Dragon*, issued without the artist's approval and quickly withdrawn from the market by order of the court.

In 1977, Gomelsky left France and relocated to New York, where he took over a three-storey townhouse in Chelsea. Installing himself on the top floor, he turned the lower floors into a rehearsal and recording studio, and a club space – primarily for music, although for a time on certain week nights it operated as an S&M bar called Paddles. Gomelsky became something of a crotchety patron to emerging artists on the new wave, punk and avant garde scenes, hosting gigs by Jeff Buckley, Richard Hell and John Zorn, among others. Bassist, producer and sonic adventurer Bill Laswell took up residence in the building for a time. (Former Velvet Underground muse Nico was another long-term house guest.) Gomelsky got involved in founding another short-lived record label, Utopia, which was mostly a US outlet for the music of Magma, although it also put out several releases by bluesman Albert King. He curated a festival of new music, hosted his own cable TV show and became an early proselytiser for personal computers and the internet. To those who knew him and worked with him, he remained equal parts inspirational and infuriating. He advised one band he was recording to drop the guitars and drive out to New Jersey to record the noise of frogs fucking instead.

* * *

In autumn 1998, to mark thirty-five years since the Rolling Stones and Yardbirds played the Crawdaddy and Eel Pie Island, local promoters Gina Way and Warren Walters, in association with the Museum of Richmond, organised a celebratory concert at York House, in Twickenham. The Yardbirds were back in town as headliners, supported by, among others, Island regulars the Downliners Sect. There was no Clapton, Beck or Page – although Eric did fax over his apologies and best wishes – and former vocalist Keith Relf had died in 1976, but Chris Dreja was on rhythm guitar and Jim McCarty on drums. Also present that evening were Twickenham residents Arthur Chisnall and Harold Pendleton, while Giorgio Gomelsky had flown over from New York especially for the occasion.

As far as anyone knows, this was the first time these three maverick shapers of the UK music industry had met together. Chisnall would have been seventy-three, long retired and suffering from ill health, but still railing against the failings of society to tackle issues relating to youth and alienation. Harold was seventy-four; he'd sold the Marquee in 1987 and stepped away from the Reading

The Station Hotel, one-time home to the Crawdaddy and its resident houseband, the Rolling Stones, derelict and boarded up in 1967.

festival in 1992, but was busy with his sound and lighting business Entec, providing technical services for touring bands including the likes of Blur, Garbage, Henry Rollins and the Sisters of Mercy. Gomelsky was a sprightly sixty-four, still with jet-black hair – obviously coloured, says Peter Moody – still exuberant, still working the angles, still dreaming. 'Hey, Peter,' he said to Moody, 'I have a job for you.' Moody was the former bassist with the Grebbels, one of the Crawdaddy house bands back in 1964 that were managed by Gomelsky. He was at York House that night with Mambo Chillum, playing support to the Yardbirds one last time.

Gomelsky wanted Moody's help in finding a rare artefact. Back in 1963, the Georgian had shot some performances by his protégés the Rolling Stones at the Crawdaddy at the Station Hotel. It was the first time the group had ever been captured on film, a bunch of young

261

men pounding out Bo Diddley in the back room of a Richmond pub. Gomelsky had deposited the footage with production facilities in Soho, but then the band had jilted him, taking up with Andrew Loog Oldham, and their now ex-manager had no need of the film any more. 'How can I get it back, Peter?' he asked. He could not remember the name of the lab or the street it was on – never mind that thirty-five years had passed.

It would be thrilling to report that after months of diligent sleuthing Peter Moody, against all odds, succeeded in unearthing that lost Rolling Stones footage. Sadly, that's not what happened. The film stayed lost. Chances are, it was junked soon after Gomelsky failed to collect it. All that survives is a tantalising story. The same is largely true of the Richmond upon Thames music scene as a whole. Other than those who were there at the time – and their numbers are fewer with every passing year – who now has heard of the Crawdaddy? In 2021, the venue that played host to the club, the old Station Hotel, is now an anodyne 'premium' pub and restaurant called One Kew Road. The only testimony to its place in rock history is a plaque on the back of the building, where the smokers gather. The clubhouse at the Richmond Athletic Association Grounds that was the second home of the Crawdaddy remains the post-match drinking venue for the Richmond and London Scottish rugby clubs. L'Auberge is a branch of Nando's chicken restaurant. The site of the Eel Pie Island hotel is now occupied by a mid-1970s housing development called Aquarius, where three-bedroom homes go for £1.65 million.

There is a revived Eel Pie Club that puts on regular blues upstairs at the Cabbage Patch next to Twickenham Station and a revived Crawdaddy Club that hires the Richmond rugby clubhouse for evenings of R&B. Meanwhile, the Swinging '60s London Bus Tour occasionally drops by the Station Hotel and then parks up opposite the Eel Pie Island Museum so passengers can walk down to Twickenham Embankment to look across at the Island and read the information board put up by the local council. It is a long way from 1963, when the upheavals of teenagers experiencing the world for the first time exploded into a chanking-guitar-led rave-up, and the world came to see what was going on down in Richmond.

NOTES AND DIGRESSIONS

Most of the quotes in this book come from interviews conducted by the author. The text also draws from a series of interviews conducted as part of an Eel Pie Oral History Project, carried out by cultural organisation digital:works in 2013. These recordings have been deposited with Richmond Local Studies Centre and the Eel Pie Island Museum; some are also available online at the project website www.eelpieisland.org.uk. Quoted material from other sources is credited below.

CARNABY STREET... KING'S ROAD... RICHMOND UPON THAMES... (pages 6–15)

1   **'Shit, that's *the Beatles!*...'** As quoted in Bill Wyman's *Stone Alone*, p127.

2   **'We're whacking our show out...'** This is from a YouTube clip, 'Keith Richards – Friends with the Beatles'. It was originally posted on Richards' website around 2003. 'We were in a pub,' he begins, 'Station Hotel, Richmond. That was our gig. It was the only one we really had.'

3   **'Mick Jagger was too embarrassed to even look...'** Twenty-five years later Mick Jagger recalled his memories of the night as he inducted the Beatles into the Rock & Roll Hall of Fame in Cleveland, Ohio: 'We were playing a little club in Richmond and I was doing this song, and suddenly I saw, there they were, right in front of me, the Fab Four! John, Paul, George and Ringo. The four-headed monster... And they had on these beautiful long, black leather trench coats. I could really die for one of those. And I thought, "Even if I have to learn to write songs, I'm gonna get this."'

4   **'It was a real rave...'** As quoted in Bill Wyman's *Stone Alone*, p127.

5   **'They just had presence...'** As quoted in *The Beatles Anthology*, p101.

6   **'They could do their stuff...'** As quoted in *The Beatles Anthology*, p101.

7   **'The Rolling Stones were playing nearby...'** From 'Elvis Costello: The Rolling Stone Interview', by David Fricke, published in *Rolling Stone* of 14 October 2004.

OFF THE COAST OF TWICKENHAM (pages 16–35)

1 **'This place became famous for its pies...'** For anyone who wants to sample this ancient Thames-side fare, Mrs Beeton's *Book of Household Management*, 1866 edition, provides the following recipe for eel pie: *Skin and wash 1lb of eels, cut them into pieces 2 inches long, and line the bottom of the pie-dish with forcemeat. Put in the eels, and sprinkle them with the parsley, shallots, nutmeg, seasoning, and lemon-juice, and cover with puff-paste. Bake for 1 hour, or rather more; make a béchamel sauce and pour it hot into the pie.* Charles Francatelli's *The Cook's Guide and Housekeeper's & Butler's Assistant* of 1861 has a geographically specific recipe for 'Richmond eel pie' that substitutes chopped mushrooms for Mrs Beeton's forcemeat and adds a glass of Harvey's anchovy sauce and two of sherry.

2 **'Born in Chelsea in 1908...'** Biographical details come from 'Go-getting Family Man', an obituary of Michael Snapper by Clara Story, published in the *Surrey Comet* of 12 January 2007.

3 **'Rutland, who grew up in nearby Isleworth...'** Trumpeter Brian Rutland, who can claim to be the person who started regular jazz sessions on the Island, still leads his own All-Star Band; he performs on the first Friday of every month on the *Tattershall Castle*, a 1930s passenger boat, now moored on the Thames in central London.

4 **'In the late 1950s, Kingston School of Art student...'** Stephens told his story to Pete Watt in June 2013 as part of the Eel Pie Island Oral History Project.

5 **'Schoolboy Robin Hunter lived on the Island...'** Hunter has written a memoir called *In the Shadow of Naked Ladies*, which includes an account of his childhood years on Eel Pie Island.

6 **'As a consequence, the water was toxic...'** The information on the foul state of the Thames sixty years ago comes from an article titled 'River Thames Home to 138 Seal Pups, Finds Annual Count', by Patrick Barkham, published in *The Guardian* of 2 September 2019.

7 **'Roy Buckley, whose family moved onto the Island in 1948...'** Buckley's childhood memories are recalled in a short text, 'Eel Pie Island 1948–1955', archived online at eelpie.org.

8 **'We left the pub and walked the few yards to the chain ferry...'** From John Lucas's *Next Year Will Be Better: A Memoir of England in the 1950s*, p188, quoted with permission of the author.

9   'a decidedly dodgy affair...' As quoted in *Eel Pie Island*, by Dan van der Vat and Michele Whitby, p43.

10 'Trombonist Mel Henry...' Henry's recollections of playing Eel Pie Island Hotel can be found on the sandybrownjazz.co.uk website.

11 'The worst thing that ever happened to jazz...' As quoted in Peter Doggett's ambitious and highly readable *Electric Shock: From the Gramophone to the iPhone – 125 Years of Pop Music*, p310.

12 'the Riverside Jazzmen, led by local clarinettist Alan Cresswell...' Cresswell is another old jazzer who won't give up the stage. In their heyday, his Riverside Jazzmen played just about every jazz club in London, including the Piccadilly Jazz Club, Ken Colyer's Studio 51, the 100 Club and Marquee. These days, he's based down in Horsham, in West Sussex, and plays with the Muskrat Ramblers and Kevin Scott's Golden Eagle Jazz Band.

13 'You felt like the floor was going to collapse...' As told to interviewer Pete Watt in June 2013 as part of the Eel Pie Island Oral History Project.

14 'This is as close as you will get to New Orleans in England...' The quote comes from the sleeve notes to *Historic Recordings Volume 1 – Ken Colyer's Jazzmen*. This was later reissued as *Ken Colyer's Jazzmen: Classic Years Volume 2*.

15 'Mod enthusiasts are usually in their 20s...' From the *Daily Mirror* of 2 March 1963.

THE EEL PIED PIPER (pages 36–49)

1   'When the poet-critic John Lucas visited Eelpiland...' Lucas's description of Arthur Chisnall comes from his memoir *Next Year Will Be Better: A Memoir of England in the 1950s*, p189.

2   'It's a draft of an article...' A draft because there are differences between the typed manuscript at the Eel Pie Island Museum and the paper as published in the *International Journal of Social Psychiatry* of summer 1969.

3   'I don't remember when I became aware of Arthur...' Biographical information about Jack Lambert and his recollections of Arthur Chisnall come from a series of emails exchanged between Lambert and Michele Whitby, in 2007 and 2008, when she was researching her book, *Eel Pie Island*. Michele kindly shared the emails with me.

4 **'Arthur would have been accepted today...'** From *Unofficial Aspects of a Life in Policy Research*, the professional autobiography of Leslie Wilkins, published posthumously by his family in 1999.

5 **'According to an obituary...'** 'Dandy of Cybernetics', by Paul Pangaro, published in *The Guardian* of 16 April 1996.

6 **'What he remembers most is Pask's eccentricity...'** Whitehouse's memories of working for Gordon Pask come from a short and hilarious account he wrote for his own amusement, which he shared with me over email.

7 **'Pask gathered many of the subjects...'** The connection between Gordon Pask and Arthur Chisnall, and the recruiting of Eelpiland club-goers for psychological research experiments is mentioned in an article titled 'Dead-Enders: Till They Got Their Chance of College through a Jazz Club!' by Mark Ottaway, published in *The People* of 13 October 1963.

8 **'As Eelpiland approached its fifth anniversary...'** This was a story with the fine title 'High Minds and Low Heels', by Peter Earle in *News of the World* of 25 June 1961.

9 **'Two clubbers reportedly lost their jobs...'** According to the article 'Eel Pie Row Raised in Parliament' in *Jazz News* of 10 December 1960.

10 **'Most amusing of the lot...'** Jeremy Sandford (1930–2003) was a television screenwriter best known for the 1966 landmark BBC TV play *Cathy Come Home*. He and his wife, Nell Dunn (author of the novels *Up the Junction* and *Poor Cow*), lived for a time on the river at Twickenham. Recollections of Eel Pie Island, drawn from an unpublished memoir, are archived online at www.jeremysandford.org.uk.

11 **'John Lucas, meanwhile, recalls the giggling and grunts...'** From *Next Year Will Be Better: A Memoir of England in the 1950s*, p190.

A GARDEN PARTY IN RICHMOND (pages 50–65)

1 **'The mic then passed to a man...'** A recording of Alan Sherriff's talk, complete with a brief word from ninety-one-year-old audience member Harold Pendleton, is archived online at the Richmond Local History Society website.

2 **'It's telling that the man who...'** When it came to writing his own drug-flavoured history of the music business (*Black Vinyl, White*

Powder, 2001), Simon Napier-Bell, who managed the Yardbirds, Japan and Wham!, among many others, recalls on his Facebook page that the first person he called was Harold Pendleton.

3   'Jones obliged...' Stones historians still debate who filled the drum stool for the group's very first gig. A press announcement in *Jazz News* of the day before gives the name of Mike Avery (sic), but Avory, who went on to drum with the Kinks for twenty years, says he didn't do it. If that's true, then it was most likely Chapman but no one can remember. There may not even have been a drummer.

4   **'What exactly happened that July day...'** The description of events comes from a story titled 'Riot at the Beaulieu Jazz Festival' that ran in *The Observer* of 31 July 1960.

5   **'Whatever the cause, the incident was met with outrage...'** For more media coverage of the events at Beaulieu see 'Unsafe Things Like Youth and Jazz: Beaulieu Jazz Festivals (1956-61), and the Origins of Pop Festival Culture in Britain', an essay by George McKay, printed in *Remembering Woodstock* (Andy Bennett, ed.; Ashgate, 2004) and free to read online through www.academia.edu.

6   **'The paper quoted one unnamed local...'** This was a story titled 'Drink Licence for the Jazz Festival', from *The Richmond Herald* of 25 August 1961.

7   **'Pendleton reassured the good people of Richmond...'** From a story titled 'Undesirables Won't Get in to Festival', from *The Richmond and Twickenham Times* of 27 August 1961.

8   **'As one interviewee pointed out...'** From a story titled 'Country's Jazzmen Come to Town – and the Beatniks Too', from *The Richmond and Twickenham Times* of 2 September 1961.

9   **'Because we knew several of the promoters...'** John Clark's recollections of the 1963 National Jazz Festival come from the website ukrockfestivals.com.

10 **'not so much a percussionist...'** Chris Welch's description of Ginger Baker at the festival comes from a piece entitled 'Ginger "the Master" Baker', archived at chriswelchonline.com. In the piece, he says Baker was playing with Alexis Korner that afternoon, but Korner wasn't on the bill at Richmond in 1963. However, the Graham Bond Quartet were and that was the drummer's day job at the time, so I've taken the liberty of 'editing' Chris's memory.

11 **'the whole audience turned round and ran…'** As quoted in *Trampled Under Foot: The Power and Excess of Led Zeppelin*, by Barney Hoskyns, p16.

DOING THE CRAWDADDY (pages 66–89)

1 **'Three things that most fascinate people…'** These are Gomelsky's opening words from an interview he gave to Chris Welch and Max Jones published under the title 'The Man Who Sold the World', in *Melody Maker* of 27 October 1973. He doesn't elaborate further on his strange pronouncement. This was a two-part interview with the second part the following week. Running an interview with one subject over two issues was usually reserved for musicians of the stature of John Lennon or Bob Dylan.

2 **'The first time I met Giorgio Gomelsky…'** From *Chelsea FC in the Swinging 60s: Football's First Rock'n' Roll Club*, by Greg Tesser, p417.

3 **'Pat Andrews thought he was "wonderful"…'** As quoted in *Rolling Stones: Off the Record*, by Mark Paytress. Pat Andrews was Brian Jones's girlfriend in 1963, and the mother of his son Julian.

4 **'Lasting impressions weren't always so favourable…'** From a story titled 'Brian Auger: Bridging the Gap', by Lin Bensley, published in *Jazz Journal* of March 2019 – Auger's exact words are, 'I made some test recordings for a notable con man and erstwhile manager, Giorgio Gomelsky.'

5 **'Harold heard about this…'** From a long, informative and highly quotable interview conducted by John Strausbaugh and George Tabb in 2015, archived online at www.nypress.com under the title 'Having a Rave Up with Giorgio Gomelsky'.

6 **'They have this nice room in the back of the pub…'** *Ibid*

7 **'One account has O'Rahilly meeting Gomelsky…'** The claim about the pair meeting at a Stanislavski acting class comes from *Changing Times: Music and Politics in 1964*, by Steve Millward, p130.

8 **'For whatever reason, Davies's tenure was a short one…'** Richard Porter of LondonRockWalks.com offers a reason why Davies quit the Dave Hunt Band: Davies told him that one evening folk legend Davy Graham, a guitarist he rated, turned up at the Station and told him he should quit the current gig and join brother Dave Davies's band – and that he should quit the guitar and concentrate on singing.

9   **'I went to see them in Sutton...'** As quoted in *The Rolling Stones: The First Twenty Years*, by David Dalton, p25.

10 **'For the Rolling Stones' debut show...'** Gomelsky told John Strausbaugh that he even remembered exactly who the attendees at that first Station Hotel Stones show were: 'These three guys who showed up, I would never forget them... One, Paul Williams, became a blues singer, another, Little H, a famous roadie who worked for Jimi Hendrix and later died in the crash with Stevie Ray Vaughn, and the third started his own venue somewhere and became an agent. They were cool guys.'

11 **'Giorgio, there's six of us and three of them...'** From the Strausbaugh and Tabb interview.

12 **'The Stones had balls...'** From an interview with Chris Chesney by Isabel Barnes, conducted in August 2013 for the Eel Pie Oral Heritage Project.

13 **'"Everybody looks up," recalled Gomelsky...'** From the Strausbaugh and Tabb interview.

14 **'A musical magnet is drawing the jazz beatniks away...'** From a story titled 'Barry May writes about the "new" rhythm and blues', published in *The Richmond and Twickenham Times* of 13 April 1963.

15 **'On Sunday 14 April, Gomelsky met with Beatles manager Brian Epstein...'** The Beatles were frequent visitors to this part of London. Between 1963 and 1965 they made around half-a-dozen visits to Teddington Studios, including at least four appearances on *Thank Your Lucky Stars*. Nearby Twickenham Film Studios, in St Margarets, saw even more Beatles activity. This is where they shot all non-location scenes for *A Hard Day's Night* (1964) and *Help!* (1965), and the first half of *Let It Be* (1969). They also used the studios for several promotional videos, including for songs 'I Feel Fine', 'Ticket to Ride', 'Day Tripper', 'We Can Work It Out', 'Hey Jude' and 'Revolution'.

16 **'As for Gomelsky's move on the Beatles...'** Giorgio recalled the tale of his attempts to get a film made with the Beatles to Strausbaugh and Tabb.

17 **'When we arrived...'** Quoted from Norman Jopling's *Shake It Up Baby! Notes from a Pop Music Reporter 1961-1972*, p69.

18 **'I thought we had a verbal understanding...'** Gomelsky's words come from 'The Rolling Stones: How It Happened', by Johnny Black,

from *Q* magazine of May 1995.

19 **'The band were rocking out on a Jimmy Reed tune...'** Quoted from Ian McLagan's *All the Rage*, pp26–27.

20 **'which is how Grimes and McDonald came to be among the grooving audience members...'** After leaving the army, Geoff Grimes became a plugger for Atlantic Records UK and a semi-pro musician. He still plays, and his band, the Beez Neez, played support for Robert Plant's on the UK dates of his Saving Grace tour in 2019. Rick McDonald, under his original name of Ian McDonald, became a founder member of first King Crimson, then Foreigner.

21 **'They were quite aggressive...'** As quoted in *Trampled Under Foot: The Power and Excess of Led Zeppelin*, by Barney Hoskyns, p16.

22 **'This has been rhythm and blues...'** As reported in the *Eltham & Kentish Times* of 16 August 1963.

23 **'It was Gomelsky who organised us...'** The Keith Richards quotes in this paragraph all come from Dora Loewenstein and Philip Dodd's *According to the Rolling Stones*, p43.

24 **'better than anybody in the world...'** *Ibid*, p45.

25 **'There is an argument...'** The theory that the Stones would have broken up if success hadn't come so quickly is put forward by John McMillian in his book *Beatles vs Stones*, p38.

HAVING A RAVE-UP (pages 90–109)

1 **'Gomelsky came to look on Hamish as his acolyte and co-conspirator...'** Gomelsky uses these terms to describe Hamish in 'Giorgio Gomelsky and the Grooming of the Yardbirds', by David First, published in *Tape Op* magazine of November/December 2007.

2 **'It was terrible to have to walk down the queue...'** From an interview with Hamish Grimes by Yardbirds historian Richard Mackay, published in *The Yardbirds World* of September 1983.

3 **'The group that caught his eye...'** When Hamish first saw the group at Ken Colyer's Studio 51 they were the Blue Sounds, a name they used for just a couple of weeks before they reverted to the name they had first given Cyril Davies, the Yardbirds.

4 **'As we're going up the stairs I hear *ta-ta-ta-ta*...'** Quoted from the John Strausbaugh and George Tabb interview, 'Having a Rave Up with Giorgio Gomelsky', archived online at www.nypress.com.

5   'On Sunday 30 June…' Sources disagree on the date for the Yardbirds' debut gig at Eel Pie Island but I've gone with the information given in Greg Russo's *Yardbirds: The Ultimate Rave-Up* (sixth edition, 2016), which stands as the definitive account of the band and everything to do with them – it's been the go-to reference for anything Yardbirds in this book.

6   '**Brock and Clapton would meet up at L'Auberge…**' Dave Brock talked about his friendship with Clapton in an interview with Rod Brakes, published on musicradar.com on 15 January 2018.

7   '**What a fabulous player…**' Ian McLagan's comments on Clapton can be found in his excellent autobiography, *All the Rage*, p37.

8   '**Eric would play faster and faster…**' Pete Townshend's reading of the Yardbirds' act comes from Will Hodgkinson's *The Ballad of Britain*, p135.

9   '**The Yardbirds performed about three songs in our garden…**' As quoted in 'It was Another Boring Day and Then the Yardbirds Knocked on the Door', published in *Classic Rock* of June 2006.

10   '**Gomelsky would also take credit for the idea of using a harpsichord…**' Paul Samwell-Smith remembers it differently: he says he had always loved Eartha Kitt's 'Just an Old-Fashioned Girl' because of its wonderful harpsichord, and that is where the idea to use the instrument on 'For Your Love' came from.

11   '**I was the one bringing in all this information…**' Quoted from 'Giorgio Gomelsky and the Grooming of the Yardbirds', by David First, published in *Tape Op* magazine of November/December 2007.

STRAIGHT OUTTA HAMPTON (pages 110–125)

1   '**And another guy called Murray Head…**' Vic Briggs was in the Animals then Steampacket; he later became a producer in California before discovering Indian music. Head was a folk rocker who found fame playing Judas in the cast of the Tim Rice/Andrew Lloyd Webber musical *Jesus Christ Superstar*. He had chart success in 1984 with 'One Night in Bangkok' from the stage musical *Chess*. He's still performing.

2   '**We were sort of the ones that got away…**' In 2012, four of the surviving members of the Others re-formed. Since then they have gigged regularly around southwest London and the Home Counties, and released new material.

3   **'How ridiculous…'** As quoted in *From Trampled Under Foot*, by Barney Hoskyns, p8. When I interviewed Jim Cregan of the Ingoes (later Blossom Toes) he told me how when Howlin' Wolf played London's Royal Festival Hall, Giorgio Gomelsky took him backstage to meet the bluesman: 'Thank goodness he introduced himself as Chester [Chester Burnett was Howlin' Wolf's real name],' said Cregan, 'because what do you call him? Howlin'? Mr Wolf?'

4   **'They were all "trainspotters"…'** As quoted in *According to the Rolling Stones*, p29.

5   **'You didn't go down there to get laid…'** *Ibid*, p31.

6   **'You were literally stepping in an inch of water…'** *Ibid*, p31.

7   **'or, as some have called it, the Surrey Delta…'** I'm not sure he coined the term, but Barney Hoskyns wrote a piece for *The Times* newspaper in 2012 titled 'Clapton, Beck, Page and the Surrey Delta of the Sixties'.

8   **'In 1964 there was more blues music being played in Kingston…'** From *Chelsea FC in the Swinging '60s*, by Greg Tesser, p329.

9   **'the only venue was the Assembly Rooms on Claremont Road…'** The Assembly Rooms did host occasional R&B gigs but much more intriguing is the story about Bob Dylan putting in an appearance at Surbiton in the first week of January 1963. The alleged performance is mentioned in *Bob Dylan in London: Troubadour Tales*, by Jackie Lees and KG Miles, but it has never been definitively verified.

10   **'Kingston and Richmond were the two key places…'** As quoted in *From Trampled Under Foot*, by Barney Hoskyns, p17.

11   **'Looking at the posters that litter the side streets of central and suburban London…'** From 'Blues in the Archway Road', by Ben Covington published in *Anarchy* 51 of May 1965. The title of the piece comes from a comment made by Rod Stewart that it was as easy to have the blues on Archway Road (where he lived, in north London) as on a Deep South railroad.

12   **'If you want to try to find somewhere…'** As quoted in *Days in the Life: Voices from the English Underground 1961–1971*, by Jonathan Green, p33.

13   **'It was better than working…'** As quoted in *Art into Pop*, by Simon Frith and Howard Horne, p80.

14   **'The simple fact is…'** Quoted from *Rock Family Trees, Volume 2*, by Pete Frame, published by Omnibus in 1983, p19.

15 **'It all came out of that art school semi-intelligentsia...'** As quoted in *From Trampled Under Foot*, by Barney Hoskyns, p18.

16 **'Everybody would bring in their own records...'** As quoted in 'Boom Boom: The Untold Story Of British R&B', by Paul 'Smiler' Anderson, published in *Classic Rock* of May 2014.

17 **'People like Wizz Jones...'** As quoted in *According to the Rolling Stones*, p14. Born in 1939 and performing since the 1950s, Wizz Jones (born Raymond Ronald Jones) is one of the unsung heroes of British folk, regularly cited as an influence by not only Keith Richards but also musicians like Eric Clapton, but a well-kept secret beyond circles of guitar aficionados.

18 **'in the band's first *Melody Maker* interview...'** This ran in the 29 June 1963 edition. Headlined 'The Rolling Stones Gather Speed', it introduced the band as 'pioneers of authentic beat music on the dangerous fringe of pop and R&B'. It notes they've built an army of followers in the clubs, have their first record, 'Come On', on the bottom rung of the Top 50 and have just signed up for the Everly Brothers' package tour of Britain in September.

19 **'Art and Ted would always have their schoolmates over...'** From Terry Rawling's *Rock on Wood*, p11.

20 **'Almost everyone I knew in Ealing ...'** *Ibid*, p22.

21 **'Pete Townshend has written...'** From *Who I Am*, by Pete Townshend, p45.

22 **'The head of the school was a chap called Osmund Caine...'** After art school, Bob Wagner would go on to work for numerous design agencies, working on over 400 album sleeves, many for Charisma, Decca and Swedish Sonet Records. He also did the film poster and publicity art for cult film *Sir Henry at Rawlinson End*.

23 **'He was an accomplished fine artist...'** The influence of Spencer is obvious in a painting like Caine's dreamlike 'Wedding at Twickenham'. The scene here is the churchyard of St Mary's on Twickenham Embankment, opposite Eel Pie Island, where a tombstone bears the artist's own name and that of his wife. St Mary's is where the funeral of the Beatles' associate Neil Aspinall took place in 2008. A schoolfriend of McCartney and Harrison, he became the Beatles' road manager, then personal assistant and, after the death of Brian Epstein, their manager. He was in the choir on 'Yellow Submarine'

and played harmonica on 'Being for the Benefit of Mr Kite'. From 1968, he lived in Waldegrave Park in Twickenham. Mourners at his funeral included Yoko Ono, Sir George Martin and Pete Townshend.

THEM RIZLA BLUES (pages 126–147)

1 **'I remember the fallout from seeing the Stones' shows...'** As told to journalist Peter Watts in a story titled 'Notes from a Small Island', published in *Uncut* magazine of January 2011.

2 **'Tom Newman's memory is that the Stones were not short of cash...'** After getting nowhere in the UK, Newman's band, the Tomcats, relocated to Spain where they became Los Tomcats and hit the big time covering hits by English groups. The Tomcats later morphed into psychedelic popsters July. In 1970, Newman built the Manor Studio in Oxford for Richard Branson, which is where Newman produced Mike Oldfield's multimillion-selling debut, *Tubular Bells*.

3 **'He wasn't a bad imitation...'** Quoted from an interview with Top Topham by Cheryl Robson, conducted in June 2013 as part of the Eel Pie Island Oral History Project.

4 **'His between-song drollery...'** Quoted from Paul Myers' *It Ain't Easy: Long John Baldry and the Birth of the British Blues*, p2.

5 **'Gingerly stepping along the platform...'** *Ibid*, p65.

6 **'First I went there as a paying customer...'** Quoted from *Rod: The Autobiography*, p42.

7 **'I saw Rod playing with Long John Baldry...'** As quoted in Peter Watts' story 'Notes from a Small Island', published in *Uncut* magazine of January 2011.

8 **'I noticed every time I returned to Eel Pie Island...'** As quoted in Paul Myer's *It Ain't Easy: Long John Baldry and the Birth of the British Blues*, p92.

9 **'We asked him why he wore girl's underwear...'** As quoted in Kevin Cann's *Any Day Now – David Bowie: The London Years 1947–74*, p42.

10 **'a steady stream of bookings at venues like the Ealing Club, Crawdaddy, Kew Boathouse, Kingston's Cellar Club...'** Kew Boathouse was next to Kew Bridge and hosted live music through the 1960s and into the early '70s, with gigs from the likes of Slade and Status Quo. The Cellar Club (formerly the Jazz Cellar), at 22a High Street in Kingston, was a buzzing R&B venue from 1962–1966.

It featured regular appearances from the Yardbirds and the Animals, among a great many others.

11   **'The Lucas brothers had noticed that the guitarist in the Nightshift...'** The Nightshift were an R&B band that gigged around London and the South East, including some coveted dates at the 100 Club. Following Jeff Beck's departure they continued through into 1965, releasing two singles, 'Stormy Monday' and 'Corrina, Corrina'.

12   **'He was so complete, so vital and inventive...'** As quoted in 'How David Bowie Helped Launch Stevie Ray Vaughan's Career', by Damian Fanelli, published in *Guitar World* of 16 May 2018.

13   **'On 25 October 1964, the BBC recorded the Tridents live at the Island...'** One track from the BBC recording, Bo Diddley's 'Nursery Rhyme', appears on the 1991 collection *Beckology*; a second track, Willie Dixon's 'Tiger in Your Tank', can be heard at thestrangebrew. co.uk/articles/the-tridents. Both capture the excitement of peak Tridents, complete with Beck's wild unrestrained guitar playing.

14   **'written by guitarist Andy Roberts and included on his 1973 album, *Urban Cowboy*...'** Middlesex-born singer-songwriter Andy Roberts played in Liverpool group the Scaffold with poet Roger McGough and Mike McCartney, brother of Paul. He has also been a member of the Liverpool Scene, Bonzo Dog Doo Dah Band, Roy Harper's Black Sheep, and Hank Wangford's Lost Cowboys. He recorded an album sharing guitar duties with Jimi Hendrix, played the Albert Hall sharing a bill with Led Zeppelin in 1969; played both 1969 and 1970 Isle of Wight Festivals and was part of the 'surrogate band' for Pink Floyd's *The Wall* tour in 1981.

15   **'We had a Hammond organ...'** All Derek Griffiths' recollections come courtesy of an interview with Ian Alderson in September 2013, conducted as part of the Eel Pie Island Oral History Project.

16   **'Two or three trips across the bridge...'** Quoted from Tim Large's *Dave Anthony's Moods: This Obscure Group*, p54.

17   **'Middle brother Ted was also a musician...'** Ted Wood was a jazzer. In the 1960s he played drums and sang with both Colin Kingwell's Jazz Bandits and Bob Dwyer's Hot Six. Kingwell's band played Eel Pie Island at least once; whether or not Ted was in that line-up is not known, but if he was it would mean all three Wood brothers played the Island in different bands.

18 'We were the biggest thing since sliced bread...' As quoted in Terry Rawlings' *Rock on Wood: The Origin of a Rock & Roll Face*, p37.

19 'You'd go and see John Mayall...' As quoted in 'Notes from a Small Island' by Peter Watts, published in *Uncut* magazine of January 2011.

20 'Keith West's Tomorrow, who had Steve Howe from Yes on guitar...' *Ibid.*

A HEADLONG RUSH TO HEDONISM (pages 148–165)

1 'At one end, the café was about five feet above pavement level...' L'Auberge makes an appearance in the 1967 Ken Loach film *Poor Cow* (based on Nell Dunn's book of the same name) – the Carol White character and friend size up passing men from the terrace.

2 'She had warts all over her fingers...' From an interview conducted by Pete Watt in June 2013 as part of the Eel Pie Island Oral History Project.

3 'It was the thing of going over the water...' From an interview conducted by Cheryl Robson in June 2013 for the Eel Pie Island Oral History Project.

4 'It was like going to someone's house, a big house, for a party...' From an interview conducted by Isabel Barnes in July 2013 for the Eel Pie Island Oral History Project.

5 'You'd walk faster...' From an interview conducted by Joy Clareburt in August 2013 for the Eel Pie Island Oral History Project.

6 'On Wednesday nights we never had enough...' From an interview conducted by Cheryl Robson in June 2013 for the Eel Pie Island Oral History Project.

7 'Most of us had read Jack Kerouac's *On the Road*...' From an interview conducted by Cheryl Robson in June 2013 for the Eel Pie Island Oral History Project.

8 'I was a sixteen-year-old boy...' From an interview conducted by Isabel Barnes in September 2013 for the Eel Pie Island Oral History Project.

9 'I was sixteen in 1964...' From an interview conducted by Cheryl Robson in June 2013 for the Eel Pie Island Oral History Project.

10 'It wasn't unusual to see couples copulating...' Don Hughes' memories of Eel Pie Island are included in his book, *Friday on My Mind*.

11 **'The filmmakers had Arthur Chisnall talking about his club's scoial-working agenda...'** I haven't seen this rare documentary but a Pink Floyd fan caught a screening on Bavarian TV and posted about it on an online fansite.

12 **'One finds it hard to imagine...'** From a story titled 'Eel Pie Shows Berlin the Way', in the *Putney and Roehampton Herald* of 7 October 1966.

13 **'Responding to the allegations...'** From a story titled 'Vicar Defends Island Jazz Club after TV Allegations', in *The Richmond and Twickenham Times* of 14 January 1967.

14 **'So, when a local woman complained...'** 'The Island of Noise', published in *The Richmond and Twickenham Times* of 8 May 1965.

THE SHAPE OF THINGS (pages 166–181)

1 **'none of the three singles and an EP the T-Bones released bothered the charts...'** When these recordings were reissued years later on a career retrospective LP called *London 1964–65*, Giorgio Gomelsky wrote in the sleeve notes: 'The big-time eluded the T-Bones only by a hair, however, in fact, their second single, a thing appropriately enough entitled "Give Him One More Chance" bubbled under the Top 50 for months on end and is even today one of the most "revived 45s" on English radio.'

2 **'Gomelsky buried the track...'** The track in question, along with another DeShannon/Page production, 'Climbing Through', eventually appeared in 1992 on the Jimmy Page rarities album *Jimmy's Back Pages: The Early Years*.

3 **'John Williams never trusted Gomelsky...'** After the Authentics broke up, John Williams was taken on by Andrew Loog Oldham, who promptly disappeared with the master tapes of Williams' debut, *The Maureeny Wishfull Album*. The tapes were eventually recovered and Williams put out a private pressing, which is now fantastically rare.

4 **'We've got our lease to think of...'** As quoted in a story titled 'Club Forced to Quit', published in *The Richmond and Twickenham Times* of 31 July 1965.

5 **'Speaking to the local press, Hamish Grimes acknowledged...'** Grimes' quotes come from a story in *The Richmond Herald* of 20 August 1965.

6   **'Sometimes I feel really sorry for them…'** Quoted from a story titled 'Wild Richmond Festival – and Meeting Two Unexpected Guests', by Keith Altham, from *New Musical Express* of 13 August 1965.

7   **'These dirty, filthy, useless, work-shy, cadging lay-abouts…'** As quoted in *The Richmond and Twickenham Times* of 28 August 1965.

8   **'There were concerns about drug use…'** Residents' drug fears were stoked by an article titled 'Pedlars Expecting Big Teenage Demand: Drug Supplies Boosted', in *The Richmond and Twickenham Times* of 8 August 1964.

9   **'Harold Pendleton responded to the festival's critics in the press…'** Pendleton's comments were reported in a piece titled 'Aspects of the Jazz Festival', published in *The Richmond Herald* of 20 August 1965.

10 **'Residents of Twickenham immediately made clear their feelings…'** Quoted from 'Jazz Festival Keeps Up Bid for New Site', published in *The Richmond and Twickenham Times* of 9 October 1965.

11 **'For some time, the band had been expressing frustration…'** A story titled 'The Quiet Revolution' in *Melody Maker* of 16 October 1965 begins, 'Depressed and frustrated. That's how the Yardbirds feel this week'. It reveals that in a bid for more exposure they've decided to have 'radical haircuts'. 'Long hair is so unmanageable,' says Jeff Beck.

12 **'I should never have been a manager…'** As quoted in *Jimmy Page: The Definitive Biography*, p87.

LIVE AT THE HANGING LAMP (pages 182–199)

1   **'There was more jazz at the Madingley Club…'** The Madingley Club was the venue, in April 1969, for the penultimate photo shoot with the Beatles. It produced a famous shot of the four lounging against Lennon's white Rolls-Royce. Further pics were taken at nearby 4 Ducks Walk, from where the Fabs rowed a boat out to an islet, where they waved for the cameras back on the bank. The Madingley burned down in the 1970s and a modern housing block called Madingley Court now occupies the site.

2   **'For reasons now forgotten…'** Richmond is identified as the centre of the British jugband scene in an article titled 'Knockin' A Jug', by Chris Welch in *Melody Maker* of 12 June 1965. It says 'much of the music seems to be emanating from that trend-setting zone Richmond, where the Rolling Stones first gave shake to maracas'.

3 **'The Richmond Folk Club had been gathering at the Richmond Community Centre on Sheen Road...'** This was an imposing building at 8 Sheen Road, dating to the 1890s, originally known as Queen's Hall. From 1901 to 1909 it was home to the local Freemason lodge. It was later converted for use as a cinema, then it became a billiards hall and during World War II it was a servicemen's club. Post war it became the Richmond Community Centre and was used for all manner of functions, from Christmas fayres to a 1963 gig by South African trumpeter Hugh Masekela. It was demolished in the 1980s.

4 **'When an unknown Paul Simon pitched up in London in 1964...'** This story, and much of the information about Theo Johnson, comes from Graeme Thomson's excellent *Small Hours: The Long Night of John Martyn*.

5 **'Creavin, whose playing was bolstered by massive amounts of charisma and gnomish charm...'** Ian Shircore remembers Creavin as an 'amazing raconteur.' According to Shircore, while in the army Creavin found himself in Malaysia stuck overnight in a pillbox somewhere in the middle of a jungle crawling with insurgents, just himself and Danny Thompson, the man who would end up playing bass with John Martyn, among others. While involved with the Hanging Lamp, Creavin's day job was at Battersea Power Station where he had to watch a dial to see that it didn't go into the red. The dial was in a little cabin, eighty feet up, reached by a metal ladder stapled to the wall. Creavin would take his mandolin and penny whistle up with him to practise and no one could hear him playing because it was so noisy.

6 **'I met lots of whizz guitarists...'** Frank McConnell's words about John Martyn come from McConnell's website, frankmcconnell.co.uk.

7 **'I could follow what he was playing...'** *Ibid.*

8 **'The owner, Gerry Southard...'** Quoted from the immensely readable *Unfaithful Music & Disappearing Ink*, by Elvis Costello, p87.

9 **'Tony Blair had left school...'** A detailed account of Tony Blair's adventures in rock promotion is given in John Rentoul's *Tony Blair: Prime Minister*.

10 **'The club had become an obstacle for both of them...'** St Elizabeth's would continue its musical associations beyond the life of the Hanging Lamp. In February 1980, Irish Catholic Phil Lynott, lead singer with

Thin Lizzy, married Caroline Crowther, daughter of TV host Leslie Crowther, at the church (the couple lived in nearby Kew, opposite the Royal Botanical Gardens). A little under six years later, in January 1986, Lynott's funeral service was held at the same venue attended by, among others, Lemmy of Motörhead and Bob Geldof.

COLONEL BAREFOOT'S ROCK GARDEN (pages 200–221)

1   'Barrett was living in a flat on Richmond Hill at the time...' This was a flat belonging to Pink Floyd's manager Andrew King that Barrett shared with fellow band member Rick Wright. Barrett said that the inspiration for his song 'Apples and Oranges' (Pink Floyd's third single) was a girl he saw walking through Richmond.

2   'He got the place a really bad name...' From a story titled 'Fight to Regain Island Hotel Licence Fails', from *The Middlesex Chronicle* of 26 April 1968.

3   'What Snapper wanted to do, he told the court...' Snapper's scheme for is reported in a story titled 'The Battle of Eel Pie Island', from *The Twickenham Herald* of 3 May 1968.

4   '"The general effect," said the officers...' Quoted from a story titled 'Council-Run Club for Eel Pie Island' in *The Middlesex Chronicle* of 31 May 1968.

5   'established by expat American Jim Haynes in 1967...' The extravagantly moustachioed and louche Haynes was born in Louisiana and arrived in Scotland as a US serviceman. He decided to stick around after his service ended and became a hugely influential figure on the UK counterculture scene. He was involved with the founding of Edinburgh's Traverse Theatre and its Fringe Festival, and ran the city's Paperback Bookshop, which he claimed was Britain's first paperback-only bookshop. In London, he co-founded alternative newspaper *International Times* and the Drury Lane Arts Lab.

6   'For example, on one side we have classical ballet...' Quoted in a story titled 'Venue Wanted for New Play', by Ron Godfrey in *The Richmond and Twickenham Times* of 11 July 1969.

7   '*The Richmond and Twickenham Times* sent along a reporter...' The visit was described in a piece titled 'Theatre Workshop Wants to Take Over Isle Hotel', published in *The Richmond and Twickenham Times* of 5 September 1969.

8 **'They played the Island again in June…'** Between the two Island dates, Free also appeared at nearby St Mary's College. The college regularly held gigs in the late 1960s and early '70s, featuring many of the same bands as the Island, including Pink Floyd, Cream, Deep Purple and Genesis. Unlike the Island, it was included on Elton John's 'World Tour' in June 1970 – squeezed between other London dates at the Lyceum, Roundhouse and Marquee.

9 **'I went to see them and I was so blown away…'** Quoted from an interview with Tony James by Steve Olson, published in *Juice* magazine in May 2010, archived online at juicemagazine.com.

10 **'It was a very friendly atmosphere…'** John Stephens was interviewed by Pete Watt in June 2013 as part of the Eel Pie Oral History Project.

SEX, DRUGS AND HEAD LICE (pages 222–241)

1 **'He told an interviewer in 2007…'** This can be found online at www.lasthours.org.uk/archive/interviews/clifford-harper/

2 **'In the mid Sixties he was living in Richmond…'** Harper's comment about Richmond having a special place in the history of English counterculture comes from an essay included in *The Education of Desire: The Anarchist Graphics of Clifford Harper*, p3.

3 **'Harper remembers an athletic girl named Sally McLean…'** The information about gaining access to the hotel comes from a series of email exchanges between Clifford Harper and Michele Whitby that took place in 2008 when Whitby was researching her book on Eel Pie Island. Michele was kind enough to share the emails.

4 **'People didn't want to know…'** Quoted from *The Education of Desire: The Anarchist Graphics of Clifford Harper*, p7.

5 **'Chris Whitehouse (also known as Weed)…'** Weed maintains the excellent Eel Pie Island Hotel website at eelpie.org, which was an invaluable resource for this book and this chapter in particular.

6 **'Afterwards, Faiers and one or two others, took a walk over to 144 Piccadilly…'** The squatting of No.144, or what was colourfully called at the time the 'siege of Hippydilly', was such compelling drama that Samuel Fuller, better known as a director of films, including *Shock Corridor*, *The Naked Kiss* and *The Big Red One*, wrote a novel based on the events, called *144 Piccadilly* (1971). Apparently, he'd been in London when the occupation was taking place and had witnessed the

initial break-in while on a late-night walk. According to his memoirs, he got 'damn mad' about the treatment of the squatters and so wrote a novel in which an American film director participates in an illegal entry in London and becomes the group's mascot, 'abandoning his hotel suite for a mattress on the floor with the flower children'.

7   **'Cliff was a big bear of a man...'** All the quotes and information about Chris Faiers, and his experiences in London and on Eel Pie Island, come from his poetic memoir *Eel Pie Dharma*, published by Hidden Brook Press.

8   **'I thought I was Henry Miller...'** This comes from a post on the website eelpie.org.

9   **'Someone who worked at the venue at the time...'** An account of the Hog Farmers at the Roundhouse can be found at ozthoughtsblog. com in a posting dated 26 February 2017.

10   **'When the Farmers left...'** A story about the Eel Pie Island commune in *Rolling Stone* of 4 February 1971 quotes hotel resident Mike ('a thin Londoner with lank, dark hair and a goatee') saying one of those who went with the Hog farmers was his wife: 'It was a good thing, as it turned out', says Mike, philosophically.

11   **'Gavin Kilty, another commune member...'** Kilty was interviewed about relations between Townshend and the commune by Richie Unterberger for his book *Won't Get Fooled Again: The Who from Lifehouse to Quadrophenia*.

12   **'and nearly killed the fucker...'** From an interview with Townshend on the CD that comes with *A Talk on the Wild Side* by Roy Carr, quoted in Richie Unterberger's *Won't Get Fooled Again*.

13   **'A WPC doctor who was part of the raid...'** The raid was reported in counterculture magazine *Friends* of 31 January 1970. Loretta Leu's comments come from an email exchange with the author.

14   **'We bubbled with the naivety that only the Sixties had...'** This comes from a short memoir posted by Gavin Kilty on the eelpie.org website.

15   **'It dawned on me it was getting ridiculous...'** From *The Education of Desire: The Anarchist Graphics of Clifford Harper*, p5.

16   **'By some accounts...'** Hotel resident Dominic McCormack posted his 'Mashed Memory of Eel Pie', in which he writes about the Hell's Angels appearance on the Island, at eelpie.org.

17 **'In January 1971, Snapper came back with a new proposal...'**
Reported in a story headlined 'Police Helped to Ruin My Island Jazz
Club Hotel Man Complains', from *The Richmond and Twickenham
Times* of 15 January 1971.

18 **'Clifford Harper quit in February...'** After Eel Pie Island, Harper
moved into squats in Camden Town and Stepney Green in the East
End. He eventually became a rent payer in Peckham in south London
but remained involved in the international anarchist movement. He
went on to work as an illustrator and graphic artist for many radical
and alternative publications. Since 1996 he has provided distinctive
woodcut-style drawings for the 'Country Diary' column in *The
Guardian*.

THE END OF THE RAINBOW (pages 242–263)

1 **'most beautiful house in the world...'** Quoted from *Ronnie*, by
Ronnie Wood, p96.

2 **'Day would turn into night...'** *Ibid*, p98.

3 **'Hogan remembers a signing...'** Pete Townshend got out of the
bookselling business in 1983, selling the Magic Bus. It remained
a bookshop, becoming part of a small Penguin chain. Five years
later, the Penguin bookshops (there were eight) became a target for
enraged protestors after the company published Salman Rushdie's
Satanic Verses, and one was even set on fire. Worried for the safety of
staff and customers, the shops closed. The Richmond shop reopened
as the independently owned Open Book, which is still going today.

4 **'When the time came, squatters got into the property first and
refused to vacate...'** Richmond upon Thames' most high-profile
squat was the former jazz venue, the Palm Court Hotel, overlooking
the river just by Richmond Bridge. Acting on a suggestion from a
musician, activist Erin Pizzey – who was running the world's first
refuge for women and children escaping domestic violence from a
two-bedroom house in Chiswick – squatted the then-unoccupied
and derelict building in 1974. For a time it was home to seventy-five
women and children.

5 **'I can hear that scream now!...'** Quoted from 'Charlie Watkins:
Audio Pioneer 1923-2014', by Gary Cooper, published in *Sound on
Sound* of February 2015.

6   **'Pendleton decided to fight…'** The full story of the National Jazz and Blues Festival's eviction from Windsor is told in an article titled 'How Quintin Hogg Made Sure the Kids Were All Right', by Martin Clemens, published in *The Independent* of 31 July 1994.

7   **'It was the coat-check girl…'** Quoted from an obituary of Harold Pendleton written by Simon Napier-Bell and posted on his Facebook page on 26 September 2017.

8   **'People kept turning up all the time…'** From 'This Little Piggy', a profile of Blossom Toes by Oregano Rathbone, published in *Record Collector* of June 2014.

9   **'Gomelsky quit London for France…'** The 'perfidious Albions' quote is from an interview with Gomelsky by Archie Paterson, year unknown, archived on the website eurock.com.

10 **'Gomelsky had already worked with two of France's biggest stars…'** According to Gomelsky, one evening after a day in the studio with Johnny Hallyday, he took the French singer's manager to dinner at Blaise's, a club in South Kensington, where Marmalade artists Brian Auger and Julie Driscoll were playing. On this particular night an unknown American guitarist was jamming with the band – this was Jimi Hendrix. Gomelsky was impressed by his performance and told Lee Hallyday that he should book him for Johnny Hallyday's forthcoming tour in France. According to Gomelsky, Chas Chandler, who was Hendrix's agent and who the Georgian knew well, was there that night and a deal was made on the spot. Which is how the newly formed Jimi Hendrix Experience came to perform their first show, in October 1966, at the Novelty in Evreaux, France, and made their first live recording five nights later at the Olympia in Paris.

TIMELINE

The dates of performances on Eel Pie Island in this timeline come from the roll call compiled by Pete Watt, Eel Pie Island Museum's music historian. Pete pieced this together largely from a stash of contracts left behind by Arthur Chisnall, and now held by the museum, with additional dates supplied by visitors to the museum. Dates for bands on the Island during the Colonel Barefoot era come from a collection of flyers that were gifted to the museum. The roll call is a work in progress, and for the most up-to-date version visit the Eel Pie Island Museum website, where you also receive the benefit of Pete's additional notes and comments.

1951	Kingston businessman Michael Snapper buys the Eel Pie Island Hotel.
1956	
Spring	Brian Rutland and his Grove Jazz Band obtain the use of the Eel Pie Island Hotel ballroom and begin using it for their own gigs.
Summer	Arthur Chisnall takes over the Eel Pie Island Hotel ballroom and uses it as a venue for free weekend parties for young people, with live jazz music.
10 Aug	Arthur Chisnall launches the Eelpiland Jazz Club with a concert by Ken Colyer's Jazzmen.
1957	
9 Feb	Cy Laurie, Bill Brunskill's Jazzmen and the Alpha Jazzmen perform at the official opening of Snapper's bridge, a first physical link between Eel Pie Island with Twickenham Embankment.
30 May	Ken Colyer's Jazzmen record their set at the Eel Pie Island Hotel and the results are later released as the album *The Classic Years Volume 2*.
1958	
19 Apr	Harold Pendleton launches the Marquee jazz club at 165 Oxford Street in London's West End.
1959	
Jan	Launch of the Ealing Jazz Club on the Broadway, Ealing.

22 May	Acker Bilk's Paramount Jazz Band celebrates the third anniversary of the Eelpiland Jazz Club.

1960

30 Jul	Crowd disturbances mar the day at the Beaulieu Jazz Festival and make national headlines, inspiring Harold Pendleton to launch his own festival with the aim of restoring the good name of jazz in the UK.
28 Sep	*Weekend* publishes an article about Eelpiland titled 'Down Among the Dead-beats'. Its libelous comments and unauthorised photography result in questions being raised in Parliament about the behaviour of the press.

1961

Jul	An article in the *Twickenham Tatler* puts the membership of Eelpiland at 8,500.
26–27 Aug	Organised by Harold Pendleton and the National Jazz Federation, the 1st National Jazz Festival is held at the Richmond Athletic Association Grounds. Headliners include Chris Barber, Ken Colyer's Jazzmen and Johnny Dankworth.

1962

17 Mar	The Ealing Jazz Club launches the UK's first R&B night, with Alexis Korner and Cyril Davies.
12 Jul	Filling a support slot at the Marquee, Brian Jones, Mick Jagger, Keith Richards, Ian Stewart, plus two others, perform together for first time as the Rolling (or Rollin') Stones.
28–29 Jul	The 2nd National Jazz Festival takes place at the Richmond Athletic Association Grounds. Headliners include Chris Barber, Humphrey Lyttelton, Kenny Ball, Johnny Dankworth and Ken Colyer.
15 Dec	The Rolling Stones play the Sandover Hall in Richmond. It's Bill Wyman's second gig, having made his debut with the group the previous night at the Ricky Tick in Windsor. They play another two shows here the following Saturday, 22 Dec.

1963

5 Jan	The Rolling Stones play the Sandover Hall, and again the

following Saturday, 12 Jan – this is possibly the first gig with both Bill Wyman and Charlie Watts in the line-up, although it will be another two weeks before they join the band on a permanent basis.

19 Jan   The last Rolling Stones gig at the Sandover Hall.

3 Feb   The Dave Hunt R&B Band with future Kink Ray Davies on guitar play the Station Hotel in Richmond. He plays the gig the following Sunday then quits.

24 Feb   The Rolling Stones play the first gig of their residency at the Station Hotel, Richmond. They will play here every Sunday night for the next sixteen weeks.

13 Apr   This Saturday's *Richmond and Twickenham Times* gives the Rolling Stones their first ever press coverage. The article includes a first mention of the 'Crawdaddy' club.

14 Apr   The four Beatles turn up to see the Rolling Stones at the Crawdaddy.

21 Apr   Andrew Loog Oldham visits the Crawdaddy to see the Rolling Stones.

24 Apr   The Rolling Stones make their first appearance on Eel Pie Island, beginning a Wednesday night residency that will run for a total of twenty-three weeks.

28 Apr   Andrew Loog Oldham revisits the Crawdaddy bringing promoter Eric Easton with him.

1 May   The Rolling Stones sign a management contract with Andrew Loog Oldham and Eric Eastman.

8 May   Norman Jopling's rave about the Rolling Stones is published in *Record Mirror*.

10 May   The Rolling Stones record their debut single, 'Come On', at Olympic Sound Studios near Marble Arch.

8 Jun   Future Yardbirds Chris Dreja, Jim McCarty, Keith Relf, Paul Samwell-Smith and Top Topham play together for the first time at a jam session in Putney.

16 Jun   The Rolling Stones play the Station Hotel for the final time.

23 Jun   The first known gig on the Island by Cyril Davies, godfather of R&B, who, with his All-Stars, settled in for a Sunday-night residency.

30 Jun	The Rolling Stones play a first gig at the new Crawdaddy at the Richmond Athletic Association Grounds. They will play here every Sunday for eleven weeks. The Yardbirds play their first ever gig, which is on Eel Pie Island supporting Cyril Davies. They play a second gig with Davies on the Island two weeks later, on Sunday 14 July.
12 Jul	The Rolling Stones play a one-off Friday night on the Island for a Twickenham School of Art end-of-year party. Support comes from the Muleskinners.
10–11 Aug	The 3rd National Jazz Festival takes place at the RAA Grounds. Headliners include Chris Barber, Acker Bilk and Humphrey Lyttelton. R&B makes a first appearance courtesy of the Cyril Davies R&B All-Stars, Long John Baldry and the Rolling Stones.
22 Sep	The Rolling Stones play the Crawdaddy for the final time.
25 Sep	The Rolling Stones play the Island for the final time.
29 Sep	The Yardbirds play their first gig at the Crawdaddy at the Richmond Athletic Association Grounds; between now and June 1965 they will play fifty-seven Sunday nights here (forty-four of those are between now and mid September 1964).
20 Oct	The Yardbirds play their first Crawdaddy with Eric Clapton in the line-up.
8 Dec	The Yardbirds play the Crawdaddy with Sonny Boy Williamson; the concert is recorded for a live album.

1964

8 Jan	Long John Baldry and the Hoochie Coochie Men perform a tribute gig for Cyril Davies, who died the previous day. Later, Baldry encounters Rod Stewart on the platform of Twickenham Station.
13 Mar	Harold Pendleton's Marquee relocates to 90 Wardour Street; the opening line-up that night is Sonny Boy Williamson, Long John Baldry and the Hoochie Coochie Men (featuring Rod Stewart), and the Yardbirds, who record their LP debut *Five Live Yardbirds* that same night.
29 Mar	Brian Jones fills in for an absent Keith Relf at tonight's Yardbirds gig at the Crawdaddy.

5 Apr	The Tridents fill in for the Yardbirds at the Crawdaddy.
25 May	The Manish Boys, featuring Davy Jones (soon to become David Bowie), make the first of several Island appearances.
7–9 Aug	The 4th National Jazz Festival takes place at the RAA Grounds. Acts include Chris Barber, Kenny Ball, Humphreys Lyttelton, Mose Allison, Memphis Slim, Jimmy Witherspoon, Georgie Fame, Manfred Mann, the Graham Bond Organisation, Long John Baldry, the Rolling Stones and the Yardbirds.
18 Sep	The Moody Blues play the first show of an eight-week Friday night residency at the Crawdaddy.
25 Oct	A Tridents show on the Island is recorded for German radio.

1965

1 Jan	Sonny Boy Williamson and the Brian Auger Trilogy play the Crawdaddy. Auger will make two more appearances here in February.
5 Feb	T-Bone Walker and John Mayall's Bluesbreakers play the Crawdaddy.
28 Feb	Eric Clapton makes his last appearance with the Yardbirds at the Crawdaddy. On the same night, Jeff Beck makes his last appearance on the Island with the Tridents prior to joining the Yardbirds.
14 Mar	The Yardbirds introduce new guitarist Jeff Beck to the Crawdaddy crowd.
11 Apr	Eric Clapton makes his first appearance on the Island with John Mayall's Bluesbreakers.
27 Jun	The final appearance of the Yardbirds at the Crawdaddy.
25 Jul	The final session of the Crawdaddy at the Richmond Athletic Association Grounds.
1 Aug	First appearance on the Island of the newly formed Steampacket, featuring Long John Baldry, Rod Stewart, Julie Driscoll and Brian Auger.
6–8 Aug	The 5th National Jazz Festival. Acts include Chris Barber, Kenny Ball, Ken Colyer, the Yardbirds, the Who, the Moody Blues, Manfred Mann, Georgie Fame, the Graham Bond Organisation, Spencer Davis, Steampacket and the

Animals. This is the last time the festival will be held in Richmond.

1966

29–31 Jul   6th National Jazz and Blues Festival takes place at the new venue of the Royal Windsor racecourse. It includes the first proper gig by the newly formed Cream, featuring Eric Clapton, Jack Bruce and Ginger Baker.

24 Aug   Cream play the Island.

14 Sep   The Herd have already played the Island on several occasions but tonight is the first time with Peter Frampton in the line-up.

1967

1 Mar   The Pink Floyd (employing the definite article at this point) make their Island debut. They will appear here again later in the month, on the 29th, and on 5 July, by which time they are just Pink Floyd.

11–13 Aug   7th National Jazz and Blues Festival takes place at Windsor. It includes the first ever appearance of Peter Green's Fleetwood Mac. Complaints about the noise mean the festival is banned from returning.

6 Sep   Local authorities close down Eelpiland for licencing violations. The last band to perform is Heart and Souls.

1968

18 Mar   The Hanging Lamp folk club launches at St Elizabeth's Church on the Vineyard in Richmond, with singer Mike Absalom.

1 Apr   First appearance of John Martyn at the Hanging Lamp, supported by Frank McConnell and Verity Stephens. Martyn will play regularly at the club over the next four years.

31 Jul   Music resumes on Eel Pie Island with a concert by Spooky Tooth and Spice. The gigs will continue (with a great run of bands including Blossom Toes, the Crazy World of Arthur Brown, the Nice, the Moody Blues, Family, Joe Cocker and Terry Reid, Jon Hiseman's Colosseum) until mid November, when suddenly they will stop again

9–11 Aug	8th National Jazz and Blues Festival takes place at Kempton Park Racecourse at Sunbury.
30 Oct	The Who make their one and only appearance on the Island.
4 Sep	Pink Floyd play the clubhouse at the Richmond Athletic Association Grounds, with Dave Gilmour now replacing Syd Barrett.
11 Sep	The Nice with Family and Peter Green play the clubhouse at the RAA Grounds in a gig promoted by the Middle Earth club.
18 Sep	Aynsley Dunbar's Retaliation play the clubhouse at the RAA Grounds.
25 Sep	The Taste and Union Blues play the clubhouse at the RAA Grounds.
27 Sep	Canned Heat, supported by Writing on the Wall, play the clubhouse at the RAA Grounds.
2 Oct	Chicken Shack play the clubhouse at the RAA Grounds.
09 Oct	Peter Green's Fleetwood Mac play the clubhouse at the RAA Grounds.
16 Oct	Blossom Toes play the clubhouse at the RAA Grounds. Sam Apple Pie play the clubhouse at the RAA Grounds.
23 Oct	Free, with the Groundhogs, Jo-Ann Kelly and Brett
25 Oct	Marvin & the Thunderbolts play the clubhouse at the RAA Grounds.
30 Oct	Steamhammer play the clubhouse at the RAA Grounds.
22 Nov	Pink Floyd, supported by Arcadium, play the clubhouse at the RAA Grounds.
29 Nov	Led Zeppelin are advertised to play the clubhouse at the RAA Grounds tonight but the gig is cancelled.

1969

17 Jan	A Benefit Ball is held on the Island for the Release organisation headlined by Jo-Ann Kelly.
31 Jan	The Nice supported by Van Der Graf Generator kick off a brief, six-week renewal of music on the Island.
28 Feb	Yes, supported by Smile, play the clubhouse at the RAA Grounds.
9 Apr	The four Beatles are photographed at the Madingley Club

	in East Twickenham and on the river at Richmond in what would be their penultimate photo shoot.
Summer	A party led by Clifford Harper gains access to the Eel Pie Island Hotel and moves in to found a commune. They pay a nominal rent to Michael Snapper.
26 Jul	Grenville Sheringham hires the unused Eel Pie Island ballroom for a twenty-first birthday party, with music by Hawkwind Zoo.
3 Oct	Grenville Sheringham's Richmond Arts Workshop organisation, which hopes to operate the hotel as a alternative arts centre, puts on a fund-raising gig with Mighty Baby; it's the first of four such Friday-night events.
27 Oct	The Hanging Lamp closes temporarily while the crypt is altered and extended.
31 Oct	The Richmond Arts Workshop has departed the Eel Pie Island Hotel and tonight's Friday gig is organised by new promoter Caldwell Smythe, launching the Colonel Barefoot's Rock Garden era – although that name is not in use just yet.
7 Nov	Free, with the Groundhogs, Jo-Ann Kelly and Brett Marvin & the Thunderbolts play the clubhouse at the RAA Grounds.

1970

20 Feb	Free play the first of two Island gigs.
4 Apr	Mott the Hoople play the Island, attracting the biggest crowd of the Colonel Barefoot era.
10 Apr	Genesis play the first of two Island gigs; this first gig is in support of Jan Dukes De Grey.
15 May	Black Sabbath play the Island, in support of their first album.
12 Jun	Deep Purple play the Island.
23 Jun	Peter Green plays a Midsummer's Eve gig for the residents of the Eel Pie Island Hotel.
20 Jul	After a hiatus of eight-and-a-half months the Hanging Lamp reopens with John James.
14 Sep	Ewan MacColl and Peggy Seeger play the Hanging Lamp.

This might be the evening that Declan MacManus, the future Elvis Costello, gave his first ever public performance, with a floorspot at the club.

21 Nov   Quintessence become the last band ever to play the Eel Pie Island Hotel as Caldwell Smythe (aka Colonel Barefoot) decides to pull the plug.

1971

30 Mar   The partially demolished Eel Pie Island Hotel is destroyed in a fire.

1972

8 May   John Martyn plays the Hanging Lamp and the gig is recorded and the tapes shelved for more than forty years before they re-emerge and are issued as the album *John Martyn: Live at the Hanging Lamp*.

19 Jun   Gryphon play the final night of the Hanging Lamp, after which the organisers close the club for good.

All the titles below were helpful to some degree in the writing of this book. Anyone interested in music in London should seek out Tony Bacon's *London Live* and John Platt's *London's Rock Routes*, both of which are long out of print but easy to find secondhand online. They cover similar ground, telling the stories of the development of the jazz, skiffle, blues, rock and punk scenes in London. The *Rock Routes* book is a good one for anyone with an interest in southwest London because author Platt grew up around Richmond and Twickenham. As mentioned in the preface, he wrote a musical history of this area in his self-published music zine *Comstock Lode*, which was invaluable in directing my own researches; his text is archived on the eelpie.org website. The other book everyone should read is Ian Marchant's *A Hero for High Times*. It interweaves the life story of David Robert 'Bob' Rowberry with a history of counterculture in the UK. In the late 1950s, Bob was sleeping rough in Soho, doing all-nighters at Ken Colyer's and marching with CND; in the 1960s he was hooking up with girls at Eel Pie Island, using parts of Long John Baldry's anatomy as a target for quoits, acting as a bodyguard for Miss Whiplash, a Scottish dominatrix wrapped up in the Profumo affair, stealing Joni Mitchell's jewellery and becoming the first person to import Afghan coats into Europe.

Bacon, Tony *London Live* (Miller Freeman Books, 1999)

Beatles, The *The Beatles Anthology* (Orion, 2000)

Bragg, Billy *Roots, Radicals and Rockers: How Skiffle Changed the World* (Faber & Faber, 2017)

Brunning, Bob *Blues: The British Connection* (Helter Skelter, 2002)

Cann, Kevin *Any Day Now: David Bowie – The London Years 1947–74* (Adelita, 2010)

Celmins, Martin *Duster Bennett: Jumping at Shadows* (JetMartin Publishing, 2007)

Clapton, Eric *Eric Clapton: The Autobiography* (Century, 2007)

Clayson, Alan *The Rolling Stones: The Origin of the Species – How, Why and Where It All Began* (Chrome Dreams, 2007)

Costello, Elvis *Unfaithful Music & Disappearing Ink* (Viking, 2015)

Cousins, Dave *Exorcising Ghosts: Strawbs & Other Lives* (Witchwood Media Ltd, 2014)

Dalton, David *The Rolling Stones: The First Twenty Years* (Thames & Hudson, 1981)

De'Ath, Wilfred *Just Me and Nobody Else* (Hutchinson & Co, 1966)

De Novellis, Mark, ed. *My Music* (Orleans House Gallery, 2005)

Doggett, Peter *Electric Shock: From the Gramophone to the iPhone – 125 Years of Pop Music* (The Bodley Head, 2015)

Du Noyer, Paul *In the City: A Celebration of London Music* (Virgin Books, 2010)

Faiers, Chris *Eel Pie Island Dharma: A Hippie Memoir/Haibun* (Hidden Brook Press, 2012)

Frame, Pete *The Restless Generation* (Rogan House, 2007)

Frith, Simon, and Howard Horne *Art into Pop* (Routledge, 1989)

Goodall, Nigel *Jump Up: The Rise of the Rolling Stones – The First Ten Years 1963–1973* (Castle Communications, 1995)

Gorman, Paul *Reasons To Be Cheerful: The Life and Work of Barney Bubbles* (Adelita, 2010)

Green, Jonathan *Days in the Life: Voices from the English Underground 1961–1971* (William Heinemann, 1988)

Harper, Clifford *The Education of Desire: The Anarchist Graphics of Clifford Harper* (Anarres Cooperative, 1984)

Haslam, Dave *Life After Dark: A History of British Nightclubs and Music Venues* (Simon & Schuster, 2015)

Hayward, Dick *Tin Pan Alley: The Rise of Elton John* (Soundcheck Books, 2013)

Heckstall-Smith, Dick *The Safest Place in the World* (Quartet, 1989)

Hjort, Christopher *Strange Brew: Eric Clapton & the British Blues Boom 1965–1970* (Jawbone Press, 2007)

Hodgkinson, Will *The Ballad of Britain: How Music Captured the Soul of a Nation* (Portico Books, 2009)

Hoskyns, Barney *Trampled Under Foot: The Power and Excess of Led Zeppelin* (Faber and Faber, 2012)

Hughes, Don *Friday On My Mind* (Armadillo, 2010)

Jopling, Norman *Shake It Up Baby! Notes from a Pop Music Reporter 1961–1972* (RockHistory Ltd, 2015)

Large, Tim *Dave Anthony's Moods: This Obscure Group* (YouCaxton Publications, 2015)

Lewis, Brian, with Arthur Chisnall and Auriol Hall *Unattached Youth* (Blond and Briggs, 1974)

Loog Oldham, Andrew *Stoned* (Secker & Warburg, 2000)

Loewenstein, Dora, and Philip Dodd, eds. *According to the Rolling Stones* (Weidenfeld & Nicolson, 2003)

Lucas, John *Next Year Will Be Better: A Memoir of England in the 1950s* (Five Leaves Publications, 2010)

MacDonald, Ian *The People's Music: Selected Journalism* (Pimlico, 2003)

Mansfield, John and Colin *As You Were: The True Adventures of the Ricky-Tick Club* (www.rickytick.com, 2019)

Marchant, Ian *A Hero for High Times* (Jonathan Cape, 2018)

McCarty, Jim *Nobody Told Me: My Life with The Yardbirds, Renaissance and Other Stories* (lulu.com, 2018)

McLagan, Ian *All the Rage* (Sidgwick & Jackson, 1998)

McMillian, John *Beatles vs Stones* (Simon & Schuster, 2013)

Melly, George *Owning Up* (Penguin, 1970)

Melly, George *Revolt into Style: The Pop Arts in Britain* (Penguin, 1972)

Millward, Steve *Changing Times: Music and Politics in 1964* (Matador, 2013)

Myers, Paul *It Ain't Easy: Long John Baldry and the Birth of the British Blues* (GreyStone Books, 2007)

Norman, Philip *Slowhand: The Life and Music of Eric Clapton* (Weidenfeld & Nicolson)

Nuttall, Jeff *Bomb Culture* (Strange Attractor Press, 2018)

Paytress, Mark *The Rolling Stones: Off the Record* (Omnibus Press, 2003)

Platt, John *London's Rock Routes* (Fourth Estate, 1985)

Platt, John, with Chris Dreja and Jim McCarty *Yardbirds* (Sidgwick & Jackson, 1983)

Power, Martin *Hot Wired Guitar: The Life of Jeff Beck* (Omnibus Press, 2011)

Rawlings, Terry *Rock on Wood: The Origin of a Rock & Roll Face – Ronnie Wood* (Boxtree, 1999)

Rentoul, John *Tony Blair: Prime Minister* (Sphere, 2001)

Rogan, Johnny *Ray Davies: A Complicated Life* (Bodley Head, 2015)

Russo, Greg *Yardbirds: The Ultimate Rave-Up* (Crossfire, 2016)

Salewicz, Chris *Jimmy Page: The Definitive Biography* (HarperCollins, 2018)

Shapiro, Harry *Alexis Korner: The Biography* (Bloomsbury, 1996)

Shircore, Ian *Loose Canon: The Extraordinary Songs of Clive James and Pete Atkin* (RedDoor, 2016)

Stewart, Rod *Rod: The Autobiography* (Century, 2012)

Tesser, Greg *Chelsea FC in the Swinging 60s: Football's First Rock'n'Roll Club* (The History Press, 2013)

Thomson, Graeme *Small Hours: The Long Night of John Martyn* (Omnibus Press, 2020)

Townshend, Pete *Who I Am* (Harper Collins, 2012)

Trynka, Paul *Sympathy for the Devil: The Birth of the Rolling Stones and the Death of Brian Jones* (Bantam Press, 2014)

Unterberger, Richie *Won't Get Fooled Again: The Who from Lifehouse to Quadrophenia* (Jawbone Press, 2011)

Van Der Vat, Dan, and Michele Whitby *Eel Pie Island* (Frances Lincoln Limited, 2009)

Wheatley, JC, ed. *The British Beat Explosion: Rock'n'Roll Island* (Aurora Metro Books, 2013)

Williams, David *The First Time We Met the Blues: A Journey of Discovery with Jimmy Page, Brian Jones, Mick Jagger and Keith Richards* (Music Mentor Books, 2009)

Wood, Ronnie *Ronnie* (Macmillan, 2007)

Wyman, Bill, with Ray Coleman *Stone Alone* (Viking, 1990)

Young, Rob *Electric Eden: Unearthing Britain's Visionary Music* (Faber & Faber, 2010)

INDEX

Numbers in **bold** refer to images.

ACKNOWLEDGEMENTS

My partner and collaborator, Gadi Farfour, put up with several years of introversion, mental absences and neglected domestic chores. I'd love to be able to promise now that the book is finished this will change but she knows better. Gadi is also responsible for how good this book looks. Thanks to my editor, Chris Wright, for his ruthless and entirely justified interventions, to Omer Ali for his diligent proofreading and to Jem Panufnik for creating the truly excellent Rick Griffin-meets-JMW Turner cover. I'm also indebted to Peter Watts, sounding board and early reader – and whose article on Eel Pie Island for *Uncut* magazine convinced me that here was a story that needed telling. Thank you, too, to two other early readers, Iain Ball and Peter Moody, for their suggestions and corrections. Thanks to Michele Whitby, founder and curator of the Eel Pie Island Museum, and to Pete Watt, the museum's music historian, for being so generous with their time and the museum's resources. And thanks to Christopher Hjort and Nick Warburton for leads and additional information.

PICTURES

Several of the photographs in this book were taken by Mike Peters. Peters used to visit the Island armed with both camera and trumpet. Born in 1933, he became a jazz fan at early age and formed his first band while doing National Service in Japan. Back in Britain he formed the Mike Peters New Orleans Jazz Band and spent a lot of time gigging on the Continent, particularly in Germany. The band did several broadcasts for the BBC and appeared (three of its members, anyway, Peters included) in an episode of *Dr Who* as the Perovian Army Brass Ensemble. They also played the Island 'dozens of times' – handy for Peters as he has always lived close by.

In the early 1960s, Peters became a professional photographer and his work subsequently appeared in a host of publications including *The Sunday Times*, *Observer* and *Telegraph* magazines. Despite the popularity (and notoriety) of Eelpiland, few photographers shot there and Mike Peters' images remain the most important visual record of the club.

p16 Britain From Above/Historic Environment Scotland; p21 the Snapper family; pp23, 26, 31, 36, 43, 47, 126, 134, 142, 143, 154, 219 Eel Pie Island Museum; p34 Alan Cresswell; pp50, 99, 104, 171 Peter Moody; p54 the Pendleton family; pp91, 166, 169 Getty; p121 Bob Wagner; p122 Stephen Goy; pp148, 157, 159, 162 Mike Peters; p152 Dave Dadswell; p182 Ian Shircore; p189 Robert Ellis; p216 Caldwell Smythe; p222 Mark Pickthall; p233 Angie Page; p248 Peter Hogan; p256 Elandra Meredith; p261 Terence Nunn.

Paradise Road publishes non-fiction books about London. Forthcoming titles include *The Marquee Story* by Robert Sellers and Nick Pendleton, and *Denmark Street* by Peter Watts.

For more information on these titles and other Paradise Road books, visit www.paradiseroad.co.uk

Thank you for reading.